Extreme Cinema

Extreme Cinema

Affective Strategies in Transnational Media

Aaron Michael Kerner and Jonathan L. Knapp

EDINBURGH
University Press

Edinburgh University Press is one of the leading university presses in the UK. We publish academic books and journals in our selected subject areas across the humanities and social sciences, combining cutting-edge scholarship with high editorial and production values to produce academic works of lasting importance. For more information visit our website: www.edinburghuniversitypress.com

© Aaron Michael Kerner and Jonathan L. Knapp, 2016, 2017

Edinburgh University Press Ltd
The Tun—Holyrood Road
12 (2f) Jackson's Entry
Edinburgh EH8 8PJ

First published in hardback by Edinburgh University Press 2016

Typeset in 11/13 Monotype Ehrhardt by
Servis Filmsetting Ltd, Stockport, Cheshire,
and printed and bound in Great Britain by
CPI Group UK (Ltd), Croydon CR0 4YY

A CIP record for this book is available from the British Library

ISBN 978 1 4744 0290 3 (hardback)
ISBN 978 1 4744 2602 2 (paperback)
ISBN 978 1 4744 0291 0 (webready PDF)
ISBN 978 1 4744 1446 3 (epub)

Contents

Figures

Acknowledgments

We would first like to thank all the people at Edinburgh University Press—namely Gillian Leslie, Richard Strachan, Eddie Clark, and Rebecca Mackenzie. Everyone at EUP was incredibly receptive to our project, and ensured that it was a smooth process from start to finish.

We would also like to thank Johnny Walker (Northumbria University, Newcastle upon Tyne), who encouraged us to reach out to Gillian Leslie at EUP.

I (Kerner) would like to thank my colleagues who served as surrogate psychoanalysts, or who simply inspired me: R. L. Rutsky, Julian Hoxter, Tarek Elhaik, Steve Choe, Daniel Bernardi.

I (Knapp) would like to thank Eugenie Brinkema for the guidance and inspiration. Additionally, I would like to thank my graduate student colleagues on the doctoral program in Film and Visual Studies at Harvard University, as well as the faculty members without whom these ideas could not have developed: Eric Rentschler, Laura Frahm, Tom Conley, and Ernst Karel. Lastly, I thank my partner, Anna Krieger, who always knows how to bring me back from the edge of the extreme.

CHAPTER 1

Extreme Cinema: Revisiting Body Genres

INTRODUCTION: WHAT IS EXTREME CINEMA?

What is extreme cinema? That is the question we intend to explore. In the decade leading up to the millennium, and in the years since then, we have witnessed the emergence of films that have pushed against, if not breached, conventions regarding the treatment of sex and violence in the cinema. For instance, self-appointed morality police, exasperated film scholars and critics decried films such as Eli Roth's 2005 film *Hostel*—charging the film with being too excessive, and dismissing it as "pornographic," "sadistic," or both. If nothing else, the near hysterical response to extreme cinema reveals that it appeals to the visceral experience of the viewer. And repeatedly, these films are accused of disregarding narrative conventions in favor of grandiose spectacles of gore and violence that play to the spectator's baser senses. Extreme cinema, then, is frequently associated with excessive brands of horror, or trends, for instance, in contemporary French cinema (or "New French Extremity" as James Quandt called it) featuring elements of brutal violence sometimes coupled with graphic sexual imagery.[1] We have no intention of disabusing the reader of these presumptions regarding extreme cinema, but would add to this, among other things, humor—the kind that makes one laugh so much it hurts. Furthermore, while the content of extreme cinema attracts considerable attention, and might be its most obvious feature, in many instances these films also experiment with form—composition, audio design, editing strategies. We survey here a wide range of international films that might be associated with extreme cinema.[2]

We take Linda Williams's landmark essay "Film Bodies: Gender, Genre, and Excess" as something of a touchstone.[3] Williams positions melodrama, horror, and pornography as the tripartite group of films that constitute the body genres. In all cases the spectator is invited to viscerally share in the experience of ecstatic screen-bodies. Melodrama might elicit tears, pornography intends to sexually arouse, and horror might startle us, making us jump from our seats, gasp, cringe, or avert our eyes at the sight of gore. In contemporary American horror, dubbed torture porn—*Saw* and *Hostel* being the most representative films of this type—bodies are torn asunder, wrenched, and contorted. Spectators obviously are not subjected to grievous bodily injury, but they are nevertheless compelled to mimic onscreen violence—flinching, tensing up, wrenching the body away from the depiction of pain. There is in that sense a degree of violence inflicted upon the viewer.

A number of scholars have taken up the subject of horror's, and extreme cinema's, capacity to affect spectators' bodies in ways that explicitly and implicitly engage Williams's concept. For instance, Angela Ndalianis's concept of the "horror sensorium" is rooted in her argument that films enable us to "extract meaning from our bodies."[4] Indeed, one of the most common threads running through many of the edited volumes on extreme cinema is the interaction between the images onscreen and the bodies of spectators.[5] What we wish to emphasize in particular, though, is the different types of responses that these films can elicit for different spectators. Take for instance the phenomena of "reaction" videos posted on YouTube (or some other hosting service)—where usually a static camera is trained on a small group of people recording their reaction to a film. In *Watching "A Serbian Film" (Reaction Video)*, posted on the TwistedChimp YouTube channel, three young men sit on a couch to watch, as the title suggests, Srdjan Spasojevic's 2010 extreme film *A Serbian Film*.[6] To start, the young men share playful fraternal banter, but as Spasojevic's film progresses (which is offscreen) the young men become increasingly agitated—anxiously bouncing their legs, mouths falling gaping open, hands thrown up over their mouth and eyes, the young man to the far right, his arms tightly folded, rocking back and forth before he retreats altogether. Reaction videos such as this exemplify the sensorial experience associated with extreme cinema. But sensorial experience is hardly a uniform phenomenon; some spectators respond quite differently—with laughter, for instance. Reaction videos frequently have nothing to do (or very little) with the films screened, but rather intend to record the visceral responses to the films. And insofar as reaction videos are preoccupied with capturing "involuntary bodily responses" on video, as Helen Hester argues—despite the fact that the "offending" material is offscreen—these might nonetheless be considered pornographic because they record the involuntary spasms of the body.[7]

Films, and this is particularly true of extreme cinema, potentially manipulate the viewing body (as documented in reaction videos), and we have established colloquialisms that express the implicit violence inflicted upon us: we refer to the weepie as a "tear jerker," in cruder terms we might say that a horror film "scared the shit out of me," and, as Williams adds, with pornography "some people might be inclined to 'jerk off.'"[8] Where we part company with Williams is her exclusion of humor from the body genres. She argues that body genres necessitate a degree of identification with the character in the throes of sensation. Comedy, Williams argues, usually features a character that we are invited to laugh *at*, not *with*. We accept Williams's position, and we would not presume to "correct" her, that is not our intention. For our purposes here we are largely concerned with the viewing body, and the ways in which extreme cinema affects it—suffice it to say that humor, and particularly its more grotesque forms, can be deeply affecting, causing the spectator to "roll" with laughter, cry, or to bend over in involuntary spasm.

Extreme cinema hosts the body at the far reaches of the human experience—from the ecstasy of pleasure to excruciating pain. And it is precisely because these experiences mark the extremities of the human sensorial spectrum that they also tend to fall outside the bounds of coded systems. Laughing is an embodied utterance without a signified, as is a furrowed brow, or the aversion of one's eyes—these are "expressions" of the body. Sexual ecstasy is expressed in animalistic terms—grunts, panting, "uh"—and if discernible words are uttered they might be "empty" of meaning as such—an expletive ("fuck," "shit," "oh god") heavily laden with artifacts of the body (*gut*tural). Sex is frequently described as an experience where one loses one's self, the temporary effacement of boundaries—the French, as is often cited, refer to orgasm as *la petite mort* (the small death).

Robert Stam, in his application of Bakhtinian ideas, suggests that the erotic encounter can be viewed as a "conversation" between bodies—physiological arousal, the involuntary spasms and eruptions might be characterized as the language of the body. And this exchange is not limited to those within the diegetic universe, but anticipates the spectator's contribution to the "conversation" as well. The erotic film invites an "interplay of sexually speaking (or listening) subjects, persons engaged in literal or metaphorical dialogue."[9] Stam pushes this further, asserting that "sex itself can be regarded as a kind of language. If we take seriously Bakhtin's idea that all human acts, including non-verbal ones, are 'potential texts'" then the possibility for a language of the body opens up. "Within the body, transmitters speed across synapses, neurons signal, and messages race from the erogenous zones to the brain and back again. Even corporeal secretions are communicative, constituting transmissions from the inner self to the outer body and to the other." The body's reflexive responses to what the subject finds arousing, while not "properly" signifying, then, nonetheless speak the body and "say" something. Stam continues, "The body in arousal exhibits indexical signs of desire; it sweats, stretches, reaches out, opens up, lubricates, thereby making way for erotic dialogue."[10]

At the other end of the spectrum is pain, but it shares similar characteristics in its corporal expressions. "Physical pain does not simply resist language but actively destroys it," Elaine Scarry insists in the opening of her book *The Body in Pain*, "bringing about an immediate reversion to a state anterior to language, to the sounds and cries a human being makes before language is learned."[11] Screams, grunts, crying, the utterances associated with pain, like laughter or sex, signify within the sensorial system, and thus "voice" nothing. The cinematic, with its aesthetic arsenal, might "articulate" or elicit that which has no intelligible "voice," through the form of the medium (color, audio design, composition, editing), rather than through conventional communicative modes (narrative). These ruptures of the expressive body in the narrative are some of the things that we would like to highlight in the present volume. And it is not necessarily as simple as *documenting* copulation, or presenting the spectator with a "disgusting object" that elicits the sensorial experience; rather, it might include the mobilization of cinematic aesthetics—in a word, stylized.[12] But to be clear, this is not to mean that there is an extreme style as such.

We might suggest, then, that what differentiates the films that we call "extreme cinema" from that which is merely violent or pornographic is an emphasis on cinematic form. Consider for a moment why Julia Kristeva gives Louis-Ferdinand Céline considerable attention. It is not simply that Céline's writing is filled with violent imagery, and laced with vicious anti-Semitic hatred; rather, what Kristeva calls our attention to is the *form* that Céline's writing takes—brimming with hyper-stylized passages. It is not just what Céline says, but *how* he says it that matters; abjection resides in form, it is not simply content that is at stake. Barbara Creed's *The Monstrous-Feminine* is a brilliant introduction to Kristeva's theory of abjection—and her landmark text undeniably helped to popularize the application of Kristeva's approach to that which prompts dread, or horror. To stop at Creed's text, though, does Kristeva's theory a fundamental disservice. As an introduction *The Monstrous-Feminine* is immensely helpful, but to locate the nuance of the abject requires that one go beyond Creed's application of it. The explanatory power of Creed's text derives from its localization of the abject in *things*, in *representations*—blood, menstruation, the undead, a corpse.[13] The abject is *not a thing*, nor is it a *representation*; it is a non-object, a feeling without a signified. It is not the corpse that prompts abjection, but rather *how* the corpse is presented. *The Monstrous-Feminine* invites us to ask the wrong question. It is not *what* is abject? Rather, what we should be asking is, *how* is it abject? The abject is not found in content; rather, it is found in form. Thus, we should take careful stock of the *form* that extreme cinema utilizes. It is not simply that extreme cinema includes highly graphic scenes of sex and violence, but rather that in certain instances these films render excessive elements in highly stylized manners. To put this into the language of Deleuze, extreme cinema operates according to the "violence of sensation."

Although the present volume is contextualized geographically—a transnational survey of extreme cinema—we have elected not to organize it according to national cinemas, or regional cinemas, but rather to consider these films under thematic headings. Admittedly this is in part an effort to sidestep the rather thorny questions of national origins.[14] Roughly following Williams's example, we have elected to partition extreme cinema thematically: the body in pain (horror), graphic depictions of sex (pornography), and crying (melodrama). In addition to this we add body-genre-inspired themes of audio design (hearing), and (grotesque) humor in extreme cinema.

EXTREME CINEMA AND AFFECT

One of the defining tropes of extreme cinema is its affective charge. As a result, in many instances extreme cinema is not governed according to narrative conventions (narrative arcs driven by character motivation), and instead emphasizes spectacles. This is certainly not true in every case, but we have found that extreme films tend to be more episodic—stringing together a series of highly embellished sequences. If not episodic in structure, then, extreme cinema might host abrupt ruptures in the diegetic narrative—experiments in form and/or composition (editing, extreme close-ups, visual disorientation, sounds that straddle the boundary between non-diegetic and diegetic registers), the exhibition of intense violence, acute intimacy with bodies in the throes of sex.[15] Like episodic forms such as the musical or pornography, extreme cinema frequently showcases set cinematic numbers that flood sensory channels with auditory and/or visual stimuli.[16] Whether an individual extreme film is episodic in nature, or plays host to a rupture in the cinematic narrative, these "breaks" generally are meant to elicit the sensual experience in the viewer. Tetsuya Nakashima's 2010 film *Kokuhaku* (*Confessions*) is particularly emblematic of this turn toward the episodic—relaying a string of confessions about the murder of a child. Strikingly similar in form, Lars Von Trier's *Nymphomaniac Volume I* and *Volume II* (2013) unfolds also as a series of confessions, or if not confessions, then "tell-all" accounts of the central character's sexual history.

Williams is particularly productive in our discussion of extreme cinema, not only for her work on horror, but also for her foundational work on pornography.[17] In *Hard Core*, Williams carefully distinguishes between hardcore porn and horror, for hardcore is "the visual (and sometimes aural) representation of living, moving bodies engaged in explicit, usually unfaked, sexual acts with a primary intent of arousing viewers."[18] Though heterosexual hardcore pornography, which Williams spends the bulk of her book analyzing, is typically oriented toward male spectators, it is the spectacle of female bodies that is the genre's focus. This is a trait that hardcore shares with horror, in which the target audience tends to be male, and the victims female, as epitomized by Carol Clover's concept of the "final girl."[19] As Clover argues, however, the nature of arousal in horror is complicated, for the male spectator's identification fluctuates between the monster/killer and the "final girl," the woman in peril who ultimately takes control of her destiny and audience identification. Williams describes this as an "oscillation between masochistic and sadistic poles."[20] This reference to sadism and masochism lends itself to an exploration of torture porn and extreme cinema, but first we shall look further at the distinction Williams draws between pornography and horror.

The primary impulse behind early hardcore pornography, Williams argues, was to make visible that which had previously been unseen: "the desire of the male performer and viewer to probe the wonders of the unseen world of the female body."[21] Ultimately, this leads to attempts to document the female orgasm. This accounts for why the female body becomes the visual and aural focus of hardcore, despite the fact that it has traditionally been geared toward heterosexual male viewers. The key to hardcore is the "unfaked, unstaged mechanics of sexual action . . . [which] is shaped . . . by techniques of confession that are applied first and foremost to female bodies."[22] This "confession" of the female body is similar to the involuntary spasms that the neurologist Jean-Martin Charcot documented in female patients who, he claimed, suffered from hysteria.[23] In other words, central to the pleasure of hardcore is the viewer bearing witness to the involuntary movements of women's bodies, confessional spasms of pleasure derived from physical stimulation. Torture porn and extreme cinema seem to work in a related way, in that they revolve around the spectacle of bodies convulsing with spasms of pain. Furthermore, by focusing on bodies being ripped apart, sometimes showing internal organs in extreme detail, torture porn also seems to "probe the wonders of [an] unseen world." There are key differences, however: in torture porn, the bodies are more likely to be male than female,[24] and the torture in these films is all simulated.

One might wonder then if "porn" is really an adequate descriptor for this particular cycle within the horror genre. Indeed, as Williams points out, part of the charge of hardcore is its indexical nature, its connection to the real. The viewer of hardcore pornography witnesses actual sex acts: real bodies in ecstatic movement, and through the "money shot," the cinematic staging of the male orgasm, the genuine "confession" of a (male) body. But the viewer of torture porn knows that the mutilation and gore, however realistic it might be, is nothing more than "movie magic." These are actors, and the carnage is created with make-up and special effects. Perhaps the key, then, is in the focus on non-narrative elements—the spectacle of bodies in pleasure/pain—and in the way that the films affect the bodies of spectators. As we will explore in

Chapter 2, sound design plays an instrumental role in giving audiences this affective charge, but so too does the presentation of the body.

The violent numbers in torture porn draw on the choreography of the pornographic genre to stage acts of extreme violence. In addition, like the episodic structure of pornography, torture porn films, as some critics and scholars are so keen to point out,[25] are little more than a string of violent vignettes with hardly a shred of narrative motivation. Following the contours of pornographic choreography, torture numbers generally begin with taunting (foreplay), the infliction of grievous bodily injury (meat shot), and culminate with the ejection of bodily fluids, usually blood (money shot). The body, which is subject to torture, is seen to writhe out of control—the victim screams, cries, pleads. And this finds certain affinities with the performances in pornography, where ecstatic bodies thrash about and vocalize verbal and non-verbal utterances. Although torture numbers are frequently devoid of sexual content, what this discloses is that the affective is not simply the product of content, but cinematic syntax—the form: "The frenzy of the visible, which Williams positions at the heart of her analysis of the pornographic," Helen Hester observes,

> might therefore be viewed as being connected less with sexually explicit images than with generalized depictions of the out-of-control body, and might be associated less with physiologic arousal than with the experiencing of a broader spectrum of intense affective responses. That is to say, some varieties of adult entertainment at times both represent and seek to elicit nongenital forms of intensity.[26]

Torture numbers capitalize on the pornographic regime to captivate its audience.

Of course, torture porn, unlike pornography, stages scenes that are simulated, and any blood spewed is not actually a physical response to stimulation (as in the "money shot" of male ejaculation). An example of extreme cinema that maintains pornography's documentary charge, unapologetically displaying the release of real bodily fluids, is Lucifer Valentine's *Slaughtered Vomit Dolls* (2006). The film, along with its counterparts in the so-called "Vomit Gore Trilogy," is regularly referenced on horror fan sites touting the "most disturbing" or extreme films.[27] Indeed, *Slaughtered Vomit Dolls* is an exemplary piece of extreme cinema, a work that seems destined to offend and/or elicit a physical response in practically any spectator; the movie showcases virtually every aspect of extreme cinema that this book attempts to trace.

Slaughtered Vomit Dolls contains scenes of tremendous violence, copious amounts of nudity (it is rare for the female performers to be wearing clothing), and, indeed, a substantial amount of vomit. The narrative—insofar as one can be pieced together—seems to revolve around a young woman named Angela Aberdeen who ran away from home as a young teenager and turned to prostitution and stripping as a means of survival (there are the fragments of a crude melodrama somewhere in here). She suffers from bulimia, claims to have once set fire to a church, and professes her devotion to satanism. These details can be gleaned intermittently from fragments of dialogue, as Angela talks frequently to the camera, or at least to the character who supposedly operates it. The film consists entirely of POV footage (though it is not necessarily clear to the audience precisely whose point of view is being offered) and, as such, bears a superficial resemblance to the "found footage" subgenre of horror that has been so prominent in recent years.[28] It would be more accurate, though, to say that *Slaughtered Vomit Dolls* adopts the cinematic syntax of "gonzo" pornography and the snuff film. Unlike the films of these categories, of course, *Slaughtered Vomit Dolls* is not a documentary as such: the women whom the audience sees brutally murdered are actors, and not actually killed (as in snuff films), and there are no hardcore sex acts like those in pornography or in the films explored in Chapter 5. Stylistically, Valentine's film also differentiates itself from documentaries and from "found footage horror" through its liberal—or perhaps "aggressive" might be a more accurate term—experimentation with form.

As we explore throughout this book, extreme cinema often demonstrates only a tangential interest in narrative, instead staging spectacular scenes of violence and/or sex in a manner that recalls the "numbers" of musical and pornography. *Slaughtered Vomit Dolls* consists of a few different numbers, of sexualized, nude or scantily clad women who are mutilated and murdered in a variety of ways, with the camera, which is supposedly held by the murderer and is therefore part of the diegesis, practically burrowing into the carnage. These scenes are constantly intercut with similar footage of Angela, who possibly took part in the killings. Or perhaps she is hallucinating them? Or is she merely another victim? (She does appear to die at the end.) It is important to highlight questions such as these not because the film invites us to try to understand the narrative that seems to be unfolding in fits and starts, or because Valentine's cinema demands serious contemplation, but rather because the act of asking of these questions is something of a rhetorical gesture. *Slaughtered Vomit Dolls* is fundamentally incoherent—and this is central to its appeal, if one wants to call it that. To be sure, there are small shards of narrative that can be gathered from the imagery and the fragments of dialogue—and they undoubtedly become clearer and perhaps even congeal upon repeated viewings. There is a line of dialogue that Angela repeats twice, presumably to the man who perpetrates the gruesome mutilations seen onscreen, but it sums up the spirit of the whole enterprise, as if the elements of the film itself were speaking to filmmaker and spectator alike: "I don't know what's left of me, but you can fuck it if you want. I don't know what I am." And, indeed, practically every image and sound in the film is manipulated such that the very form of narrative cinema is pushed to its limit. This is cinematic form that can only be characterized as "extreme."

The cross-cutting mentioned above, between footage of Angela and the various numbers in which other women are brutalized, is frenetic and jagged. It can be difficult for the viewer to discern who or what is being seen, as the handheld cinematography adheres strongly to the first part of Williams's famous description of pornography—"frenzy"—but only just barely to its object: "visible."[29] Flickering, shuddering black and white footage from a scratched filmstrip suddenly jumps to grainy color video, with harsh white light washing over the frame—and back again. This is not to say, however, that gore is invisible in the film. On the contrary, violence is shown in extreme detail: eyes are gouged, flesh is stripped, throats are slit, brains are eaten. But this gore—this violence of representation—is always accompanied by the violence of sensation. To be clear, Valentine's aggressively gruesome film is a far cry from the refined form of painting violence—"painting the scream"— that Gilles Deleuze praised in the work of Francis Bacon.[30] Nevertheless, Valentine constantly attacks the very form of his film—doing violence to, and with, image and sound. In addition to the constantly moving camera, jagged editing, and murky imagery, the film also employs visual devices such as freeze frames and slow motion, not as tools to create dramatic tension but rather as a means of further disorientation. As in the films discussed in Chapter 2, noise is a prominent feature of the soundtrack, both literally and figuratively, as that which disrupts the signal, the source of communication and meaning. Characters, particularly Angela, talk repeatedly to the camera, but their state-ments, as a result of the editing, are fragmentary and jumbled. Moreover, speech and other diegetic sounds are distorted, slowed down, played back-wards, and subjected to all manner of manipulation. Subterranean rumbles, scrapes, and beeps saturate the soundtrack; these non-diegetic noises shoot in and out, overwhelming image and sound alike.

Through these many layers of visual and audio grime, the spectator sees an acute attention to the body. This is particularly true of the female body, as women's breasts, lips, and labia are all displayed prominently and repeatedly. As stated above, though, *Slaughtered Vomit Dolls* does not contain any explicit scenes of penetration. Where the film most clearly approaches the choreogra-phy of pornography—with the display of its "meat shots" and the "physical evidence" of pleasure coming through the "cum shot" of male ejaculation—is in its obsession with bodily evidence of a different sort. Vomit is spewed con-stantly throughout the film: bulimic characters stick their fingers down their throats, gagging and hurling viscous chunks, while others hack up blood. There is an extended sequence of vomiting that is notable for several reasons.

Most obviously, it is the first scene to focus primarily on a man, who may or may not be the man responsible for all the carnage that has preceded (it is not clear). The scene also features relatively linear editing and, as such, seems more oriented toward display than the majority of the film. After having hacked off a woman's arm, the man begins vomiting, inducing this bodily spasm by sticking the dismembered limb's fingers down his throat. Vomit mixes with the blood from the arm, and it becomes difficult to differentiate between the liquid from his body and the dead woman's body. The bloody, milky substance flows—in seemingly endless supply—away from his body into a plastic-lined box below and, most notably, into a beer mug that he holds out in front of him. The man drinks his vomit, which of course induces further vomiting—and the cycle continues, with the entire image at points being enveloped in vomit.

This is the point in the film where, for this viewer at least (Knapp), involuntary spasms of disgust—the gag reflex—gave way to another reaction entirely: laughter. It is hard to say with certainty that Valentine was aiming for this type of fluctuating reaction, culminating in amused disbelief (although the very fact that the vomiter in question is a pasty, chubby white man with a prominent belt buckle spelling out "HENRY" suggests that there is indeed a sense of humor at work, however twisted). But this matters little: the point is that, as we will see throughout our exploration of extreme cinema, the physical responses of spectators are not uniform, and do not always adhere to logic or morality. It is worth noting that laughter for this viewer (Knapp) once again gave way to disgust, back to laughter, and ultimately to an uneasiness that bordered on boredom. *Slaughtered Vomit Dolls*—like many of the examples of extreme cinema discussed in this book—on some level pushes cinema to its limit, exposing realities of the body in extreme detail and striving to affect the bodies of spectators through graphic content and abrasive form, taking the basic elements of image and sound and rendering them at their most primal.

Extreme cinema *is* pornographic. But not in the ways in which this intentionally provocative statement might suggest. Although it is presumed that the pornographic engages with sexually explicit material anticipating sexual excitation in the spectator, Hester insists that the pornographic need not elicit sexual "arousal, sexual pleasure, and orgasmic climax." She views the pornographic in expanded terms, associating it with material (e.g. memoir, novels, television) that is intensely affecting. For instance, the highly affecting *2 Girls 1 Cup*, an infamous internet sensation that will be discussed in Chapter 4, "represents something of a displacement of the sexual. Just as the gag reflex comes to stand for another bodily paroxysm in the *2 Girls 1 Cup* reaction videos, so an interest in the authentic bodily experience of sex is displaced onto a fascination with the authentic bodily experience of illness in [the British television series] *Embarrassing Bodies*." The program features a compendium of abject human ailments. Thus, when the notion of the pornographic is expanded, it becomes clear that we no longer need "the act of external ejaculation" in order to elicit the label "money shot"—"pus, mucous, or inflammation might just as easily come to stand in for semen."[31] Where we diverge from Hester's argument is her insistence upon "authentic" performances "with real bodies really experiencing corporeal phenomena on screen."[32] For instance, Eli Roth successfully appropriates the syntax of pornography in his staging of torture numbers in the *Hostel* films.[33] Where our arguments might reconverge is in the "authentic" experience of the spectator—a spectator that is affected, be that in the form of tumescence, sweat, goosebumps, laughter, tears, nausea.

Because extreme cinema generally does not subscribe to conventional narrative regimes (e.g. character development/motivation, plot, narrative arc), instead privileging cinematic embellishments, this demands appropriate modes of cinematic assessment. And this calls to mind the very critical prejudice that Tom Gunning exposes in his seminal essay, "The Cinema of Attractions." Gunning is largely concerned with the historical context that gave rise to "the narrativization of the cinema," which he places between 1907 and 1913.[34] Prior to this, Gunning argues, the cinematic elicited a different sort of pleasure from the spectator—one closer to the amusement park ride, or attraction. The cinema of attractions offered visual spectacles (relatively) unencumbered by the obligations of narrative, as Gunning states, "emphasizing the direct stimulation of shock or surprise at the expense of unfolding a story or creating a diegetic universe. The cinema of attractions expends little energy creating characters with psychological motivations or individual personality." Rather than directing attention toward the interior world of the diegetic text (whether fictional, or not), the cinema of attractions "moves outward towards an acknowledged spectator."[35] Extreme cinema, to one degree or another—in an effort to viscerally address its audience—mobilizes the cinematic attraction.

We might find affinities between our examination of extreme cinema and Martine Beugnet's exquisitely nuanced volume on the cinema of sensations. She observes: "The cinema of sensation is an approach to filmmaking (and, by extension, to the analysis of film) that gives precedence to the corporeal, material dimension of the medium." She finally concludes that the trend of extreme cinema—and in her case she is specifically addressing French cinema—necessitates a paradigmatic shift in our "critical and theoretical approaches and, possibly, different viewing habits."[36] This is explicitly evident when she takes the critic James Quandt to task for his assessment of *Trouble Every Day* (Claire Denis, 2001), in which he laments, "An enervated Denis barely musters a hint of narrative to contain or explain the orgiastic blood letting."[37] Quandt's assessment reveals, like David Edelstein's dismissal of contemporary American horror, the prejudicial criterion on which he evaluates film, privileging narrative that in his view should "contain or explain" the exhibition of violence.

Beugnet, though, is quick to point out that shock for its own sake, "and the voyeuristic harnessing of the effect of verisimilitude towards the pornographic accumulation of 'realist' images," earned the disdain of otherwise amenable proponents of the cinema of sensations (namely, Deleuze).[38] Beugnet observes that pornography necessitates "authenticity" in its performance, whereas

> art cinema traditionally draws its legitimacy from a recognised ability to balance stylisation with representation mediated by a critical vision. Narrative construct and characterization, thus, generally become useful crutches, allowing for the integration of unusual formal techniques and sensory effects within a more distanced framework that can be, in turn, more easily identified in terms of underlying message or referred to an underpinning discursive strategy.[39]

In other words, Beugnet places art cinema—in its balance of style and the crutch of narrative constructs—in the realm of "tamed attractions" as Gunning termed them, cinematic spectacles nested within a narrative diegesis.[40] We find these nested embellishments in extreme cinema as well.

Extreme cinema tends to adopt the pornographic regime to play to the sensorial experience, and does not necessarily appeal to a spectator's emotions. Where conventional narratives invite the spectator to make an emotional investment into a character's arc, extreme cinema frequently appeals to other experiences: gut reactions and involuntary spasms. Brian Massumi has distinguished this realm of experience, affect, from the realm of emotions: "Affect is most often used loosely as a synonym for emotion." Rather, for Massumi, affects "follow different logics and pertain to different orders."[41] He continues:

> An emotion is a subjective content, the sociolinguistic fixing of the quality of an experience which is from that point onward defined as personal. Emotion is qualified intensity, the conventional, consensual point of insertion of intensity into semantically and semiotically formed progressions, into narrativizable action-reaction circuits, into function and meaning. It is intensity owned and recognized. It is crucial to theorize the difference between affect and emotion.[42]

While affect theory or the affective potential of the cinematic currently enjoys significant critical interest, thanks in part to figures such as Massumi, some critics and scholars alike either conflate or fail to substantially differentiate between emotions and sensations, making it all that more difficult to offer a judicious reading of extreme cinema.

Finding affinities with Massumi's thinking here, William Ian Miller in his *Anatomy of Disgust* makes a similar observation:

> Emotions are feelings linked to ways of talking about those feelings, to social and cultural paradigms that make sense of those feelings by giving us a basis for knowing when they are properly felt and properly displayed. Emotions, even the most visceral, are richly social, cultural, and linguistic phenomena . . . Emotions are feelings connected to ideas, perceptions, and cognitions and to the social and cultural contexts in which it makes sense to have those feelings and ideas.[43]

Where we part company with Miller is his alignment of disgust with emotions: "Disgust is a feeling *about* something and in response to something, not just raw unattached feeling. That's what the stomach flu is."[44] We are more inclined to keep open the possibility of sensations, such as disgust, emerging from the relation to a *non-object*—more in keeping with the Kristevan paradigm.

While there might be certain visceral affects associated with emotions—crying prompted by sadness, giddy elation (or even happy tears) spawned by a "happily ever after" resolution, anxious exhilaration perhaps even making one literally sweat over a nail-biting thriller—emotions in the end tend to be directed toward codified categories, feelings that can be defined as such. The sensual experience, on the other hand, is not necessarily bound to signification. Hair standing up on end, the physical gesture of averting one's eyes, heaving or nausea, laughing—these affective "expressions" are, at least in the realm of traditional linguistics, "meaningless." Teresa Brennan's book *The Transmission of Affect* goes a long way in attempting to lend a voice to the language of the body. Although she uses different terminology from ours, Brennan also differentiates between emotions and sensation when she notes that "Feelings are thoughtful, and affects are thoughtless. Feelings are meant to be information about whether a state is pleasurable or painful, whether one is attracted to something or averse to it. This is the classic and only basis for distinguishing feelings and affects."[45] Affect for Brennan, then, is affiliated with what she calls the "language of the body," or "codes of the flesh," those things that stimulate the senses, but go uncaptured by (properly) signifying systems.

Affect and emotions might be co-present, but this is not to suggest that they are the same. Tarja Laine similarly views affect as "the pre-reflective bodily mechanism that underlies all emotion and that gives pre-semantic meaning to information that originates from our bodily system, and more in particular from our senses."[46] Laine might take issue, however, with our (too neat) partitioning of affect and emotion:

> In film theory the emphasis often seems to be either on the affect (the Deleuzian tradition) or on the emotion (the cognitivist tradition) as separate, rather than unified states. By contrast, I attempt to approach

cinematic emotions as unified evaluations, affect being an implicit quality of the stream of emotion. Therefore I employ the concept "cinematic emotion" as an umbrella term that covers both affective appraisals and emotional evaluations.[47]

We certainly appreciate Laine's careful consideration and parsing out of the differences between emotion and affect. And we have no intention of refuting Laine's assertions (really quite the opposite); rather, we focus on the subject of affect, while at the same time acknowledging that the human experience is heterogeneous (semiotic/Symbolic; feeling/sentient).

Briefly, let us consider Tetsuya Nakashima's 2010 film *Confessions*, which uses many of the tropes associated with extreme cinema. It is relayed in a series of confessions, and thus unfolds as a string of episodic vignettes. In short, it is a revenge narrative—a mother and teacher, Yuko Moriguchi, seeks revenge for her daughter's murder. The audio design is full of elements that straddle the diegetic/non-diegetic register. The musical score is equally affecting, sometimes using melodic drones, in other instances moody or ethereal music (The xx and Radiohead), and at other points grating distorted guitars. Nakashima manipulates the image in a number of different ways: through slow motion "pillow shots" (rain, rose buds, junior high students jumping in puddles, clouds and sunsets), extreme close-ups (blackened teeth, matted hair), and stylized editing. Two boys in Moriguchi's class are responsible for her daughter's death. Shuya, who openly flouts his arrogance and violent predilection, believes that he has killed the girl, but he has only rendered her unconscious. The other boy, Naoki, threw her in a pool where she drowned. The police ruled the drowning an accident. The film leads us to believe that Naoki threw the girl into the pool thinking she was dead already; however, in his confession, the boy reveals that, as he held her, she regained consciousness and he knowingly threw her into the pool. Moriguchi, in the opening confession, reveals that she is HIV-positive, and has injected her blood into the milk served to her classroom. An extreme close-up of a hypodermic needle injecting spumes of presumably infected blood are (particularly once we know the context) affecting. In this case narrative does amplify the affecting exhibition of blood—it is not simply gruesome, or splatters of crimson red, but a contaminating agent. *Confessions* is a gripping revenge thriller that invites our emotional investment in characters that are cold-blooded killers and in a mother's quest for vengeance. In keeping with extreme cinema, though, this emotional investment is amplified by the affecting elements, which are elicited through the highly embellished audio design, its play with editing, and composition.

The affecting numbers in extreme cinema are not entirely devoid of narrative. As Williams observes, "it is commonplace for critics and viewers to ridicule narrative genres that seem to be only flimsy excuses for something else—musicals and pornography in particular are often singled out as being *really* about song and dance or sex."[48] This is not to say, however, that the episodic spectacles—song and dance routines in musicals, sex in pornography, or exhibitions of violence in horror—are completely devoid of narrative. "Narrative informs number," Williams insists, "and number, in turn, informs narrative."[49] Williams adds later that "as in the movie musical, the episodic structure of the hard-core narrative is something more than a flimsy excuse for sexual numbers: it is part and parcel of the way the genre goes about resolving the often contradictory desires of its characters."[50] Musicals frequently work out these contradictory desires—usually between male and female characters—through the song and dance numbers ending in a heterosexual union.

While different in certain respects, these genres—musicals, pornography, horror—rely on the exhibition of bodies. In musical numbers the channels of sensation are loaded up with aural and visual stimulus; on display are bodies that gyrate, writhe in pain, contort, and are thrown into ecstatic motion—bodies that wail, howl, and scream. In these moments narrative progression slows down, and much of this holds true for extreme cinema; however, the visceral numbers in extreme cinema are not necessarily devoid of meaning, but rather potentially elicit from the viewing body complex (perhaps even morally contradictory) sensual experiences—erotic arousal from scenes of disgust (*Wetlands*), sublimity in blood (*Inside*), raucous laughter in the politically incorrect (*Borat*).

THE CONTOURS OF EXTREME CINEMA

What follows in this book is our effort to locate representative examples of extreme cinema and to chart its topography. We make no claim that the present volume is exhaustive, that the selected films represent *the* body of extreme films. Rather, we prefer to view the selected films as examples, from which we might extrapolate further the contours of extreme cinema. We acknowledge, as well, that the films discussed here come from many different contexts—from different nations, from different industrial structures, each with its own socio-economic and cultural realities and traditions. Thus, scholars more versed in these local nuances might provide quite different insights—a prospect that we welcome enthusiastically. What we aim to do is to trace a current of extremity that runs through many contemporary films, regardless of their geographic or industrial context. Thus, we sample an array of international films that treat graphic content—sex and/or violence—in a highly stylized manner that "speaks" (to) the "language of the body."

The following chapter, "Hearing: With a Touch of Sound," considers the significance of audio design in extreme cinema. Audio design, perhaps even more so than the visual image, wields the most potential to elicit an affective response in the viewer. And it is not simply that sound fuels the imagination, but that sound can easily be unhinged from its signified, slipping into the realm of the non-object, the abject. Sounds that are in-between, composites, signifying the instability or the violation of borders—these instances are pregnant with affective potential. Sound is paramount in horror; as realistic as a film's graphic images might be, they are never fully satisfying, for the spectator understands them as simulation. In the pornographic genre the meat shot is intended to deliver proof of penetration. In horror, however, the meat shot—the forensic close-up (e.g. the drill bit boring into Josh's leg in *Hostel*)—does not command the same evidentiary weight; clearly it is a cinematic prosthetic. The "meat sound" might be just as important, or maybe even more so in horror, delivering what the forensic shots cannot. The meat sound is not necessarily indexical in the manner of the meat shot, but it gives the viewer a similar affective charge, precisely because the origin of the sound is more difficult to discern. It is slippery; it is a non-object, abject. The "meat sound," particularly in something like "art cinema," might also be an important feature in the exhibition of sex. The exchange of bodily fluids, which cannot be shown (for whatever reason—visual discretion, physical impossibility), can be conveyed through the audio design. The films explored include: *Dumplings* (Fruit Chan, 2004), *127 Hours* (Danny Boyle, 2010), *Inside* (Alexandre Bustillo and Julien Maury, 2007), and *Calvaire* (Fabrice Du Welz, 2004).

Chapter 3, "Pain: Exploring Bodies, Technology, and Endurance," considers the exhibition of the body in pain. We probe the apparent fascination with forensic knowledge of the body that is frequently displayed in horror films and thrillers. From the rending of a body to tests of endurance, the trope of the medical is abundant in these films (the *Saw* franchise, *The Human Centipede*, *Martyrs*). The spaces and tools employed to execute pain, particularly in the torture porn cycle, exhibit a melancholic nostalgia—the vast accumulation of tools and mechanisms with a rusted patina, abandoned factories, the machinery and facilities associated with (mid-twentieth-century) industrial production. What is "lost" is not industrialization *per se*, but rather the physicality of labor—the "blood, sweat, and tears" of work. We posit that torture porn, in its intense (some might say "excessive") focus on bodies in pain and in its constant return to the tools of the industrial age, is yet another manifestation of the passion for the Real (Slavoj Žižek). The experience of pain potentially brings the subject to the threshold of what it is to be human. Where a film like *Martyrs* examines the semiotic debt (Kristeva) to the symbolic subject—exposing the naked universe of the drive economy—*A Serbian Film* depicts the meat-flesh (Deleuze) of the subject. Some of the films to be discussed: *Saw III* (Darren Lynn Bousman, 2006), *Martyrs* (Pascal Laugier, 2008), and *A Serbian Film* (Srdjan Spasojevic, 2010).

Extreme cinema that invites the spectator to laugh is the subject of the fourth chapter, "Laughter: Belly-Aching Laughter." These films frequently evoke the carnivalesque—characterized by "feasting, riotous revelry, or indulgence."[51] Like the historical medieval European carnival examined by Mikhail Bakhtin, extreme cinema offers a venue to experience the cathartic possibilities of laughter usually prompted by exhibitions of transgression. Comedy, humor, and jokes generally necessitate narrative contextualization, but in this chapter we examine other avenues that lead to laughter—as a response to disgust for instance. Affective responses documented in reaction videos, bodies tortured (*Jackass*), and images of gluttony (*Taxidermia*) wield the potential to cause the spectator to "roar" with laughter. Some of the films to be discussed: *Taxidermia* (György Pálfi, 2006), the Fox Network's *Family Guy*, reaction videos (typically posted to YouTube), Larry Charles's 2006 film *Borat: Cultural Learnings of America for Make Benefit Glorious Nation of Kazakhstan*, and films from the *Jackass* franchise.

The fifth chapter, "Arousal: Graphic Encounters," negotiates the use of graphic sexual imagery. Graphic sex has been a part of popular filmmaking since the 1970s—from hardcore pornography like *Deep Throat* (Gerard Damiano, 1972) to sexually explicit "arthouse" fare like *In the Realm of the Senses* (Nagisa Oshima, 1976). Yet, at the beginning of the twenty-first century, international filmmakers began depicting explicit sex with far greater frequency. These films—which have typically been associated with international "art cinema"—demonstrate a deep interest in making the body visible in a manner that shares affinities with pornographic cinema, as well as the body horror of torture porn. In these sexually explicit films, we frequently see an exploration of the boundaries between pleasure and pain. Some of the films to be discussed: *Baise-Moi* (Virginie Despentes and Coralie Trinh Thi, 2000), Michael Winterbottom's 2004 film *9 Songs*, *The Piano Teacher* (Michael Haneke, 2001), David Wnendt's 2013 film *Wetlands*, Mika Ninagawa's 2012 film *Helter Skelter*, *Romance* (Catherine Breillat, 1999), *Clip* (Maja Miloš, 2012), Lars Von Trier's *Nymphomaniac Volume I* and *Volume II* (2013), and *The Wayward Cloud* (Tsai Ming-liang, 2005).

Brutal though *A Serbian Film* is, at its heart it is a melodrama—one of the key tropes of the melodrama being the temporal dimension of "too late," which results in some injury to, if not the destruction of, the familial unit. Chapter 6, "Crying: Dreadful Melodramas—Family Dramas and Home Invasions," examines the mobilization of melodramatic elements, namely in relation (usually threats) to familial units, in extreme cinema. These films exhibit many of the elements discussed in the previous chapters—graphic depictions of the body in pain and a commitment to eliciting a physical response in the body of the viewer—but frame these spectacles within the familiar narrative category of the melodrama, a body genre that Linda Williams suggestively referred to as the "tearjerker." Some of the films to be discussed are Kim Jee-woon's 2010 film *I Saw the Devil*, *Inside*, and Shion Sono's 2005 film *Kimyo na sakasu* (*Strange Circus*), as well as his *Why don't you play in hell* (2013), Lars Von Trier's 2009 film *Antichrist*, and *Funny Games* (Michael Haneke 1997/2007).

NOTES

1. Although this trend toward the extreme might seem new, Andrea Butler reminds us, at least in the French context, that its roots go back to the Grand Guignol French theatre of terror. Andrea Butler, "Sacrificing the Real: Early 20th Century Theatrics and the New Extremism in Cinema," *Cinephile* 8, no. 2 (Fall 2012): 27.
2. We acknowledge that distributors, in order to market films, have applied the term "extreme." See for instance Jinhee Choi and Mitsuyo Wada-Marciano's discussion of Metro Tartan's "Asia Extreme" line of films. Jinhee Choi and Mitsuyo Wada-Marciano, "Introduction," in *Horror to the Extreme: Changing Boundaries in Asian Cinema*, eds. Jinhee Choi and Mitsuyo Wadra-Marciano (Hong Kong: Hong Kong University Press, 2009), 5–7.
3. Susanna Paasonen observes that, particularly in the realm of porn studies, "relatively little has happened in conceptualizations of porn and its fleshy, sensuous appeal since Linda Williams's 1991 article on body genres and Richard Dyer's 1985 consideration of pornography as a genre 'rooted in bodily effect' and involving bodily knowledge." Our approach in this book is to make a modest contribution to this deficit—accentuating the body's senses in response to extreme cinema. Susanna Paasonen, *Carnal Resonance: Affect and Online Pornography* (Cambridge, MA: MIT Press, 2011), 13. Paasonen cites Richard Dyer's *Only Entertainment Second Edition* (London: Routledge, 2002), 140.
4. Angela Ndalianis, *The Horror Sensorium: Media and the Senses* (Jefferson, NC: McFarland, 2012), 6.
5. See for example Tanya Horeck and Tina Kendall (eds.), *The New Extremism in Cinema: From France to Europe* (Edinburgh: Edinburgh University Press, 2011), as well as the special issue of *Cinephile*, 8, no. 2 (Fall 2012): "Contemporary Extremism." Also see Xavier Aldana Reyes, *Body Gothic: Corporeal Transgression in Contemporary Literature and Horror Film* (Cardiff: University of Wales, 2014); and Laura Wilson, *Spectatorship, Embodiment and Physicality in the Contemporary Mutilation Film* (New York: Palgrave, 2015).
6. *Watching "A Serbian Film" (Reaction Video)*, originally uploaded October 12, 2011.
7. Helen Hester, *Beyond Explicit: Pornography and the Displacement of Sex* (New York: SUNY Press, 2014), 50.
8. Linda Williams, "Film Bodies: Gender, Genre, and Excess," *Film Quarterly* 44, no. 4 (Summer 1991): 5.
9. Robert Stam, *Subversive Pleasures: Bakhtin, Cultural Criticism, and Film* (Baltimore: Johns Hopkins University Press, 1989), 183.
10. Ibid., 181.
11. Elaine Scarry, *The Body in Pain: The Making and Unmaking of the World* (New York: Oxford University Press, 1985), 4.
12. See Julian Hanich, "Toward a Poetics of Cinematic Disgust," *Film-Philosophy* 15, no. 2 (2011): 13, 31.

13. In her discussion of disgust, Eugenie Brinkema makes a similar observation: "Historically, film theory (in particular horror studies and work indebted to Kristeva's theory of abjection) have concretized disgust into specific and singular things, images, or icons (*that* corpse; *this* rot; *these* maggots) . . . To concretize the excluded—to point, stark deixis, and insist 'this is this' or 'this is it'—is to avoid having to think disgust by only ever thinking the disgusting." Eugenie Brinkema, "Laura Dern's Vomit, or, Kant and Derrida in Oz," *Film-Philosophy* 15, no. 2 (2011): 61.

14. Kevin J. Wetmore expresses a similar concern in his discussion of post-9/11 horror: "'American' [film] as a term fails to represent the complexity and transnational nature of contemporary cinema production and reception, as well as the global nature of 9/11. In the case of the former, the United States's two most lucrative exports are weapons and films. As a result, both are emblematic of American culture and have far-reaching influences and implications on the world stage. There is an international visual language and influence of film that has developed over the last few decades. Asian cinema has profoundly influenced Quentin Tarantino, who then has a reciprocal influence on Asian cinema . . . Furthermore, the economics of film production has reduced Hollywood's geographic importance. Films are made with American money and some American actors, but filmed in Toronto or Vancouver, or in Eastern Europe in order to become more profitable." Wetmore goes on to explain: "I am not suggesting that American popular culture does not continue to dominate, merely that cultural flow is not unidirectional and that 'American' is not an uncomplicated term." Kevin J. Wetmore, *Post-9/11 Horror in American Cinema* (New York: Continuum, 2012), 5–6. For instance, a torture porn film like *Steel Trap* (2007) is difficult to situate: its director, Luis Cámara (Silva), is Mexican, the production largely a German enterprise (shot in Cologne), the cast multinational (though all acting as American characters), and the money American. The dialogue is in English (with standard American accents), intended to capitalize on the biggest possible international market-share.

15. See Catherine Zuromskis, "Prurient Pictures and Popular Film: The Crisis of Pornographic Representation," *The Velvet Light Trap* 59 (2007): 5.

16. Building off Rick Altman's work on the musical, Linda Williams has analyzed the structure of pornography as being one of staged "numbers." See Linda Williams, *Hard Core: Power, Pleasure, and the "Frenzy of the Visible"* (Berkeley: University of California Press, 1989), esp. 126–36.

17. For the remainder of this chapter, we will use "hardcore" to refer to pornography in the traditional sense of sexually explicit material. This is in an attempt to distinguish it from torture porn, which we understand as being a cycle within the genre of horror, not pornography.

18. Williams, *Hard Core*, 30.

19. Carol J. Clover, *Men, Women, and Chain Saws: Gender in the Modern Horror Film* (Princeton: Princeton University Press, 1993).

20. Williams, "Film Bodies," 6.

21. Williams, *Hard Core*, 192.

22. Ibid., 48.

23. Ibid.

24. Steve Jones states: "In the 45 films that have been referred to by three or more major international English language publications as 'torture porn' . . . 244 males and 108 females are killed. 293 male characters and 144 female characters are severely injured." Steve Jones, *Torture Porn: Popular Horror after* Saw (New York: Palgrave, 2013), 133.

25. See for example David Edelstein, "Now Playing at Your Local Multiplex: Torture Porn,"

New York 39, no. 4 (February 6, 2006): 63–4; and Christopher Sharrett, "The Problem of *Saw*: 'Torture Porn' and the Conservatism of Contemporary Horror Films," *Cineaste* 35, no. 1 (Winter 2009): 32–7.

26. Hester, 75.

27. For a typical, and useful, example, see <http://horrornews.net/6527/extreme-cinema-top-25-most-disturbing-films-of-all-time-part2/> (last accessed September 5, 2015).

28. Perhaps the most famous examples of this subgenre are *Cloverfield* (Matt Reeves, 2008) and the *Paranormal Activity* movies.

29. See Williams, *Hard Core*.

30. See Gilles Deleuze, *Francis Bacon: The Logic of Sensation*, trans. Daniel W. Smith (Minneapolis: University of Minnesota Press, 2004).

31. Hester, 60.

32. Ibid.

33. On the choreography of pornography and torture porn see Aaron Kerner, *Torture Porn in the Wake of 9/11: Horror, Exploitation, and the Cinema of Sensation* (New Brunswick, NJ: Rutgers University Press, 2015), 133–40.

34. Tom Gunning, "The Cinema of Attraction[s]: Early Film, Its Spectator and the Avant-Garde," in *The Cinema of Attractions Reloaded*, ed. Wanda Strauven (Amsterdam: Amsterdam University Press, 2006), 385.

35. Ibid.

36. Martine Beugnet, *Cinema of Sensation: French Film and the Art of Transgression* (Carbondale: Southern Illinois University Press, 2007), 32.

37. James Quandt cited in Beugnet, 37.

38. Beugnet, 24.

39. Ibid., 38.

40. Gunning, 387.

41. Brian Massumi, *Parables for the Virtual: Movement, Affect, Sensation* (Durham, NC: Duke University Press, 2002), 27. Tarja Laine similarly submits, "Affective experience is situational, the 'with-ness' in the midst of the world, whilst emotional evaluation is contextual, subject to reflective interpretation." Tarja Laine, "Imprisoned in Disgust: Roman Polanski's *Repulsion*," *Film-Philosophy* 15, no. 2 (2011): 41–2. Laine cites both Erin Manning and Brian Massumi here. See Erin Manning, *Politics of Touch: Sense, Movement, Sovereignty* (Minneapolis: University of Minnesota Press, 2007); and Massumi, *Parables for the Virtual*.

42. Massumi, 28.

43. William Ian Miller, *Anatomy of Disgust* (Cambridge, MA: Harvard University Press, 1997), 8.

44. Ibid.

45. Teresa Brennan, *The Transmission of Affect* (Ithaca: Cornell University Press, 2004), 116.

46. Laine, 1–2. Susanna Paasonen discusses the difference between emotion and affect, but ultimately decides that "isolating affect from emotion amounts to an impossible task." Paasonen, 26.

47. Laine, 2.

48. Williams, *Hard Core*, 130.

49. Ibid.

50. Ibid., 134.

51. "Carnivalesque," s.v. *OED*.

Hearing: With a Touch of Sound—The Affective Charge of Audio Design

INTRODUCTION: FROM A GRIND TO A SCREAM

It has been, as the film's title reminds us, nearly 127 hours. Aron, a thrill-seeking climber, is deep in the backcountry of Canyonlands National Park, in southeastern Utah, trapped at the bottom of a slot canyon, his right arm stuck between a boulder and the canyon wall. Various attempts to dislodge the boulder have failed, and an earlier effort to slice through his arm with a cheap pocketknife ended when the dull blade came up against a material it could not cut: bone. Aron's last hope for survival is to break these bones, so he thrusts his body up and away from the wall, a forceful movement that the camera mirrors by quickly jolting from the boulder to the empty corridor behind him. A sharp snap penetrates the space. The image cuts back to a close-up of Aron's face as he gasps in pain. To fully get the bone out of the way requires more precise work: he digs into his ripped flesh, wraps his left hand around the broken bones, and physically pulls the dense tissue away from his forearm, which marks the boundary between his living flesh and what he will soon leave for dead. The camera focuses in close-up on Aron's face as he does this, clenching his teeth, grunting and grimacing with pain. A loud pop bursts forth as Aron jerks his head back, allowing sunlight reflecting off the canyon wall to completely envelop the image. Aron's gasps of pain quickly turn into howls of laughter: he has successfully cleared the bone.

After removing tears from the corners of his eyes, Aron prepares the blade. The camera cuts constantly between different angles of the scene, as he slices open his flesh, digging his fingers into the gash to remove gobs of bloody skin, muscle, tendon, and vein. The procedure moves along slowly, but steadily, until the knife meets a thin, stringy, white fiber: a nerve. From a high angle, the camera peers over Aron's shoulder, down at the arm, flayed open, nerve exposed. As the blade touches the nerve, an electronic grinding noise overtakes all other sound. The camera swerves upward to Aron's shocked face, as if in response to this sudden eruption of noise. This unnerving, inorganic sound has no precedent within the film, which mixes loud non-diegetic pop songs with more "realistic" scenes that emphasize how the vast, wild landscape dwarfs Aron's calls for help. When Aron tries lifting the nerve with his finger, the grinding again dominates the soundtrack. The camera swerves up to Aron's face, his mouth agape. Does he hear this sound, too? Does the nerve connect to his ears as well as his brain? Is he hearing the destruction of his own body? Is this the sound of pain? The camera shudders back and forth, as if in anticipation of the intense pain and harsh grinding noise that will soon return. Aron tugs the nerve, and the grind now begins to take on a higher, more recognizable pitch, like a blade being sharpened by a spinning metal wheel. The nerve is ripped out, and the grinding trails off, overtaken by Aron's repeated screams.[1]

Such is the buildup to the uplifting conclusion of *127 Hours*, a film about endurance, devoting roughly an hour of its 90-minute runtime to the ordeal of this immobilized man. Released in 2010, the film came at the end of a decade of film that was regularly discussed for its turn to extreme violence, particularly in horror and in certain segments of art cinema.[2] But this film was by no means from the fringe; it was directed by Danny Boyle, whose previous work, *Slumdog Millionaire* (2008), won numerous Academy Awards. And, like its predecessor, *127 Hours* is ultimately meant to inspire, being based on the "true story" of a man who triumphed over adversity. Though it garnered six Academy Award nominations, it was not without controversy, as the press widely reported that the amputation scene drove some spectators to faint and vomit.[3] The film does not avoid gore, but it frequently calls upon other elements to convey its violence. Aside from a few, brief direct shots of the sliced-open arm (most notably those with the exposed nerve), the scene is primarily shot from angles that obscure the action, relying instead on James Franco's acting and the context to communicate the horror. It also depends heavily on sound: the crack and pop of broken bones and, most intriguingly, the overpowering electronic grinding that communicates the pain of an exposed nerve. This chapter will take this grind, and its attendant scream, as its departure point, exploring how films of extreme horror—in particular *Inside* (Alexandre Bustillo and Julien Maury, 2007), *Calvaire* (Fabrice Du Welz, 2004), and *Dumplings* (Fruit Chan, 2004)— use sound as an instrument of violence, to convey ruined bodies on the screen and to unnerve bodies via it.

TRANSSENSORIAL RHYTHM AND GUT REACTIONS

Michel Chion would be unsurprised that *127 Hours* relies so heavily on sound in this crucial scene and, further, that the images and sounds apparently had such a profound effect on the bodies of some spectators. Chion is arguably the scholar who has done the most sustained work on the theorization of cinema as an *audiovisual* medium, and he has argued that films appeal to the human sensorium beyond merely looking and listening. Instead, for Chion, the eye and ear work in a complicated, interrelated manner, perceiving elements that are not strictly related to the eye's capacity for vision and the ear's capacity for hearing. Rather, Chion's model is a "transsensorial" one, in which "the senses are channels," and "[w]hen kinetic sensations organized into art are transmitted through a single sensory channel . . . [they] can convey all the other senses at once."[4] The ear might hear things that the brain registers as images, and the eye might see things that are interpreted as sounds. And, further, a film can use image and sound to appeal to other senses, such as touch, smell, and taste. Central to this process is rhythm, a musical term that of course also has a long history in cinema theory, particularly with respect to editing. Chion describes rhythm as "neither specifically auditory nor visual," but rather what reaches the brain through the channel of the eye or ear.[5] Thus, the spectator does not merely hear a sound and picture its source; the sound triggers feelings that are beyond cognition. Chion's concept seems particularly relevant to a discussion of non-diegetic sounds, most conventionally the use of music to communicate the emotion of a scene. But it can also help illuminate the function of non-musical sounds, such as the electronic grinding that accompanies the slicing and ripping of an exposed nerve. The sound not only has no visible diegetic source within *127 Hours*; it cannot be attached to any signified. It is harsh, grating, and used to communicate affect: to express a character's intense pain and to unsettle the spectator, to make him or her feel, or at least come up against, the intensity of a violence that cannot be fully comprehended.

In his work relating sound to fear, Steve Goodman builds off Chion's notion of transsensorial rhythm to argue that spectators, or listeners, receive stimuli through the channels of the eye or ear, and these stimuli are then felt, and transformed, within the body. The way the body internalizes the stimuli overpowers the external stimuli themselves: "Where there is a visceral perception initiated by a sound and in a split-second the body is activated by the sonic trigger, then the gut reaction is preempting consciousness."[6] In other words, intense affect can overpower cognition. This may help explain what makes the amputation scene so difficult for some viewers, even if they know it is simulated. For instance, as reported in the *Los Angeles Times*, "Phelps fainted on the restroom floor, and was treated by paramedics who had been called when another moviegoer suffered an apparent seizure. 'I have never had, even remotely, an experience like this,' she said. 'I'm a television producer. I know this stuff is not real.'"[7]

Goodman's connection of sound to gut reactions, or irrational fear, also points toward one of the reasons horror films rely so heavily on their soundtracks, a topic that has generated a fair amount of commentary.[8] The horror genre has been celebrated for its innovative use of music, from the piercing strings of Bernard Herrmann's iconic *Psycho* score to the throbbing synthesizer of John Carpenter's films. And, of course, there is the scream of the "final girl" in slasher films, "whom we see scream, stagger, fall, rise, and scream again."[9] Carol Clover uses the verb "see" in this instance, but the sonic dimension of these screams is as important as the visual one, if not more so. For some scholars, such as Greg Hainge, it is noise, above all, that is "indelibly associated with horror."[10] What Hainge means here is, essentially, those sounds that cannot be attributed to dialogue or to the conventional musical score: humans' screams and monsters' roars, but also other diegetic sounds like doors creaking and twigs snapping, and the strange, unidentifiable non-diegetic sounds that build suspense and generate negative affect. The electronic grinding is such a noise. What makes its use in *127 Hours* so remarkable is that Boyle's film is not a horror movie, but rather a film that "is intended to be, and critics are singling it out as, a highbrow drama for sophisticated moviegoers."[11] Setting aside the incredibly problematic assumptions this makes about genre, demographics, and cinematic style, the industry spin is nonetheless revealing: violent negative affect has its place—and that is in horror. Or, rather, perhaps it signifies that the extreme violence of horror films and international art cinema had truly infiltrated mainstream Hollywood; even Oscar winners could now revel in gore and negative affect.

The discussion of affect, senses, and the body calls to mind the work of Gilles Deleuze. Anna Powell has argued that, although Deleuze's writings do not have anything particularly kind to say about horror films per se, his philosophy nonetheless offers much that is applicable to the genre. Powell claims that the sense of disorientation and sensory assault that are so central to horror cinema undermine spectators' "projected coherence," thus causing them to "slide into a molecular assemblage with the body of the film."[12] Angela Ndalianis makes a similar argument in her concept of the "horror sensorium," observing that new horror films viscerally assault spectators, directly and synesthetically affecting their minds and bodies with intense images and sounds, such that "we ingest the disgusting material presence that's onscreen into ourselves so that our bodies are forced to respond physically."[13] Though using different language, Chion's transsensorial rhythm and Goodman's gut reactions convey a similar idea: spectators on some level absorb the stimuli into themselves—a process that is particularly suited to sound and hearing. Also writing on the subject of cinematic violence, Marco Abel has turned to Deleuze's work on the painter Francis Bacon. What Abel appreciates within this work is that Bacon's painting comes to be understood for its violent sensations, not for its violent representations. Following this, Abel does not "frame the encounter with violent images in terms of signification and meaning (mediation) but, instead, in terms of affects and force—that is, asignifying intensities."[14] Put differently: the violent power of images lies not in *what* they represent, but in *how* they do it, how they elicit affect. "The violence of sensation is opposed to the violence of the represented (the sensational, the cliché)."[15] Thus, for Deleuze, Bacon's paintings do not gain their power because they depict scenes of violence. Rather, Bacon does violence to the image itself: through color, through a technique of blurring that Deleuze calls "scrubbing," and, above all, through rhythm.[16] These are the techniques available to the painter, which of course differ from the techniques available to the filmmaker. The latter can use, for instance, techniques of camera movement, sound, light, duration, distance, and—just as in painting—color and rhythm.

Rhythm, as we have seen, is a central concept in Chion's and Goodman's work on sound. What rhythm means here, though, is not the conventional definition pertaining to music: "The systematic grouping of musical sounds, principally according to duration and periodical stress; beat; an instance of this, a particular grouping or arrangement of musical sounds."[17] Deleuzian rhythm is not unrelated to this definition, as it does include the concepts of duration and stress. And further, Deleuzian rhythm can certainly be found in music. The distinction is that Deleuzian rhythm, which is one of intensity, is not necessarily grouped systematically; it cannot easily be categorized as something like meter, or beats. This rhythm is a question of movement, of making invisible forces visible and palpable: it comes through not in figuration, or narrative content, or a clearly depicted scene, but rather through the sensual techniques that are at play. Bacon's project is "to make spasm visible."[18] He does not paint a scene of a body in spasm, but instead paints the spasm itself. The painting, composed of colors and lines, *is* the spasm. We might extend this, then, to the concept of making a spasm audible—a notion that is suggestively hinted at in a famous passage in which Deleuze quotes Bacon: "'I wanted to paint the scream more than the horror.'"[19] This notion resonates strongly with a notion of writing that Deleuze explores in his essay "He Stuttered," where he singles out writers who make the very form of language strange, making the syntax itself stutter and tremble: Franz Kafka, Herman Melville, Samuel Beckett.[20] If we extend this concept to our exploration of violence in extreme horror films, we might productively think of a film that not only depicts screams and strives to induce them, but a film that itself screams. For the moment, however, we will continue our exploration of rhythm and the audible spasm.

Rhythm and audible spasms are peppered throughout Tetsuya Nakashima's 2010 film *Confessions*. Characters wail at instances when they are overcome with the guilt associated with the abject crime of infanticide. Many of these feral screams penetrate the viewing body as archaic utterances. Unsocialized, pre-linguistic, and perhaps akin to the screams of a newborn child, these screams resonate within the spectator—they are, in short, stomach-turning. Almost as animalistic as Lucie's bestial apparition in *Martyrs* (discussed in Chapter 3), Naoki, an unbathed, unkempt adolescent boy responsible for killing his teacher's daughter, darts in and out of his room, and belts out uncontrollable screams. The non-diegetic audio design recedes into the background, muted, and then emerges at the fore—stressing not only background/foreground, but also internal subjective diegetic sound/non-diegetic sound, and inside/outside. The editing, sharp and jarring, embodies the spasms of a body at the threshold of what is human. Naoki's mother, when she too comes to realize the truth about her son, is shattered and screams—rendered multiple times in an overlap edit generating a spastic rhythm.

By staging a self-amputation scene, *127 Hours* could be said to participate in the violence of representation—but this does not necessarily mean that it cannot also engage the violence of sensation. For Deleuze, the violence of sensation is "inseparable from its direct action on the nervous system, the levels through which it passes, the domains it traverses."[21] This mention of the "nervous system" of course resonates with the images of Aron's exposed nerve. The film visibly represents this violence—it makes it part of the narrative—but this does not foreclose its affective power. The camera shows Aron touching the nerve with his finger and his knife, and each time he shudders and screams in pain. But the film presents this in a manner that is far from the "realistic, documentary style" that has been attributed to it.[22] The camera jerks along as Aron shudders, as if to mirror his pain, and the editing is forceful and conspicuous, one might even say rhythmic, rapidly cutting between different angles. Above all, the noise of electronic grinding does violence to the film's soundtrack, overpowering the music, announcing its presence, and defying narrative logic. It is as if the film thematizes the violence of sensation: showing how images and sounds directly affect the nervous system. It gives form to this violence through an aggressive, harsh noise, which on the one hand communicates a character's unbearable pain, and on the other hand assaults the spectator with its radical unfamiliarity. One can never predict how different spectators will react to such scenes, of course, but the scene clearly stimulated intense physical reactions in the bodies of some spectators. Above all, it is the sound, which gives abrasive form to the plucking of a nerve, that communicates the scene's intensity. It is a dramatic presentation of cinema's capacity to generate affect through image and sound.

NOISE, INTENSITY, AND THE SLIPPERY NATURE OF SOUND

The use of sound in extreme cinema has been provocatively explored by Lisa Coulthard, who uses Chion's keen interest in Dolby digital surround sound—and the way it facilitates experimentation with silence and noise alike—as a springboard for an exploration of what she terms "haptic noise in new extremism."[23] In films such as Gaspar Noé's *Irreversible*, Claire Denis' *Trouble Every Day*, and Philippe Grandrieux's *Sombre*, Coulthard traces what she calls the "dirtying" of sound, a process of sonic manipulation that uses noise and drone to convey violence, decay, and death. Interestingly, according to Coulthard, in *Irreversible*, Noé and his sound designer employ a low-frequency rumbling in order to literally impact the bodies of spectators physically, to create vibrating resonance in their guts, and to make them feel nauseous.[24] As Michel Serres has pointed out, noise and nausea are etymologically related in French, as are "nautical" and "naval."[25]

We might say, then, that noise flows to the human body, where it is registered physically, and can induce feelings of nausea. Much of the theoretical writing on noise, including Serres as well as Jacques Attali, draws from information theory, with its discussion of signal and noise.[26] Noise is that which disrupts the signal; as static or interference, noise does violence to communication. Thus, for Attali, noise harbors radical potential, for noise "makes possible the creation of a new order on another level of organization, of a new code in another network."[27] In other words, noise can be simultaneously destructive and constructive. Crucially, for Attali, music—which we might think of here as a signal—depends upon noise for its existence, for "*music is a channelization of noise*."[28] Thus, communication, or language, is not separate from noise, but rather part of the same system, with noise being the frequently suppressed, or channeled, aspect of it. Through its disruptive power, though, noise can bring forward elements that might otherwise be relegated to the outside of the system. Though not interested in information theory, Deleuze's notion of the "outside of language"[29] is relevant here, for it too theorizes a force that transcends conventional modes of communication, creating something new. Here, language—the form that holds the system together—murmurs and trembles; it creates a new system, one of feelings and intensities.[30]

Coulthard has explored how the interaction between noise and music might affect spectators: "The blurring of noise and music works to construct cinematic bodies that move beyond their filmic confines to settle in shadowed, resounding form in the body of the spectator."[31] This is literally true in the case of *Irreversible*, which, when screened in a theater with a proper sound system, employs a low rumble that can be felt physically in the spectator's body. However, as we will see later through the work of Jean-Luc Nancy and

Douglas Kahn, the material of sound always on some level affects the auditor's body, resonating within it. The music that blurs with noise in Coulthard's formulation occurs within the context of films that fall under the category of the European New Extremism. *127 Hours* would not fit her classification for reasons beyond geography, as its aesthetic choices are too conventional. This extends to the musical score, which employs pop music, rather than the moody, experimental drones typically associated with European Extremism. But the grinding noise does blur with the musical score in *127 Hours*, over-powering it. Here, the pain of the character becomes all-consuming, drowning out all else and commanding the audience's attention. Perhaps it would be most productive to think of the musical score as an example of non-diegetic material, which might also describe the grinding noise, which is not audible within the world of the film. Or is it? Might the character be hearing this noise, as an index of his pain? Regardless, the noise seems to straddle the diegetic and the non-diegetic just as it seems to straddle the inside and outside of his body; it is a rupture between the two that, in its abrasiveness, has the capacity to affect the bodies of spectators just as it communicates the pain of characters.

Inside uses sound in a similar fashion, though this film fits comfortably within the more experimental confines of Coulthard's European New Extremity category. It is a remarkably violent, gory film and, as such, could be accused of wallowing in the violence of representation. However, its depiction of bodies, *in utero* and *in extremis*, is of great interest sonically. It is through sound, in particular, that the film approaches the violence of sensation. The scenes of visual violence are extremely auditory, maximizing the sonic potential of scissors piercing bellies and slicing throats, of blood spurting onto walls, and of lifeless bodies smacking into wooden floors. They are an excellent illustration of Chion's claim that "some kinds of rapid phenomena in images appear to be addressed to, and registered by, the *ear that is in the eye*, in order to be converted into auditory impressions in memory."[32] Hearing does in fact have the capacity to be intercepted by our visual cortex. For instance, neurological studies have shown that the practice of echolocation employed by some blind people (clicking, and listening to how it reverberates in their environment) stimulates not only auditory processing but visual processing as well.[33]

The film's plot is simple: an unnamed Woman violently kills everyone who stands in the way of her efforts to steal the fetus of a widowed pregnant woman named Sarah. These violent events all transpire over the course of a single night at Sarah's house, and the terrified young woman spends a good portion of the night hiding (or trapped) inside her bathroom. In one scene, while Sarah's boss tries to climb upstairs to come to her aid, the Woman stabs him from behind, the blade loudly puncturing his flesh. The blade repeatedly jabs his battered body as he gushes blood and screams in pain. The fleshy physicality of these sounds, which draw attention to the body's affinity with meat, a topic explored by Deleuze, would alone suffice to elicit negative affect for many spectators.[34] However, the invisible force of violent rage takes sonic form, too: as the Woman slashes and stabs, her motions are accompanied—and eventually overtaken—by an electronic scraping noise. It bears a faint family resemblance to the grinding in *127 Hours*, but here it takes on a distinctly anthropomorphic, or animalistic, character. But, if this sound has its origin in organic material, it is life that has been violently altered: it is as if vocal chords, vibrating rapidly, are aggressively scraped. But this would still sound too much like organic life; the scraped scream has been transmitted through a distorted amplifier.

The reader may note that the description of sounds, in *Inside* and *127 Hours*, is slippery, failing to declare definitively what a sound is. Instead, something "sounds like . . ." or "is akin to." Jean-Luc Nancy explains that sound "does not stem from a logic of manifestation."[35] Rather, "it stems from a different logic, which would have to be called evocation . . . a call and, in the call, breath, exhalation, inspiration, and expiration."[36] In terms of cinema, particularly when it comes to violent scenes in narrative films, this is doubly true, insofar as the sounds of violence are not indices of real violence that was done to real bodies. Of course, this also applies to visual representations of violence: the bodies that are stabbed, ripped apart, maimed, and consumed in horror films are not real human bodies, or at least the violence done to them is simulated, using all manner of analog or digital effects. Still, vision and audition operate quite differently. Even if a spectator recognizes that what he or she sees is not "real," the eye registers objects as a manifestation, a display, a "making evident."[37] With the ear, by contrast, there is "withdrawal and turning inward, a making *resonant*."[38] Images appear as objects, with a material surface that we can recognize, even if we understand that any violence done to living objects in a film is not actually occurring. According to Rey Chow and James A. Steintrager, "[s]ound, on the other hand, does not appear to stand before us but rather to come to or at us . . . objects as sonic phenomena are points of diffusion that in listening we attempt to gather."[39] We cannot so easily apprehend the source of sounds, and the way we experience them depends a great deal on how our bodies receive them and our minds process them. Sounds depend on affect, cognition, and—in the case of film, certainly—visual context.

Chion initiates a discussion of this contextual aspect of film sound in a description of Liliana Cavani's *The Skin* (1981). Chion recalls a scene in which a tank runs over a young boy, and the soundtrack contains "a ghastly noise that sounds like a watermelon being crushed."[40] Though he assumes that most spectators have never experienced the sound of a body destroyed in this manner, Chion suggests that "they may imagine that it has some of this humid, viscous quality."[41] At the same time, he points out, this exact sound could take on very different qualities in a comedy film: "[t]he same noise will be joyful in one context, intolerable in another."[42] He continues by describing a torture scene in Tarkovsky's *Andrei Rublev* (1966), in which boiling oil is forced down someone's throat, a violent act rendered sonically by the "atrocious sound of gargling," which could theoretically be put to very different use by Peter Sellers "in a Blake Edwards comedy."[43] These descriptions articulate the slippery nature of sound: it is difficult for the source of sounds to be self-evident, as further suggested by Chion's description of the noise not *as* the sound of a watermelon, but rather as something that sounds *like* a watermelon.

We may very well be suspicious of the claims above about the evidentiary nature of images and mutable nature of sounds. This might be particularly true in the cinematic context, even more so if one subscribes to Sergei Eisenstein's theory of montage as collision and conflict, a technique that uses the juxtaposition of images to create something greater than what the images would contain in isolation.[44] Imagine, however, that we were to alter Chion's scenario with the watermelon: what if Cavani's film were completely silent, without sound effects and without musical accompaniment? Would we still recognize the scene in question as a boy being smashed by a tank? Would it be as affective? Chion would certainly argue that it would not be—that the Foley work gives resonance to the scene, enabling the audience to "hear" the sound of a body being destroyed. Now, imagine a film that consists completely of black leader with a looped audio track of something that sounds "like" a watermelon being smashed. There are, in other words, no representational images and no objects that are self-evident. What might we make of this sound? Would it seem violent? Disgusting? Funny? Now imagine that the sequence of the boy and the tank is edited into the black leader and, several frames later, is followed by a comedy sequence. What qualities might the watermelon sound have now? Would we find it upsetting, and then find it funny? If the images were looped through again, or run in the inverse order, how might that alter our experience? What if we were now to continue watching the black leader with the looped sound of the watermelon? How might we hear the sound at this stage? Would it still sound like a watermelon?

An exemplary horror film that investigates the affective power of smashed fruit—and, more generally, the disorienting nature of sound—is Peter Strickland's *Berberian Sound Studio* (2012). A film about an English sound engineer hired to record and design the sound for a gruesome 1970s Italian horror movie called *The Equestrian Vortex* (think a Dario Argento or Lucio Fulci *giallo*), *Berberian Sound Studio* is notable for its absence of visual violence: the violent content in the film all takes place in the film within the film, which the audience never sees, except for an abstract opening credit sequence. Instead, *Berberian Sound Studio* consists primarily of scenes of the sound engineer, Gilderoy, doing Foley work while he watches scenes from *The Equestrian Vortex*. Sometimes the Italian director or producer explains to Gilderoy what he is about to see—with a particularly lurid example being a flaming poker shoved inside the vagina of an alleged witch—while at other times the audience must infer what Gilderoy sees on the basis of the evocative sound effects he generates. Either way, those scenes of Gilderoy sizzling grease, stabbing cabbages, and smashing melons all take on a sinister tone when one imagines the gory visuals they are meant to accompany, or perhaps stand in for. The process clearly takes a toll on Gilderoy himself, as his world (the diegetic world of *Berberian Sound Studio*) and that of *The Equestrian Vortex* begin to blur. *Berberian Sound Studio* cuts liberally between spaces and times, from the sound studio to Gilderoy's sleeping quarters, after the workday, where he continues to tinker with his recordings. The sounds of Gilderoy's recordings—screams, stabs, sizzles, and smashes—serve as the bridge between these different spaces and times, playing on the soundtrack as the image cuts from one setting to the next, and, eventually, between the different registers of diegesis. Sound becomes something that can break out of, transcend, and even rupture diegetic space, for Gilderoy becomes unable to determine whether he is a character in the film he is working on or the film that we, as the audience of *Berberian Sound Studio*, are watching. Gilderoy is disturbed by images, surely, but it is sound that truly unnerves him, that sticks with him and causes worlds to collapse.

A related idea is explored in Brad Anderson's *Sounds Like* (2006), an entry in the Showtime network's horror anthology series *Masters of Horror*, in which the protagonist has hyper-sensitive hearing such that he is incapacitated by the aural stimuli that surround him. As in *Berberian Sound Studio*, the protagonist begins to lose his grip on reality; the intrusion of noise seems to infect him, leading to irrational, dangerous behavior. This is sound literally doing violence to a human body—a gruesome consequence of the adage that "the ear has no eyelids."[45] Further, it is a forceful thematization of the ability of sound to penetrate space, to transcend and destroy barriers.

As Kiva Reardon has argued, *Inside*'s focus on the fleshy material of birth and the maternal body make the film highly attuned to questions of barriers, borders, and their permeability: inside/outside, life/death, self/other, subject/abject.[46] These questions are taken up in a very different fashion in *Dumplings*, Fruit Chan's entry in the 2004 omnibus film *Three Extremes*.[47] Like *Inside*, *Dumplings* is concerned with fetuses, although in this instance, fetuses are something to be aborted and consumed by women in order to defy the physical processes of aging. The theme of cannibalization has been connected by Winfried Menninghaus to "splatter videos," which "present . . . disgust-horror-porno excesses and seem bent on establishing cannibalism as the quintessence of exciting visual entertainment."[48] By linking horror and pornography, Menninghaus seems clearly to be referring to what we now call extreme cinema—and the focus on the disgusting taboo of cannibalism

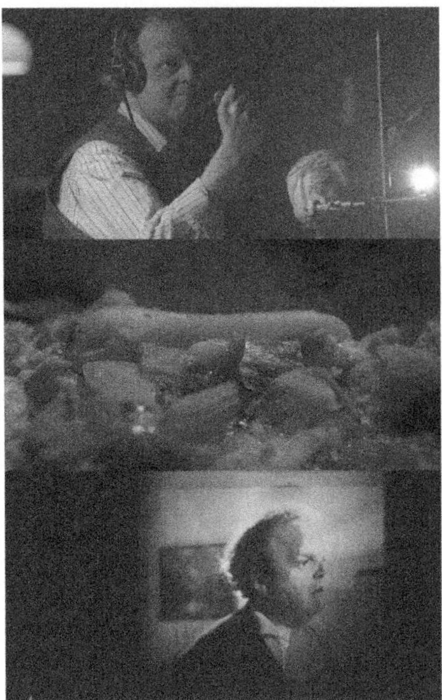

Figure 2.1 *Berberian Sound Studio*, Peter Strickland, 2012

does indeed place *Dumplings* within a rich tradition of extreme films.[49] Part of what sets *Dumplings* apart from earlier examples of exploitation cinema and from a film like *Inside*, which has a fairly stark palette, is its exquisite color photography. Shot by Christopher Doyle, who is most famous for his vibrant collaborations with Wong Kar-wai, *Dumplings* makes the disgusting palatable, as Doyle's camera moves freely throughout the space of the film, lovingly capturing every sensual detail. This attention to detail is particularly evident in the lush colors—of the sets, of the costumes, and of flesh.

Dumplings contains a few food preparation scenes, as Mei, the peddler of edible fetal matter, mashes and dices piles of tiny fetuses, which seem to have the color, consistency, and translucent quality of gelatin, intermingled in a polychromatic pile of red, white, and pink. In the preparation scenes, as she chops this formless mass of flesh, blood seeps out over the white cutting board, and the soundtrack features exaggerated noises of the cleaver slicing through gushy, gooey muscle and skin, and tiny, crunchy bones. Underpinning all of this noise is a non-diegetic sound, a rhythmic metallic screeching, like a wavering drone that echoes each successive chop of the cleaver. The colors are, quite simply, beautiful, but unnervingly so—a quality that the dissonant music underscores. Sound is most emphasized in scenes of eating, where Mei's client, Mrs. Li, slides the fetus-filled dumplings into and out of her mouth, every slurp amplified. As she chews the food, the soundtrack contains loud crunching sounds, as if to remind audiences and Mrs. Li alike that what she eats are the tiny bones, tendons, muscles, and decimated flesh of fetuses. Her slurps have an intriguing analog in the film's sole abortion scene, in which Mei relieves a teenage girl of her unwanted pregnancy, as bloody fetus and placental debris slop and splash into a tub. Thus, sonically, Mrs. Li's life is connected to this unnamed, stillborn fetus's death. The abortion is shot in a manner that obscures the most graphic imagery, as the film relies primarily upon sound to elicit disgust.[50]

Extreme cinema often calls upon sound to articulate what might simply be too explicit to render visually. The American horror films that have been labeled torture porn, such as the *Hostel* and *Saw* franchises, for instance, frequently convey the destruction of characters' bodies through sound: the crack and snap of broken bones and the pounding and ripping of meaty flesh. These sounds amplify the images that the films do show, and they provide evidence for the violent imagery that the film withholds. Thus, we might think of these fleshy noises as "meat sounds," to borrow from Linda Williams's discussion of "meat shots" in early pornographic stag films.[51] The sounds provide evidence of extreme physical acts, in this instance of bodies being hacked, sliced, twisted, and penetrated.

In Shion Sono's 2009 film *Love Exposure* a young woman, Koike, assumes a leadership role in a gang after her father vacates the position. We learn that as a child her father beat her. Following her father's stroke, Koike finds him unconscious, but she notices that his penis is erect. Grabbing ahold of her father's member, she snaps it; we see very little but the audio emphasizes the sounds of "cracking" sinews. Despite the restrictions to the visual field, the "snapping" serves as a meat sound, and the audio element is deeply affecting, likely to cause any number of different responses—anxious laughter, a non-linguistic utterance, cringing, or some combination of these. Koike, in the literal acquisition of phallic power, finds a pair of scissors and proceeds to cut off her father's penis. The castrated stump ejects jets of blood that drench Koike and the room. Although it is more fantastically exaggerated (in the spirit of manga), Koike's dismembering of her father finds certain affinities with scenes in *Antichrist* where there is a conflation of sexual discharge with blood (see Chapter 5). The jetting blood serves as a displacement for the money shot in porn—a climax to the earlier meat sounds.

More than the subjects of the other chapters, which negotiate some form of bodily expression—sexual emissions, laughter, tears—the topic of the present chapter, hearing, is nearly synesthetic in nature. Moreover, hearing is something that is *done* to the body, as opposed to being *from* it. Nonetheless, we contend that sound wields tremendous affective potential. The horror genre

Figure 2.2 *Love Exposure*, Shion Sono, 2008

relies heavily on non-diegetic sound to elicit a sense of dread in the spectator. Diegetic sounds in the horror genre—the tearing of sinew, the cracking of bones—have the power to induce disgust. The pornographic genre, or films that incorporate sexual content, all but demand the inclusion of orgasmic utterances—particularly from the female character, as the female orgasm is (typically) not visible. Like the meat shot, the supposed paroxysmal utterances, particularly during climax, lend evidence to what is invisible. Although orgasmic utterances, which can be faked or exaggerated, "meat sounds," like meat shots, still offer further evidence that the sexual encounter is genuine; the slop/slurp sounds serve as an index of the exchange of fluids, or penetration. "In one sense," Linda Williams agrees, "we could say that the close-up sound of pleasure attempts to offer the 'spectacular' aural equivalent of the close-ups of 'meat' and 'money.'" Williams, though, underscores that what we are calling "meat sounds" offers "none of the same guarantee of truth that the visual ejaculation does."[52] Nonetheless, bodily utterances are inherently intimate precisely because they come from *within* the subject that utters, and penetrate the one that hears:

> The allure of the sounds of pleasure resides at least partly in the fact that they come from inside the body and are often not articulate signs (meaningful combinations of sound and sense) but, rather, inarticulate sounds that speak, almost preverbally, of primitive pleasures. Although they seem to arise spontaneously, they are not involuntary as the "frenzy of the visible" of the male orgasm is.[53]

While our culture prizes visual erotics, sound greatly enhances the potential for arousal in the spectator. Music, singing, and incantations possess the seemingly mystical capacity to make the spectator's body run flush with goosebumps, to have hairs stand on end, to cause the spectator to inexplicably shed tears.

LISTENING TO *INSIDE*, AND THE OUTSIDE OF CINEMATIC LANGUAGE

As mentioned above, Nancy argues that listening is internalized. It is important to note that he distinguishes between hearing and listening. Hearing is a process of understanding and, as such, is something like the aural equivalent of "seeing" described above, in that it allows us to objectively recognize a sound: "to hear a siren, a bird, or a drum is already each time to understand at least the rough outline of a situation, a context if not a text."[54] Listening, on the other hand, is a more exploratory, open-ended process, wherein we are "straining toward a possible meaning, and consequently one that is not immediately accessible."[55] The use of the word "straining" is telling in this case, as it suggests a fully embodied action, a topic that we will return to later. Nancy's concept of listening aligns with Rey Chow and James Steintrager's articulation of sound as an "emanation" that "fill[s] the space around us. Objects as sonic phenomena are points of diffusion that in listening we attempt to gather."[56] Because this act of gathering takes work, Chow and Steintrager argue, it implies that listening is a personal, subjective experience. The listener tries to make sense of what he or she is listening to, to find context as well as text. This is especially relevant to sounds that have no obvious source, such as the grinding in *127 Hours* and the electronic scraping of *Inside*. The listener might struggle to find meaning in these sounds if they were heard in isolation. But, when paired with imagery, the sounds give the film a charge that the images alone would lack. Furthermore, they are sounds that are difficult to *hear*, both in common usage and in Nancy's usage. Put differently: these sounds are unpleasant and unsettling and, following Nancy, they are nearly impossible to attribute to a particular object. Perhaps they sound like something that can be articulated, or approximated, through descriptive language. What is most important, though, is what they *feel* like: intense pain and violent rage.

The scraping noise occurs at several points throughout *Inside*, and it is typically associated with the Woman's fits of violence. A notable exception is its final appearance, when a policeman, whom audience and characters alike had presumed dead, suddenly reappears, stumbling and with eyes gouged, as if he were a zombie. When Sarah approaches him, he screams and lurches forward, and the scraping noise—a sort of distorted amplified scream—shoots forth from the soundtrack, becoming intermingled with the diegetic screams of attacker and attacked. The cop smashes Sarah's belly, and the image cuts to a shot inside the womb, of the fetus cringing while the sound of rushing amniotic fluid washes over the loud crack of the nightstick. Fluid gushes from between Sarah's legs and hits the floor with a sloppy splash: did her water break, or is she having a miscarriage? The scraping continues, pulsating rhythmically, as Sarah, cop, and the Woman all scream. The Woman attacks the man with a blade, as the tight jabs of metal piercing flesh punctuate the screams and scrapes. The scraping continues, pulsing, until a close-up of the Woman's hand picking up the scissors. The sharp metallic sound of blade hitting blade rings out, abruptly stopping all other sounds.

This description hopefully communicates the idea that the sound design of *Inside* is sophisticated and complex, weaving together many layers of diegetic and non-diegetic sounds. The film depicts violence visually and explicitly, to be sure, but its use of sound is more nuanced: this is the violence of sensation. Perhaps the most exemplary sequence in this regard is one that occurs just after a scene of violent representation. After an intense struggle, Sarah has stabbed the Woman in the arm. After she flails and screams, the Woman sits outside the bathroom, attempting to calm down. She breathes heavily, as the camera shoots her in close-up. She lights a cigarette, and we hear the sound of singeing, crackling tobacco. The camera work becomes jagged and the image shudders. We hear rips and tears—is this the filmstrip being torn? Overlapping and intercut with these rips, crackles, and agitated breaths are subterranean rumbles, electronic clicks, and burns, the latter being echoed in the image by flames and flashes of color (a blue skull?). Image and sound surge and shudder irregularly until the loud clap of thunder silences all. This is filming the scream, not filming the horror—violence done to, and with, image and sound. Or, to borrow from another of Deleuze's essays, it is an instance in which the very language of cinema is made to "scream, stutter, stammer, or murmur."[57] For Deleuze, a work thus approaches the limit of representation and figuration; crucially, this is "the *outside of* language, but is not outside it."[58] Thus, the configuration of image and sound that is cinema—here shuddering and on the verge of rupture—approaches a form of language that is "as if the words could now discharge their content: a grandiose vision or a sublime sound."[59] This is art that trades not in concepts or meanings but in feelings— the expression of pleasure or pain.

A remarkably similar scene comes near the end of *Calvaire*, in a sequence that is particularly interesting because it is so clearly a homage to Tobe Hooper's *The Texas Chain Saw Massacre* (1974). The protagonist, Marc Stevens, has been trapped by Bartel, a lonely innkeeper who has decided, inexplicably, that Marc is his estranged wife. Dressed in the absent woman's clothes and tied to a chair for Christmas dinner, Marc sobs, squealing in pain and desperation. The camera spins around, and Bartel and his friend Boris, who is holding his pet "dog" (actually a cow), mock him, laughing. Marc begins to scream, which Bartel and Boris imitate, alternating between laughs and screams. The camera swirls around with increasing speed, and we hear what sounds like a rush of wind. Images blur and the voices overlap—it becomes difficult to distinguish who is screaming and laughing, and the sounds become increasingly guttural. Is the cow making sounds, too? As the camera continues swirling, we begin to hear clicking sounds and tight, compact whooshes of air, as streams of fluorescent color (presumably the Christmas lights) shoot across the screen, in very prominent counterpoint to the film's generally subdued color palette. The camera cuts to an extreme close-up of bloodshot eyes darting back and forth, as the soundtrack adds layer upon layer: muffled grunts, subterranean rumbles, and metallic clanging—perhaps Boris is clinking silverware to glass, making a perverted holiday toast? Images and sounds alike speed up, and a deep, buzzy bleat (the cow?) begins to drone until, suddenly, a gunshot and the shatter of glass halt the macabre reverie.

The scene remains very true to the spirit of the famous dinner scene in *The Texas Chain Saw Massacre*, which shows that horror films have been experimenting with form, and doing violence to image and sound, for far longer than the films of the New French Extremity.[60] This should not detract from *Calvaire*'s achievement, however. The scene differs radically from the style of the remainder of the film, which features muted colors, fairly static camera work (which is not to say no camera movement), and a relatively "realistic" sound design, which contains absolutely no non-diegetic music and tends to emphasize the ambient sounds of the landscape. The first inkling that something else is afoot comes in a scene when Marc has temporarily escaped from Bartel. Marc runs through the forest, as shown in a stunning (and fast!) tracking shot, in which many layers of trees stream across the frame—passing in front of, next to, and behind Marc's blurry figure. The whooshing of air seems to give sound to these blurs, but the sound cannot be easily located: it shifts, repeats, elongates, and becomes intermingled with an ominous rumble.

The sound that occurs just after the dinner scene is notable in a different way: a group of villagers besiege the house, killing Bartel and Boris, and raping Marc. They bring with them a pig, which squeals loudly and incessantly, as if in great pain. The animal's squeals are relentless, making it difficult to listen to anything else on the soundtrack (and there are other sounds: screams, and the sounds of dozens of footsteps sprinting across fields and forests). Again, this seems to be a continuation of the *Chain Saw* homage; after the dinner scene, the prototypical final girl, Sally, screams constantly as she runs from Leatherface, who howls and swings his ever-roaring chainsaw.[61] The pig's squeal in *Calvaire* might thus be understood as another scream, one that mixes with and enhances (and, perhaps, even stands in for) Marc's. The use of the scream in *Calvaire* does not only resemble *The Texas Chain Saw Massacre* in this instance, however. The macabre reverie of the dinner scene—with Marc's cries intermingling with Bartel's and Boris's mock screams and laughs—

strongly echoes the dinner scene in Hooper's film. But screams, cries, and laughs do not only blend on the level of multiple characters. In a sequence shortly after Bartel first mistakes Marc for his estranged wife, the former ties the younger man to a chair so that he can cut his hair. Marc pleads with Bartel, sobbing and convulsing in a manner that could easily be mistaken for laughter, or at least pleasure. The context suggests that Marc cries out of fear and pain, but this could not be determined from sound alone. There is resonance here with discussions of the sound of female orgasms in pornography, which are designed to provide evidence for female pleasure (to complement the "money shot" of male pleasure).[62] But, as John Corbett and Terri Kapsalis argue, it can be unclear if the "moans, shrieks, and cries [are] evidence of pleasure or pain."[63] Thus, the lines of representation become blurred, unable to cleanly convey meaning. Again, sound can be used to disrupt communication. This brings us, once again, to Chion, where we find that the scream can function in a manner similar to noise, overpowering all other sound and representing an intensity at the outside of language.

"THE SCREAMING POINT" AND THE BODY AS A RESONANCE CHAMBER

Chion articulates the concept of "the screaming point," which is ultimately a film's *raison d'être*, that instant where all elements converge in a single scream: "it is seen to saturate the soundtrack and deafen the listener."[64] Chion insists upon the scream being gendered—it must be a woman's—but let us qualify this and not fully accept it, for he is assuming a male filmmaker and a female character, operating under the traditional dynamics of patriarchy. It is, as he says, a question of mastery. The films we are discussing here were all directed by men, but in the case of *Calvaire*, the protagonist is a man mistaken for a woman and his/her scream becomes bound up with that of a pig. What is most interesting about Chion's description of this screaming point are the ways in which it resembles Deleuze's violence of sensation—Bacon's painting of the scream, and not the horror. Chion writes: "The screaming point is a point of the unthinkable inside the thought, of the indeterminate inside of the spoken, of unrepresentability inside representation."[65] He continues that it "gobbles everything up into itself . . . it is where speech is suddenly extinct, a black hole, the exit of being."[66] The scream, in other words, is something that defies narrative, language, structure; it is an invisible force made visible, it is the full flowering of rhythm. Through this black hole, the film consumes the spectator and the spectator consumes the film. It is, to borrow from Deleuze, "in direct contact with a vital power that exceeds every domain and traverses them all."[67] Chion insists that the screaming point is a singular event; it "explode[s] at a precise moment."[68] What happens, then, in cases such as *Calvaire* and *Chain Saw*, when the scream does not stop, when it is elongated into something that must be endured, by character and audience alike?

Nancy traces the various ways in which one can say "listening" in French: from *écouter* ("to listen") to *auscultare* ("to lend an ear"). He concludes: "To listen is *tender l'oreille*—literally, to stretch the ear . . . it is an intensification and a concern, a curiosity or an anxiety."[69] Thus, the act of listening becomes both an action of nervous intensity and one that connotes the movement of the body. The ways in which sounds affect their sources as well as the bodies of their auditors is already implicit within the phrase "to lend an ear," but it becomes clearer when Nancy further elaborates the differences between vision and audition. He explains that "the visual is tendentially mimetic, and the sonorous tendentially methexic (that is, having to do with participation, sharing, or contagion)."[70] We might productively link this to an earlier discussion, in which Nancy contrasts the image's logic of manifestation with sound's logic of evocation. But methexis brings additional elements, putting the creator of sound and the listener(s) to sound into a circuit with one another. Most provocative is the suggestion of "contagion," which may help illuminate the ways in which the relentless squeal of the pig not only signifies that animal's agitation, but comes to infect the mind and body of an agitated listener/ spectator.

A scream is also the most extreme iteration of a person's voice—one might say that it is a vocalization that takes the form of noise—and, for all its communicable elements, is experienced as a singular phenomenon by the one who utters it. A screamer may very well hear the scream through his or her ears, as the sound waves reflect off nearby surfaces and travel back, but he or she— above all—hears it in his or her body.[71] Douglas Kahn has suggested that the origin of modernist hearing is Comte de Lautréamont's *Le Chants de Maldoror* (1868), in which a deaf man gains the capacity to hear only after experiencing a scene of unbelievable horror. As Kahn explains, "[t]he scream created his hearing."[72] Building off this notion of a fully embodied hearing (and one that is linked to horror no less), Kahn explains that speakers hear their own voices "conducted from the throat and mouth through bone to the inner regions of the ear. Thus, the voice is . . . propelled through the body."[73] The body becomes, therefore, not only the place where sounds originate; it is also an organ for the reception and transmission of sound. It is a space of resonation.

We began to approach this concept, of the body as a vessel for sound, in Goodman's discussion of sonic triggers and gut reactions. But it is Nancy who fully explores the implications of the body as a "resonance chamber."[74] For Nancy, this resonance is something "beyond sense" and "beyond signification."[75] Though Nancy does not say as much, this "beyond signification" and "beyond-meaning" could be understood as the invisible forces of sensation, of color and rhythm. This link becomes more forceful when Nancy, following Deleuze, invokes Antonin Artaud's concept of the body "without organs."[76] This body is, for Deleuze, one of "flesh and nerve," a suggestive phrase for our discussion of the sound of flayed bodies and exposed nerves.[77] For Nancy, this resonant chamber, the body without organs, is opened up, vibrating, echoing, bringing the listening subject close to that which is "beyond-meaning."[78] What lies "beyond meaning" is inherently difficult to grasp: life, death, pain. Yet sound seems to bring us close to these things, through the grinding of an exposed nerve, through noise, through the scream. Allen Weiss explains that Artaud saw the scream as a gesture of violence through which life and death alike could be accessed and worked through: "The scream is the expulsion of an unbearable, impossible internal polarization between life's force and death's negation, simultaneously signifying and simulating creation and destruction."[79]

CONCLUSION: WHEN A SCREAM BECOMES A CRY

Is this not similar to Chion's "screaming point," the black hole where all elements converge? *Inside*, as we have seen, is full of screams, but if there is an ultimate moment, it is Sarah's death/her child's birth—where one being's final scream leads to another's first cry. Nancy describes the body's resonance as "womb-like," going further to conclude: "it is always in the belly that we—man or woman—end up listening, or start listening. The ear opens onto the sonorous cave that we then become."[80] It is through sound, then, that we come into being. We hear what is outside, through another's body, and when we exit, we cry. *Inside* begins, literally, in the womb, in this sonorous cave, as a fetus swims in amniotic fluid. There is the sound of a woman's voice, muffled, through a rumbling barrier of liquid and solid, meat and flesh. She claims ownership, stating that no one can take this tiny creature away from her, and then, suddenly, come the sounds of a rush of air and fluid, a crash, and the smack of the baby's head. Blood trickles into the amniotic fluid. It is in this womb that we hear life become death.

A spectator is born in his or her encounter with a film. Extreme horror films stage scenes of incredible violence, of bodies being sliced, pummeled, eviscerated, and extinguished. These images resonate with the sounds of meat being cut and flesh being ripped, of harsh scraping and subterranean rumbling. And, of course, with screams. Cinema history has no shortage of references to Plato's Allegory of the Cave.[81] In the twenty-first century, people still gather in vast dark spaces to experience projected images and sounds—though in far smaller numbers than in decades past. People now consume movies through many different screens and in many different settings. Perhaps, then, the darkened chamber that is most important is not the theater, but the body of the spectator. He or she sees images of extreme violence, and takes the sounds within. The sounds echo and reverberate; they pulse throughout the body, and are felt in the gut. The film and the spectator share these sounds; they come together and share the scream.

NOTES

1. Eugenie Brinkema first brought this scene to my (Knapp) attention. This chapter developed out of a series of conversations with Brinkema and, as a result, it was shaped considerably by her insights.
2. See, for instance, on horror, David Edelstein, "Now Playing at Your Local Multiplex: Torture Porn," *New York*, <http://nymag.com/movies/features/15622/> (last accessed May 19, 2015). On art film, see James Quandt, "Flesh & Blood: Sex and Violence in Recent French Cinema," in *The New Extremism in Cinema: From France to Europe*, eds. Tanya Horeck and Tina Kendall (Edinburgh: Edinburgh University Press, 2011), 18–25.
3. For an example, see John Horn, "Some Viewers Need a Hand after the Forearm Amputation in '127 Hours,'" *Los Angeles Times*, <http://articles.latimes.com/2010/oct/31/entertainment/la-et-arm-movie-20101031> (last accessed May 19, 2015).
4. Michel Chion, *Audio-vision: Sound on Screen*, trans. Claudia Gorbman (New York: Columbia University Press, 1994), 137.
5. Ibid., 136.
6. Steve Goodman, *Sonic Warfare: Sound, Affect, and the Ecology of Fear* (Cambridge, MA: MIT Press, 2010), 48.
7. Horn.
8. For an edited volume devoted solely to the subject, see: Philip Hayward (ed.), *Terror Tracks: Music, Sound and Horror Cinema* (London: Equinox, 2009).
9. Carol Clover, *Men, Women, and Chain Saws: Gender in the Modern Horror Film* (Princeton: Princeton University Press, 1992), 35.
10. Greg Hainge, *Noise Matters: Towards an Ontology of Noise* (New York: Bloomsbury, 2013), 85.
11. Horn.
12. Anna Powell, *Deleuze and Horror Film* (Edinburgh: Edinburgh University Press, 2005), 5.
13. Angela Ndalianis, *The Horror Sensorium: Media and the Senses* (Jefferson, NC: McFarland, 2012), 6.
14. Marco Abel, *Violent Affect: Literature, Cinema, and Critique After Representation* (Lincoln: University of Nebraska Press, 2007), x.
15. Gilles Deleuze, *Francis Bacon: The Logic of Sensation*, trans. Daniel W. Smith (Minneapolis: University of Minnesota Press, 2003), 34.
16. Ibid., 9.
17. "Rhythm," s.v. *OED*.
18. Deleuze, xxix.
19. Ibid., 34.
20. Gilles Deleuze, "He Stuttered," in *Essays Critical and Clinical*, trans. Daniel W. Smith and Michael A. Greco, 107–14 (London: Verso, 1998).
21. Deleuze, *Francis Bacon*, 34–5.

22. Horn. Also see an interview with Aron Ralston, in which he claims: "The movie is so factually accurate it is as close to a documentary as you can get and still be a drama." Quoted in Patrick Barkham, "The Extraordinary Story behind Danny Boyle's *127 Hours*," *Guardian*, <http://www.theguardian.com/film/2010/dec/15/story-danny-boyles-127-hours> (last accessed May 20, 2015).

23. Lisa Coulthard, "Dirty Sound: Haptic Noise in New Extremism," in *The Oxford Handbook of Sound and Image in Digital Media*, eds. Carol Vernallis, Amy Herzog, and John Richardson (New York: Oxford University Press, 2013), 115–26.

24. Ibid., 117–18.

25. Michel Serres, *Genesis*, trans. Geneviève James and James Nielson (Ann Arbor: University of Michigan Press, 1995), 12–13. There is something quite interesting here in the etymology: Lucien Castaing-Taylor and Verena Paravel's 2012 film *Leviathan* is a documentary set on a fishing vessel. Much of the film was shot on a Go-Pro camera, allowing the filmmakers to get extreme close-ups of bins filled with fish guts, bulging fish eyes, blood and seawater. The sloppy, slurpy diegetic sound design emphasizes the indiscernibility of inside/outside, the geography of fish bodies. *Leviathan* has the potential to elicit queasiness, and thus shares certain affinities with the "nautical" and its close proximity to "sea sickness."

26. For a useful introduction to Serres's ideas, including his use of this information theory, see Cary Wolfe, "Introduction to the New Edition: Bring the Noise: *The Parasite* and the Multiple Genealogies of Posthumanism," in *The Parasite*, trans. Lawrence R. Schehr (Minneapolis: University of Minnesota Press, 2007), xi–xxv.

27. Jacques Attali, *Noise: The Political Economy of Music*, trans. Brian Massumi (Minneapolis: University of Minnesota Press, 1985), 33.

28. Ibid., 26

29. Deleuze, "He Stuttered," 112.

30. This invites an intriguing analogy with Kristeva's heterogeneity of language: where the semiotic and the Symbolic are intertwined. Where noise finds affinities with the semiotic, and signal with the Symbolic.

31. Coulthard, 121.

32. Chion, *Audio-vision*, 135.

33. See the incredible story of Daniel Kish, a blind person who uses echolocation, on the NPR program *Invisibilia*. Kish claims that he is able to see, despite the fact that he has no eyes. The neuroscientist Lore Thaler reminds us, "In the end, the image, it's something that your mind constructs." See "Batman Pt. 2," *Invisibilia* (January 22, 2015). Available at <http://www.npr.org/2015/01/23/379134701/batman-pt-2> (last accessed November 29, 2015).

34. See Deleuze, *Francis Bacon*, especially 19–24.

35. Jean-Luc Nancy, *Listening*, trans. Charlotte Mandell (New York: Fordham University Press, 2007), 20.

36. Ibid.

37. Ibid., 3.

38. Ibid.

39. Rey Chow and James A. Steintrager, "In Pursuit of the Object of Sound: An Introduction," in *differences: The Sense of Sound* [Special Issue] 22, nos. 2 and 3 (2011): 2.

40. Chion, *Audio-vision*, 22.

41. Ibid.

42. Ibid., 23.

43. Ibid., 23–4.

44. See Sergei Eisenstein, "A Dialectic Approach to Film Form," in *Film Form*, ed. and trans. Jay Leyda (New York: Harvest, 1949), 45–63.
45. This statement has been variously attributed to Malcolm de Chazal and Pascal Quignard.
46. Kiva Reardon, "Subject Slaughter," *Cinephile* 8, no. 2 (Fall 2012): 18–25.
47. Other than the film by Chan, who is from Hong Kong, the other two films in *Three Extremes* are *Cut* by Park Chan-wook, from South Korea, and *Box* by Takashi Miike, from Japan.
48. Winfried Menninghaus, *Disgust: The Theory and History of a Strong Sensation*, trans. Howard Eiland and Joel Golb (New York: SUNY Press, 2003), 12.
49. See, for instance, the heyday of 70s/80s exploitation: *Last Cannibal World* (Ruggero Deodato, 1977), *Emmanuelle and the Last Cannibals* (Joe D'Amato, 1977), *Cannibal Holocaust* (Ruggero Deodato, 1980), *Eaten Alive!* (Umberto Lenzi, 1980), *Mondo cannibale* (Jesus Franco, 1981), and *Cannibal Ferox* (Umberto Lenzi, 1981). For a more recent example that sits more comfortably under contemporary Extreme Cinema, see *Trouble Every Day* (Claire Denis, 2001).
50. Consider also the birth of the central character, Jean-Baptiste Grenouille, in Tom Tykwer's 2006 film *Perfume: The Story of a Murderer*, where the birth of the child is rhythmically cut with sloppy sounds of animal guts, maggot-infested meat (amplifying the sound of burrowing maggots), and other moist objects.
51. Linda Williams, *Hard Core: Power, Pleasure, and the "Frenzy of the Visible"* (Berkeley: University of California Press, 1989), 72–3.
52. Ibid., 124–5. Analyzing *The Sounds of Love* (Alan Vydra, 1981)—featuring a protagonist on a quest to record "the most powerful, natural, and spontaneous of orgasms"—Williams finally concludes that the film "merely underscores the fact that visual and aural voyeurism are very different things. The attempt to 'foreground' the sounds of pleasure fails. As Mary Ann Doane points out in 'The Voice in the Cinema' (1980, 39), sound cannot be 'framed' as the image can, for sound is all over the theater, it '*envelops* the spectator.' It is this nondiscrete, enveloping quality that, when added to the close-miked, nonsynchronous sounds of pleasure, seems particularly important in the hard-core auditory-viewer's pleasure in sound." Williams, 125.
53. Ibid., 126. Williams continues: "This apparent spontaneity is particularly important in the pornographic quest to represent the female desires and pleasures that come from 'deep inside.' *Deep Throat* is but one of many films and tapes to pose this problem, in which 'depth' becomes a metaphor for getting underneath deceptive appearances. Thus depth of sound does not lend itself to the same illusion of involuntary frenzy as that offered by the visible. Nevertheless, although there can be no such thing as hard-core sound, there remains the potential . . . for performers to converse with one another, in articulate or inarticulate vocables, about their pleasure." Williams, 126.
54. Nancy, 6.
55. Ibid.
56. Chow and Steintrager, 2.
57. Deleuze, "He Stuttered," 110.
58. Ibid., 112.
59. Ibid., 113.
60. It should be noted that *Calvaire* is actually a Belgian film.
61. It seems likely that the combination of a man, raped in the backwoods by other men, and the squealing of a pig is also a homage to the (in)famous scene in *Deliverance* (John Boorman, 1972), in which the character played by Ned Beatty is forced to "squeal like a pig!" by his rapist.

62. See Williams, *Hard Core*.

63. John Corbett and Terri Kapsalis, "Aural Sex: The Female Orgasm in Popular Sound," in *Experimental Sound and Radio*, ed. Allen S. Weiss (Cambridge, MA: MIT Press, 2001), 103.

64. Michel Chion, *The Voice in Cinema*, trans. Claudia Gorbman (New York: Columbia University Press, 1999), 77.

65. Ibid.

66. Ibid., 79.

67. Deleuze, *Francis Bacon*, 37.

68. Chion, *The Voice in Cinema*, 77.

69. Nancy, 5.

70. Ibid., 10.

71. It is worth noting here that the term "screamer" in the common vernacular can refer to a woman who vocalizes her orgasms particularly loudly. This would be yet another iteration of a scream that is felt in the body.

72. Douglas Kahn, *Noise, Water, Meat: A History of Sound in the Arts* (Cambridge, MA: MIT Press, 1999), 6.

73. Ibid., 7.

74. Nancy, 31.

75. Ibid.

76. Ibid.

77. Deleuze, *Francis Bacon*, 40.

78. Nancy, 31.

79. Allen S. Weiss, *Phantasmic Radio* (Durham, NC: Duke University Press, 1995), 24.

80. Nancy, 37.

81. For a recent example, see Nathan Andersen, *Plato's Cave and Cinema* (New York: Routledge, 2014).

CHAPTER 3

Pain: Exploring Bodies, Technology, and Endurance

The unleashed desire to kill that we call war goes far beyond the realm of religious activity. Sacrifice though, while like war a suspension of the commandment not to kill, is the religious act above all others.[1]

— Georges Bataille

INTRODUCTION: TORTURE CHAMBERS, TORTURE PORN, AND THE NOSTALGIA FOR BODIES

The torture chamber is a common trope associated with the American torture porn cycle. A space specifically designed for the execution of pain is also present in many extreme films. The cinematic torture chamber—like the spaces used for sacred rituals—is frequently associated with the transformation of a character. The torture chamber tends to be a hermetic space, and more than this a non-place, sequestered from the day-to-day civilized world— what Michel Foucault called a heterotopia. Set in contrast to utopias, heterotopias are "sites with no real place"; they exist contiguous with the inhabited world, and yet are set apart, sequestered.[2]

In the spirit of earlier generic horror conventions, the torture chamber can also be read as an uncanny site, along the lines of the haunted house, or "terrible place."[3] Interestingly, Evangelos Tziallas observes that torture porn replaces horror's (and particularly the slasher film's) typical preoccupation with phallic weapons with "the overwhelming presence of 'vagina dentata' or 'vaginal weaponry.'"[4] The torture chamber threatens to (re)absorb the body, to consume it, and in that sense returns us to the site of the generative mother.[5]

In torture porn the torture chamber-cum-womb witnesses the transformation of characters as (perverse) paternal agents—and they generally emerge, like a baby, from the monstrous site bloody, gasping, and crying. In extreme cinema, characters very well might emerge transformed, and surface from their ordeal like a gangly baby, but more often than not they are completely wrecked subjects. *The Human Centipede* ultimately produces a (dying) "centipede," and *Frontier(s)* concludes with Yasmine's blood-drenched spasmodic walk. In *Martyrs* Lucie is wracked with haunting visions and Anna is brought to the threshold of life and death, while Milos in *A Serbian Film* destroys everything he loves.

The cinematic torture chamber is the stage upon which painful spectacles are executed—and the excesses of these violent pageants generally overwhelm conventional narrative regimes.[6] The overripe spectacles of pain intend to elicit a visceral response in the spectator. In many ways, the *meaning* of torture porn—if one wants to call it that—*is* the spectacle and the way that it affects viewers, making them shudder and cringe at the scenes of pain and mutilation; the spectator's involuntary spasms echo (however faintly) those of the bodies onscreen. But the films do not completely disregard narrative; rather, as Matt Hills argues, they fuse form and content: "part of *Saw*'s success . . . lies in [the] extreme condensation of narrative and spectacle via traps."[7] A key element of the narrative embedded within these traps—and within the torture scenes in the *Hostel* films as well—seems to be a story of cultural loss, a nostalgic longing for a past America of industrial prowess. The gateway to this past, it would seem, is a return to the body and to signifiers of the industrial era. Linda Williams's analysis of the "body genres" offers an entry into the narratives embedded within the traps and torture scenes of *Saw* and *Hostel*, the two film series at the heart of the torture porn cycle and, indeed, in American horror film at the beginning of the twenty-first century.

Williams argues that the systems of excess that one finds in the genres of hardcore (pornography), horror, and melodrama are not gratuitous, but instead serve very specific functions, for the "deployment of sex, violence, and emotion is . . . a cultural form of problem solving."[8] In hardcore, she argues, the problem is sex and the solution is "more, different, or better sex," while the problem and solution in horror both revolve around "violence related to sexual difference."[9] "In women's films," Williams finds, "the pathos of loss is the problem, repetitions and variations of this loss are the generic solution."[10] Williams roots her analysis in issues related to gender identity; though torture porn does not avoid questions of gender, this is not the primary focus of the films, as men are just as likely as women to be the tortured—and thus have their bodies on display. If we were to construct a statement about torture porn in terms of problems and solutions, it would read something like: "The problem is a disconnect from the body, and the solution is a radical return to the body, as seen through displays of torture and mutilation." Though gender is perhaps not as important to torture porn as it is to hardcore pornography, melodrama, and slasher films (the type of horror Williams focuses on in her essay "Film Bodies"), torture porn is nonetheless rooted strongly, almost defiantly, in the body. Williams discusses the body genres in terms of fantasy, temporality, and loss, which proves illuminating in this context.

In her essay, Williams makes a "connection between [Jean] Laplanche and [J. B.] Pontalis's structural understanding of fantasies as myths of origins which try to cover the discrepancy between two moments in time and the distinctive temporal structure of these particular genres."[11] In making this connection, Williams argues that the body genres are all a means to explore childhood fantasies and loss. Hardcore explores "the enigma of the origin of sexual desire," solved by seduction (or sex), horror explores sexual difference, solved by castration, and melodrama explores "our melancholic sense of the loss of origins."[12] Torture porn is ultimately also concerned with melancholic loss, but in this case the origin in question is not childhood, but a collective American past, when Americans were more connected to their physical bodies and when "work" meant physical labor, not the less visible or abstract forms of today that revolve around digital technologies. In other words—to borrow from Slavoj Žižek's analysis of the terrorist event of 9/11—torture porn is a cinematic "strategy to return to the Real of the body" and it achieves this by displaying bodies in pain, which in turn causes spectators to become more aware of their own bodies.

This is yet another iteration of Williams's argument that horror is one of the "body genres" (as well as pornography, and melodrama), in which "the body of the spectator is caught up in an almost involuntary mimicry of the emotion or sensation of the body on the screen."[13] The visceral affects of body genres rely not only on what is seen, but also on what is heard. The aural signifiers that slop/slurp generally signify, whether in pornography or horror, the traversal of boundaries, and the exchange/expulsion/loss of bodily fluids. In torture porn, then, we witness highly embellished audio designs: dripping blood, the splash of vomit, seeping pipes in ruined industrial sites, and the ever-present cliché of dripping water in subterranean torture facilities. All these things work to embellish the scenes of torture and amplify the sensational experience for the spectator.[14]

To elaborate how time works in the various body genres, Williams argues that hardcore corresponds to the temporal structure of "on time," horror corresponds to "too early," and melodrama corresponds to "too late." Hardcore is "on time" because it depicts characters coming together "now" through sex, while the "too early" in horror refers to the fact that the monster frequently catches the victim off guard and attacks before he or she is ready. The "too late" of melodrama comes about because "the quest for connection is always tinged with the melancholy of loss."[15] Torture porn seems to be a strange confluence of all three temporal structures: the victims are captured because they are not ready (too early), while the physical suffering that results from their capture, which the films depict in excruciating detail, correlates to the pleasure of hardcore's "now." And infusing it all—as is made evident through an emphasis on rust, abandoned factories, and other modern (mid-twentieth-century) industrial signifiers—is a nostalgic tinge of melancholy (too late).

Haunting torture porn's rusty, abandoned factories is the specter of past labor, the physicality of human bodies, a notion that becomes clearer when the films are put into dialogue with Slavoj Žižek's response to 9/11. In response to the destruction of the World Trade Center, Žižek and Jean Baudrillard each suggested that the terrorist event *fulfilled* an American fantasy, or at least erupted from the ideological system that governs it. Unsurprisingly, these ideas sparked anger, which was perhaps a reasonable reaction, but one that served to obscure the content of Baudrillard's and Žižek's arguments. Both scholars suggest that contemporary culture—which is characterized by the US-dominated global capitalist system—had become a numbing void that only an event (such as the terrorist event) could puncture. Baudrillard argues that the desire for the destruction of the global superpower exists not only within the powerless, but also within those who benefit from the system: "no one can avoid dreaming of the destruction of any power that has become hegemonic to this degree."[16] One of the ways in which Americans "dreamed" of this event was through movies: "The countless disaster movies bear witness to this fantasy . . . [and] the universal attraction they exert . . . is on par with pornography."[17] Žižek argues something similar: "And was not the attack on the World Trade Center with regard to Hollywood catastrophe movies like snuff pornography versus ordinary sadomasochistic porno movies?"[18]

This shared linkage to pornography finds a strong echo in torture porn—and, indeed in extreme cinema more generally. If, per Žižek, we can understand 9/11 as "a violent return to the passion for the Real,"[19] perhaps we might also understand torture porn and other forms of extreme cinema in this way. The parallels become particularly strong through Žižek's brief discussion of "cutters"—those individuals, typically young women, who lacerate their skin with razors or knives. This form of physical mutilation, of the destruction of the body, clearly resonates with the violence of the torture porn cycle, particularly the *Saw* series, which revolves around the figure of John Kramer, a.k.a. Jigsaw, a serial killer who technically does not kill anyone; rather, he entraps his victims and compels them to play meticulously constructed, violent games in which they harm themselves and one another.[20] Žižek finds the phenomenon of cutting "strictly parallel to the virtualization of our environment" that led to the rupture of the terrorist event: "it represents a desperate strategy to return to the Real of the body." Torture porn, it would seem, is a cinematic strategy to return to this Real of the body, too. And many critics would not hesitate to call it "desperate." We are not concerned here with the level of artistry found in torture porn and other forms of extreme cinema. At the center of extreme cinema is the human body, both the bodies of the actors onscreen and those of the spectators who react to the visual and aural stimulation. If, as Žižek argues, the beginning of the twenty-first century is characterized by feelings of dislocation or alienation from the body, then extreme cinema is a violent return to it.

While violently returning to the body, many torture porn films—particularly the *Saw* series, but *Hostel* as well—fetishize old, rusty technologies that predate the digital era. "Newer" technologies, most typically surveillance technology, video, and audiotape (the way that Jigsaw communicates to all his victims), are frequently depicted as either useless or deceptive. Catherine Zimmer argues that the *Saw* films use surveillance footage to blur the boundaries between torturer and tortured and to confuse Jigsaw's victims as well as the audience.[21] In *Saw II*, Detective Eric Matthews tries to save his son from one of Jigsaw's games, which he sees play out on a computer monitor in Jigsaw's lair. At the end of the film, we learn that the surveillance footage came from a pre-recorded tape used to manipulate and misdirect Matthews. Zimmer argues that this "temporal ambiguity opens up the space for—even demands—torture as a wishfully ahistorical call to violent bodily presence . . . [for] in *Saw* and torture films, violence is a moment of clarity."[22] Zimmer's language here bears a striking resemblance to Žižek's: "the 'postmodern' passion for semblance ends up in a violent return to the passion for the Real."[23] Postmodern ambiguity has led to confusion and numbness, which can only be resolved through a violent embodiment. Zimmer speaks of a violent moment of clarity, while Žižek explains that "authenticity resides in the act of violent transgression, from the Lacanian Real . . . to the Bataillean excess."[24] Žižek then describes this passion for the Real as it manifests in hardcore (in extreme close-ups of female anatomy); we might posit, then, that torture porn, in its intense (some might say "excessive") focus on bodies in pain and in its constant return to the tools of the industrial age, is yet another manifestation of this passion. And, as we have learned through Williams's discussion of body genres, the spectacle that is in "excess" of the narrative is actually integral to the system through which the films function.

The *Hostel* films hint at twenty-first-century technology's ability to confuse most directly in the first film, in which the three males who become commodities within the torture economy are repeatedly duped by staged digital photographs displayed on cell phones. Digital photographs lead them to Slovakia, where nubile women will supposedly offer their bodies for sex, and digital images convince the two Americans that their Icelandic friend has left the hostel (when in fact he has already been tortured and killed). In *Saw V*, it is the use of a cell phone that allows Detective Mark Hoffman to frame Special Agent Peter Strahm as Jigsaw's accomplice. These films seem to suggest that newer, digital technologies are best used to confuse, deceive, and disconnect.

The spectacle of people tortured with mechanical traps and tools, by contrast, offers a violent form of embodiment, a sudden connection to the Real.

One might ask what, if anything, torture porn films propose as the constructive solution to our contemporary alienation. Jigsaw certainly seems to believe that his games are a gift to his victims, a "second chance" at life. Yet the games almost always—even if played correctly—result in horrific pain and disfigurement. At best, his approach amounts to construction through destruction.[25] Jigsaw's philosophy seems, then, to be quite reactionary and conservative. As Matt Hills argues, torture porn is best understood as politically incoherent.[26] One of the ways in which the *Saw* franchise achieves this incoherence, Hills suggests, is by allowing audiences to read themselves within the figure of the torturer or the tortured—and perhaps both simultaneously. Jason Middleton argues that the key to the *Hostel* films is an inversion of the typical American position of dominance (although he explains that the films ultimately undercut their critique): "both [*Hostel*] films' narrative structures are premised upon a reversal of positions between exploiter and exploited."[27] Middleton compares this inversion to that which occurs in *The Texas Chain Saw Massacre*, wherein "the consumers and exploiters of working-class labor, literally become the consumed: hung up on meat hooks, they take the place of the fetishized commodity."[28] Following this line of thought, Middleton argues that the repressed that violently returns in the *Hostel* films is not labor (as in *Chain Saw*) but "the United States' dirty business in the 'war on terror'—the abuses that are intended to stay hidden from view."[29] Middleton notes, however, that *Hostel*, like *The Texas Chain Saw Massacre*, likens its characters to commodities and, in fact, images of meat were used in the films' promotion.[30] Of course, by focusing so intently on bodies being ripped apart and mutilated, *Saw*, *Hostel*, and other examples of extreme cinema show the human body as just another form of meat.

Interestingly, meat plays a significant, if subtle, role in the narrative of the *Saw* series. Each of Jigsaw's victims has a critical flaw, and the rationale behind his torture is that those who succeed and survive will be rehabilitated; they will come to cherish their lives. Jigsaw's traps are highly elaborate, and each one seems to offer more spectacular scenes of pain and death, a major part of the franchise's appeal to fans.[31] In one of *Saw III*'s main storylines, Jeff must traverse a series of rooms containing people who were either responsible for his son's death or in some way aided the perpetrator's early release from prison. To advance, and succeed, he must forgive each person and save him or her from death. In one room, the judge responsible for the killer's brief sentence is chained to the bottom of a vat rapidly filling with liquefied pig guts. As Jeff decides whether to save the man, one rotting pig corpse after another streams in on a conveyor belt, drops into a grinder, and spews out as brown sludge that envelops the judge. As only one of many torture scenes throughout the *Saw* series, this is not as pointed a return of the repressed as one sees in *The Texas Chain Saw Massacre*, but it is nonetheless a dark reminder of the "dirty business" of the meat industry, which most Americans would prefer to ignore. It bears mentioning here that the idea of consumers having lost touch with the origins of their food—meat—is verbalized, twice, in *Hostel* by a Dutch businessman, a client of the torture syndicate with a penchant for eating with his hands rather than a fork.

The *Saw* films do not draw as direct a parallel to the meat industry, and thus the labor class, as *The Texas Chain Saw Massacre*, but the specter of labor—indeed of modern industry in general, and its decline—seems to hover over the films. Jigsaw's former profession was that of a civil engineer, and his first completed project was the Gideon Meat Packing building. It was so important to him, evidently, that he had planned to name his son (who died in utero) after it; the Gideon building, now abandoned, serves as the site for many of the torture games, including the above-mentioned pig scene. In the second *Saw* film, the police track down Jigsaw at his headquarters, the abandoned Wilson Steel Factory. It is as if Jigsaw forces his victims, and the audience, to remember the American industries of yesteryear, which—in the information-based global economy—have now been abandoned in favor of cheaper labor abroad and the "start-up" culture of Silicon Valley.

Jigsaw's traps bear the mark of his background in civil engineering. They are, more often than not, *mechanical*; he frequently describes the torture devices as the "tools" to his victims' salvation. Though the series takes place in the present day—a culture bombarded with technology—the *Saw* films, and Jigsaw's schemes, are defiantly low tech. This does not mean that Jigsaw's traps are simple, however; on the contrary, they are quite intricate. Their function revolves around pulleys, pendulums, and gears—the machinery of the industrial age. Each game, or test, is strictly timed, with the countdown on a clock always prominently displayed. Jigsaw seems to be obsessed with time; in a flashback sequence in *Saw IV*, he shows his wife the elements of his new work space, particularly marveling at the still-ticking "mechanism inside" a 300-year old clock, which has "stood the test of time." Jigsaw's fetishization of clocks resonates with Williams's discussion of temporal structures in body genres, and particularly with the "too late" of melodrama.

Even though the clock is a pre-modern technology, it still has great usefulness in the "now": all of Jigsaw's games include a clock counting down, and the elegantly constructed mechanism of clocks seems to inspire many of his torture devices, which operate on a similar system of gears that, once set in motion, are self-propelled (electricity is used from time to time, but the typical Jigsaw device operates with older technology). The metal that Jigsaw uses for his traps is almost uniformly rusted, which matches the decaying industrial spaces that house his torture games. This rust and decay has a strong visual echo in the *Hostel* films, where wealthy individuals pay money to torture abductees in the ruins of a factory in rural Slovakia.

The device that Jigsaw proclaims as his favorite is an elaborate network of gears and pulleys that connect to a sort of industrial crucifix. Hanging from it is Timothy Young, the man who killed Jeff's son (mentioned above in the pig conveyor belt scene in *Saw III*). To save Timothy, Jeff must remove a key that is attached to a shotgun. If time runs out, the gears will twist Timothy's head and limbs until they break. The camera shows many of the gears and bolts of the mechanism in extreme close-up, capturing every rusty millimeter in fetishistic detail. As almost always happens in the *Saw* series, Jeff does not succeed in time, and Timothy's body is twisted and snapped, his bones shattering and piercing through his skin. Distraught, Jeff kneels before Timothy's lifeless body hanging from this rusty crucifix, an image that suggests Jeff has succumbed and accepted Jigsaw's call for a violent return to an embodied Real.

Of course, the key characteristic that binds all torture porn films together is right there in the name: torture. All the films associated with American torture porn—the *Saw* and *Hostel* franchises, as well as films such as *Turistas* (John Stockwell, 2006) and *Captivity* (Roland Joffé, 2007)—privilege scenes of torture. Quite often, the characters being tortured are ostensibly the protagonists, although this becomes murky when, as often happens, the tortured becomes the torturer.[32] Regardless of who is torturing whom, the films tend to feature long, drawn-out scenes of bodies being beaten, sliced, dismembered, and otherwise mutilated. These bodies in pain are on display in a manner that shares affinities with the display of bodies in the throes of pleasure, as found in hardcore pornography. This is not a phenomenon exclusive to American films; similar torture scenarios are found in films such as Australia's *Wolf Creek* (Greg Mclean, 2005), France's *Martyrs* (Pascal Laugier, 2008), and The Philippines' *Kinatay* (Brillante Mendoza, 2009). Like their American counterparts, these films feature extended scenes of torture; one might say that it is this spectacle that is the most salient characteristic of these films—not any narrative elements. The display of bodies in pain is at the heart of this strand of extreme cinema, which is highly attuned to the physicality, and the fragility, of human flesh. This focus on bodies and sensation is reminiscent of Gilles Deleuze's discussion of the work of Francis Bacon, a topic that will be particularly relevant to our discussion of *A Serbian Film*.[33]

The torture porn cycle came after a period in which American horror had moved away from violence and the body: supernatural horror inspired by trends in Asian cinema (such as *The Ring* (Gore Verbinski, 2002)) and the postmodern self-referentiality of *Scream* (Wes Craven, 1996). Torture porn certainly connects to the horrors of torture that came to light in the "war on terror," but it also seems to fill another void. It violently returns the horror genre to the body and forces us, as viewers, to face our physical essence during a time in which technologies seem to disconnect us from it. "Is not its goal also to awaken us, Western citizens, from our numbness, from immersion in our everyday ideological universe?"[34] Žižek writes here of the rationale behind fundamentalist terrorism, but he could just as easily have been talking about Jigsaw, the premier icon of the torture porn cycle and a true believer in the power of steel and of the human body, both to create and to withstand punishment. These films seem to suggest—whether consciously or not, and however crude and misguided their messages may be—that we need to reconnect with our bodies, with one another, and with the architecture and tools that constructed our society: the labor, the muscle, and the mechanisms that have been abandoned to rust and decay.

MARTYRS: PAIN AT THE THRESHOLD OF THE HUMAN/ANIMAL

"In the beginning was emotion," Louis-Ferdinand Céline proclaims, counter to the biblical inscription "In the beginning was the Word." Reading Céline, Julia Kristeva notes, "one has the impression that in the beginning was discomfort." Or perhaps in more pointed terms we might say, "In the beginning was pain and suffering." Discomfort is the very primer of culture, of a properly signifying subject. The subject emerges from suffering, from *want* (not desire), and it is discomfort that the not-yet-subject begins to differentiate "from chaos," as Kristeva argues. "An incandescent, unbearable limit between inside and outside, ego and other. The initial, fleeting grasp: 'suffering,' 'fear,' ultimate words sighting the crest where sense topples over into the senses, the 'intimate' into 'nerves.' Being as ill-being."[35] Pascal Laugier's 2008 film *Martyrs* (re)presents the violent return of the maternal, engulfing subjects and bringing them to the collapse of meaning—a universe of uncoded sensations. But *Martyrs* does not go far enough; while we witness the utter destruction of characters onscreen, the *film itself* does not sufficiently experiment with form. If the film truly approached abjection, "one would find neither narrative nor theme but a recasting of syntax and vocabulary—the violence of poetry, and silence."[36] The conclusion of the film does touch on this in its climactic moment, and *Martyrs* is instructive in its "being as painful-being," to recast Kristeva's terms.

Unfolding in three parts, Laugier's film bears some of the hallmarks of torture porn, but diverges quite radically from its American counterpart in very distinctive ways—namely, metaphysical inquiries.[37] The tripartite plot unfolds around Lucie Jurin and Anna Assaoui: in the opening act we learn that our characters are being raised in an orphanage (or boarding school), and that Lucie was subject to abuse; the median narrative details Lucie's violent revenge ending with her death; and finally, Anna is tortured to the brink of human endurance ending in her "rapture," as it is called in the film. What is not revealed until the latter third of the film is that a cult has been systematically subjecting young women/adolescent girls to torture with the objective of revealing the mysteries of life and the hereafter. Although Lucie as an adolescent girl escapes her tormentors (this is what we witness in the opening of the film), having to leave at least one other victim behind, she is presumably haunted through her adolescence and young adulthood by the ghost of the girl she abandoned. The cult runs its systematic torture operation in the Chamfors industrial zone in an abandoned slaughterhouse, similar to the Slovak factory in the *Hostel* films and the Gideon plant, designed by Jigsaw, as discussed above.

At the orphanage Lucie arrives deeply traumatized—withdrawn and wary of others. Anna, a girl of the same age, with a nurturing personality, helps to slowly bring Lucie out of her shell, befriending her. Lucie exhibits wounds on her arms, in what appear to be self-inflicted lacerations, but begs Anna, "Don't tell anybody." Anna comforts her and implores Lucie not to hurt herself, but Lucie insists, "It wasn't me." A figure haunts Lucie; ghostly and animalistic, it lurks in the shadows and is (supposedly) responsible for her injuries.

Lucie, intent on exacting revenge, believing she has discovered the individuals responsible for her torment, arrives at the Belfond household and guns down the entire family. After this brutal exhibition of violence, Lucie waits for Anna to arrive, but discovers that she is not alone. Her faithful and haunting companion lurks in the house. The pale gangly figure snarls, more animal than human, before bellowing a barking howl and leaping on Lucie's back like a feral beast. In these instances the specter is never completely in frame, nor viewed in full light, and subsequently its body-geography is not entirely clear. Nonetheless, the figure is recognizably female, unclothed, and covered in bruises and laceration scars. (Its form is revealed in more detail later.) Having dispatched her tormentors, Lucie believed that the haunting specter, which has shadowed her most of her life, would be sated by the bloodletting and finally set free. This proves incorrect.

The gait of Lucie's specter is more quadrupedal than bipedal—something akin to a feral non-human primate. Though the specter has all five digits, the way it clutches objects suggests an un-socialized body; it is, in a word, animalistic.

It is naked, literally and figuratively—and tears at the border between human and animal. The composition, editing, and audio design emphasize the abject. The spectral figure is lent a ghostly character prior to its assault, its furtive presence indexed by swaying blinds and a door that creaks open and suddenly slams shut. From shot to shot, the camera (from Lucie's perspective) attentively darts around, searching for the monstrous figure. The audio

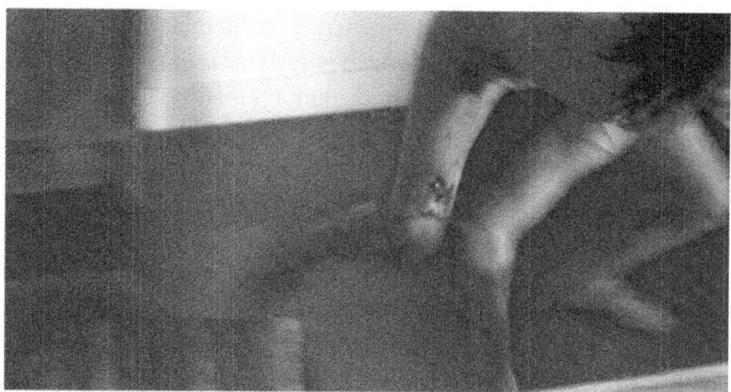

Figure 3.1 *Martyrs*, Pascal Laugier, 2008

similarly serves as an index of its ghostly presence—hissing, the pattering of bare feet, the jostling of things in the house. When the specter first pounces, the camera is positioned low, looking up at Lucie as she searches the house; it is presumed that the low angle view is the specter's gaze. However, the specter leaps from the top of the frame, the editing conceit working to evoke fright in the spectator. Astride Lucie, the ferocious specter, with a straight-razor, cuts X's onto Lucie's back, or, seen differently, crosses—marking her as a martyr? A martyr for what exactly will not be answered until the third part of the film. Forensic shots, close-ups of the razor running across Lucie's back, show crimson sparks of blood exploding outward. The violence, the breaking of skin, the spray of blood—that which should be inside ejects outside—elicits dread in the viewer.

Though sickened by Lucie's violence, Anna loves her and comes to her aid, stitching up the deep lacerations on her back. Like its counterparts in American torture porn, *Martyrs* includes medicalized gore, in the form of brief forensic shots of Anna's procedure suturing Lucie's gaping wounds. The tug of the needle and suture pulls at Lucie's skin as she winces in pain. The open wounds, the blood, the needle—which at once transgresses the bounds of the flesh and in the same instance endeavors to close the laceration—locates the wellspring from which the abject materializes: the partition between inside and outside. The laceration violates the integrity of this most integral border— skin. Anna, as nurturing-mother-nurse, attempts to repair the breach, to make the body clean and proper. But the violence exercised on Lucie's body is too much; Anna's efforts to close the gaping wounds will never be sufficient. And the exhibition of the wounded body demonstrates its fragility, how easily it might be torn open.

This tearing at the skin's surface, whether it is Lucie's wounds, or the mauled flesh of her specter, signifies an abomination, like leprosy, where it finds affinities with the discourse of impurity: "intermixture, erasing of differences, threat to identity."[38] The violence visited upon Lucie's body is evidence of impurity—a corrupted, contaminated, damaged subject—because it is later revealed that the specter is a figment of her imagination, as her wounds are self-inflicted. The specter then manifests as an "expression" of Lucie's own body—a brutal eruption of semiotic violence. "The body must bear no traces of its debt to nature," Kristeva states; "it must be clean and proper to be fully symbolic." Lucie's specter is feral and animalistic, it howls guttural utterances and hisses—it is outside the Symbolic. The socialized body, the body that is clean and proper, "should endure no gash other than that of circumcision, equivalent to sexual separation and/or separation from the mother [the navel]. Any other mark would be the sign of belonging to the impure, the non-separate, the non-symbolic, the non-holy."[39] The inability of the viewer to read the specter's corporal geography (non-symbolic), its non-communicative utterances (non-symbolic), and the fact that it is a manifestation of Lucie's aggression (non-separate) firmly place the specter in the realm of the impure.

The discovery that the haunting specter was little more than a projection of Lucie's feelings throws the narrative into jeopardy—her credibility as a character comes under question, and finally one begins to question if the Belfonds had anything to do with Lucie at all.[40] In the final act of the tripartite narrative, though, Anna discovers a heterotopic basement in the Belfond home, hidden behind a cabinet. A state-of-the-art torture facility lay beneath the bourgeois home the whole time. The main hall of the facility is lined with backlit images of tortured victims, an exhibition of morbid curiosa. Some images are historical—for instance, a photograph taken by Georges Dumas of Fou-Tchou-Li. Found guilty of murdering Prince Ao-Han-Ouan, Fou-Tchou-Li was sentenced to be buried alive, but the advisors of the child-emperor, believing the punishment too cruel, determined that he should die by Leng-Tch'e—what in colloquial English terms we call, "a death by a thousand cuts." In Beijing on April 10, 1905, the condemned man—given opium to withstand his torture and to prolong his death—was executed by literally being cut into pieces. Georges Bataille takes from this image the existence of "perfect contraries, divine ecstasy and its opposite, extreme horror."[41] And by plumbing the depths of abject horror it is possible to arrive at a reversal. Bataille establishes "a fundamental connection between religious ecstasy and eroticism—and in particular sadism. From the most unspeakable to the most elevated."[42] Within the diegetic world of *Martyrs*, Lucie's tormenting specter comes into clearer focus: it embodies the *incomplete* project of transcendental suffering/violence, never passing from "the most unspeakable to the most elevated."

At the far end of the basement, a locked portal leads to yet another level below. Lowering a ladder Anna descends into the dark cell and finds a woman chained to the floor. The woman looks very much like Lucie's specter: she has a pale complexion, bruised and scarred, a metal shield covers her eyes, another metal shield covers her genitals—a chastity belt—and barbwire circles her waist. (The chastity belt corresponds to the traditions of sacrificing virgins, Anna and Lucie too are coded as largely sexless, and even when Anna makes a romantic gesture toward Lucie she is rebuffed.) Seemingly incapable of speech, the woman whimpers, crawling toward Anna, shivering. Anna escorts the woman to the home and grabs a first-aid kit, but the wounds on the woman's body are so numerous, the damage to her body so thorough, she does not even know where to begin. "I can't help you," Anna says helplessly. Anna draws a bath for the woman, who writhes in agony, the water quickly discolored by her seeping wounds. Taking a flat-head screwdriver, Anna pries loose the metal shield, which is literally bolted to the top of the woman's head. In tight close-up, and to emphasize the gore, blood oozes from the holes. This is very similar to the surgical procedure performed on Jigsaw in Darren Lynn Bousman's 2006 film *Saw III*, which—though improvised with available home power-tools—was still situated within the medical regime and the scientistic discourse, thus buffering the spectator from the raw texture of meat and bone. Anna's role as "first responder" similarly situates the procedure in *Martyrs* loosely within the realm of scientistic discourse, but for whatever buffering there is in the *Saw* film, and there is not much, *Martyrs* offers even less. As in *Saw III* the sound design emphasizes gore, the scrape of the metal screwdriver against the metal plate, the squishy gush of oozing blood, and the anguished scream of the woman as she writhes in pain. Once the shield is removed, Anna covers the woman's head with a towel, and caresses her, saying gently, "Calm down," precisely in the same manner that she used to comfort Lucie. Anna returns to Lucie's corpse, and pleads for forgiveness—realizing that she in fact suffered terribly at the hands of the Belfonds.

Blood from the woman's festering sores, the discharge of pus and blood from the torn away metal shield, fills the tub, turning the water putrid red. Anna, just as she did with Lucie, attempts to enact the maternal and make the damaged body clean and proper. The horrific sight brings *Carrie* to mind. After the prom, Carrie, drenched in pig's blood, retreats home and takes a bath. As Barbara Creed recounts:

Carrie takes off her bloody gown and huddles in a foetal position in the bath, where she washes away the blood and make-up, both signs of her womanhood. The bath filled with bloody water suggests a rebirth and a desire to return to the comforting dyadic relationship. As in many horror films, the pre-Oedipal mother is represented as a primary source of abjection. Unlike the young girl we first saw enjoying her body in the shower [in the opening of the film], Carrie is once again reduced to a trembling child as she was when the girls pelted her with tampons.[43]

The tub-cum-womb signifies a retreat to the maternal. Like Lucie's specter, the tortured woman is non-communicative, seemingly regressed to a pre-linguistic state, anything but a clean and proper body. *Martyrs* exhibits the full fury of maternal revenge—bringing young women to the threshold of human life, returning them to a state prior to the erection of the boundary between inside and outside, self and other, to the chaos of the unsocialized nervous system. Lucie's specter, which is nothing more than a projection of her own suffering, lends form to the collapse of the subjective that exceeds its bounds.

Exhausted, Anna falls asleep at the side of Lucie's lifeless body, but is awoken by the ghastly moans of the woman from the torture chamber. Anna finds her with a knife cutting herself. The woman scurries away like a wild animal, but is suddenly struck dead with a single shotgun blast to the head. A woman clad in black lowers her weapon and is flanked by others, also dressed in black—members of the cult re-establishing control of the Belfond home. They detain Anna, who is eventually interrogated by the eccentric leader of the mysterious cult. The woman explains the cult's endeavor to "create martyrs" by chaperoning young women through the transcendental experience by means of torture, citing, among others, Georges Dumas's photograph of Fou-Tchou-Li as an example.[44] The madam presents other images of women in the "ecstasy" of extreme suffering, telling Anna to look at their eyes—all exhibit the same sublime stare. Mademoiselle concludes that the female sex is "more responsive to transfiguration. Young women."

Anna's hair is shorn, and she is bound in chains. Days, weeks, perhaps months go by where Anna is subjected to beatings, deprivation, and humiliation. She is spoon-fed a greenish-yellow gruel, and in her first feeding spits it out; her stoic female "care-giver," dressed in plain grey-black garb, slaps her, yanks her hair to pull her head back, and continues to feed her. Michel, a stocky bald man (similar to Rasa in *A Serbian Film*), pays Anna regular visits, silently beating her. Without remorse, without anger, without any emotion whatsoever, he delivers devastating blows. Daily, Anna is systematically abused until, broken, she hears Lucie's voice coaxing her to "Let yourself go." The woman who feeds Anna notices a change, and reassures her, "You'll be all right, Anna. Your suffering is almost over. There's one more stage. The last one. You'll be all right. You won't have to protect yourself ever again."

Michel, in addition to being a torturer, is also a surgeon and carries her to an adjacent surgical room. He straps her to a device, cuts her clothes away, and flays her alive—her flesh is completely removed from her body, save her face. After seeing Anna in the pose of a crucifixion, the woman who feeds her screams, apparently startled by Anna's raptured expression. The woman calls the cult madam and explains, "She's let go, completely let go. Her face is like—Mademoiselle—her eyes—I swear, she no longer sees anything around her." Cutting back to Anna, the camera slowly zooms in on her blank expression, finally closing in on Anna's left eye; the reflection of light in her iris consumes the frame and the film is enveloped in a cloud of milky white before being completely overcome with what appears to be a celestial body—a hot white gaseous star. The non-diegetic accompanying sound (or is it internal-diegetic?) suggests a hail of angelic voices. The sound design and the use of white to evoke the sublime find affinities with the conclusion of Gaspar Noé's 2002 film *Irreversible*.[45] The milky white suggests a return to the maternal as well. The camera zooms out to witness Anna's quivering body—presumably in a state of ecstasy. In this instance we locate Laugier's attempt to approach abjection in the cinematic form: where the film is suffused in hot white, and narrative for all intents and purposes ceases, giving way to the "meaningless-ness" of color, and the highly embellished audioscape.

The *Saw* franchise delivers suffering as a gift—a return to the Real, reac-quainting those (un)fortunate souls within the diegesis with the experience of the body, and perhaps those outside the diegesis too—and *Martyrs* does something similar, but with an element of the sacred. Recalling Bataille, Susan Sontag observes that the exhibition

> of suffering, of the pain of others . . . is rooted in religious thinking, which links pain to sacrifice, sacrifice to exaltation—a view that could not be more alien to a modern sensibility, which regards suffering as some-thing that is a mistake or an accident or a crime. Something to be fixed. Something to be refused. Something that makes one feel powerless.[46]

Indeed, Anna's transfiguration is an effort to repatriate the sacred and its tra-ditional relationship to human suffering and sacrifice. What *Martyrs* does is to register the historical intimacy between (human) suffering and the sacred.[47]

Because the first two thirds of the narrative are heavily invested in Lucie's story, what might go unnoticed with the first viewing of *Martyrs* is that the film actually documents Anna's transformation. If the transformation of a character is the dramatic imperative for narrative progression, it is Anna who fulfills it. Lucie does not change—she is every bit as damaged as she is from the begin-ning; there is no transfiguration for Lucie. There is another "problem" within this narrative. Beyond the conceit of whose narrative this really is, it is also matriarchal in nature—whereas patriarchal narratives work toward placing characters in their "proper place," rectifying violations or prohibitions, in *Martyrs* characters regress into abjection.[48]

In this matriarchal narrative the torture chamber is less about destroying a person, and more about creating something—a martyr. And from this perspec-tive the torture chamber finds affinities with Victor Frankenstein's laboratory, which is similar to the basement-cum-surgical room in *The Human Centipede*. The cult conducts experiments, like Frankenstein, to unlock the mysteries of life. And while Frankenstein strives to re-animate the dead, the cult seeks to cross the boundary between the living and the dead. While Frankenstein knows what it is like to play God (as he exults in the classic 1931 James Whale film), the cult attempts to open a direct channel to the sacred, the vital force (if viewed from a somewhat secular perspective) that lies behind the veil of death. Frankenstein creates life in his laboratory, and in so doing transgresses a taboo, for he enlists the generative power that only God and women are allowed to possess. Again, like *The Human Centipede*, the torture chamber in *Martyrs* is an artificial womb like Frankenstein's laboratory.[49] The torture chamber is a dark removed space, hidden from view, passable through a small opening, and as Amy Green observes,

> the images of the mother often coincide with images of water, and also with cavernous, womblike spaces. The torture chamber exists in an underground portion of the family's home, accessed through a hidden room and a ladder. These labyrinthine, hidden spaces are "associated with a loss of orientation, the failure of the sense of sight, and the elevation of lower-order senses," and most importantly, they become reminiscent of the womb and the birth canal.[50]

This evokes the heterotopic staging of the torture chamber and its affinities with the womb—where the maternal site is viewed as a cavernous void that threatens to absorb the victim, the torture chamber as a vaginal weapon.

The women who are tortured regress, and this is particularly true of Anna's transformation over the course of the film. In the first third of the film, although Anna is only a child, she effectively takes on the role of mother for the deeply traumatized Lucie. As a young adult, Anna continues to act as Lucie's maternal figure (or lover), caring for her wounds, stitching up the lacerations, and cleaning up Lucie's mess. In fact, the cult only captures Anna precisely because she is "too motherly"—tending to the gravely wounded Gabrielle Belfond, the victim she discovers in the Belfond basement, and of course Lucie. In the final part of the tripartite narrative, Anna regresses into childhood and beyond. In the torture chamber Anna is punished like a little girl, she is spoon-fed mush, she stops speaking, and her hair is shorn like an infant's. In the last stages of her torture Anna's sex is stripped away with her skin; she is effectively little more than bio-mass.[51] Rather than progressing through the conventional thresholds of femininity (loss of virginity associated with the marital union, and motherhood) she "physically appears to regress to the fetal stage. While she is being beaten, the group keeps her chained to the wall, in effect an umbilical cord leading to death, not nourishment."[52] Finally, she is suspended in a gelatinous substance, analogous to the way in which a fetus is suspended in-utero. In the first few weeks of development, the human fetus is sexless; if the gonads go up they become ovaries, and if they go down they become testes. In Anna's "unsexing" and her suspension in the translucent gelatinous fluid, she effectively regresses to the earliest recognizable pre-gendered human form. And in these encounters with the boundaries between form and formlessness, between male and female, between life and death, between self and other, *Martyrs* approaches ontological concerns that are generally absent from torture porn narratives.

A SERBIAN FILM: PAIN AT THE THRESHOLD OF MEAT/FLESH

Human beings are animals—this fact is made abundantly clear in Srdjan Spasojevic's *A Serbian Film* (2010). The central character, Milos, has not worked in the porn industry for years, and Vukmir, a porn filmmaker, attempts to lure him out of retirement with the promise of a substantive payday. Milos is particularly uneasy with Vukmir's proposition, because the contract does not specify the acts to be filmed, nor does the smut peddler provide Milos with a script, let alone a basic scenario. Vukmir claims that he wants to capture "Truth." "Real people, real situations, real sex—minimal editing. There's a serious script. We know it, you don't!" After further philosophizing, Vukmir finally presents a contract telling Milos, "No need to read it all, just the numbers." The mise-en-scène—the large conference table, and the window—echo the opening moments of Pier Paolo Pasolini's 1975 film *Salò, or the 120 Days of Sodom*, where the libertines sign their pact; with all the signatures collected, the Duke declares, "All is good if it's excessive." Milos hesitates, unwilling to commit to a project that explicitly keeps him in the dark. He consults with his wife, Marija, unsure of what to do, but the pair agree that the financial benefits outweigh any potential negative repercussions. (They could not be more wrong.)

Salò, which turned out to be Pasolini's last film—the filmmaker was murdered a couple of weeks following its release—also earned the ire of critics and self-appointed morality police. Supposedly the most infamous film ever made (perhaps *A Serbian Film* owns that title now?), *Salò* closely follows the Marquis de Sade's novel on which it is based, but sets the film in the waning moments of the fascist regime in Italy. Counter to our colloquial understanding of sadism, the libertine is not capricious. The libertine—the clinical sadist—does not act upon erotic feelings, or bestial passion; rather, the sadist is scrupulously calculated.[53] Jean Baudrillard, in his response to the 9/11 terrorist attack, "The Spirit of Terrorism," observes that Western philosophy operates according to a complete misunderstanding, "on the part of the Enlightenment, of the relation between Good and Evil." He continues by noting:

> We believe naively that the progress of Good, its advance in all fields (the sciences, technology, democracy, human rights), corresponds to a defeat of Evil. No one seems to have understood that Good and Evil advance together, as part of the same movement. The triumph of the one does not eclipse the other—far from it.[54]

Indeed, and despite Baudrillard's strong assertion otherwise, someone did understand this all too well: the Marquis de Sade. His novels can be read as cautionary tales. As the streets ran red with blood, which Sade witnessed with his very eyes, barbarity shadowed the progress of liberal human values that in the same stroke cast off the yoke of aristocracy.

Read through the lens of allegory, Sade's work is a critique of the Enlightenment, and specifically the autonomy of reason—human agency unbound from the governing sovereign, or theocracy. In short, Sade's literature envisions the logical end of reason unbound by ethics. The sadist eroticizes the execution of law (or duty in the Kantian paradigm). And subsequently the sadist's stringent adherence to the laws of libertinage decouples him/her from any ethical obligations. At its core, then, sadism is the practice of reason divorced from ethics. For instance, understood from this perspective, the eugenics project might be a sadistic enterprise insofar as it is the application of Darwinian science without regard to ethics, to humanitarian compassion. Few have truly appreciated the philosophical significance of Sade, but Pasolini does so astutely in *Salò*.

Spasojevic's film is nowhere as sophisticated as Pasolini's film, but they do possess affinities in their appropriation of sadism. Spasojevic strove to make a film that reflected the experience of his native Serbia, beset by years of war and economic hardship, and not to approach the subject with "kid gloves," but to portray the realities of victimization in what he describes as an "unrestrained and direct manner." The explicit nature of the material is such that "the violation, humiliation, and ultimate degradation of our being," Spasojevic insists,

> must be *felt* and experienced by every viewer. So that it cannot be ignored. Every victim in the film represents us and everyone else whose innocence and youth have been stolen by those governing our lives—for purposes unknown. We only painted a literal metaphor of how we feel: you are raped from birth, and the raping doesn't even stop after you're dead.[55]

The metaphor of "being fucked" is made explicit. Whether or not a viewer can stomach the violent debauchery, Spasojevic's film emerges from a war-torn culture that frightens Western viewers to their very core—because the Balkans Conflict exhibited the naked brutality of European neighbors turning against neighbors—in what Wes Craven called the "Kosovo Effect." This was not a far-flung conflict, where the brutality of the "other" might well be "expected"; in this case, we witnessed Europeans perpetrating barbarous acts—the images of which called to mind the catastrophic violence seen just half a century prior. Like *The Last House on the Left* (Wes Craven, 1972), *A Serbian Film* potentially exposes the consequences of the erasure of all moral codes and reveals the animalistic nature of humanity that lurks just below the surface. Along these lines, Mark Featherstone and Beth Johnson argue that the pornographic violence in "*A Serbian Film* . . . exposes the real of Serbian ethno-nationalism to the harsh light of day and makes it entirely dominant over normal symbolic reality."[56]

Perhaps one of the things that makes this film so disturbing is its explicit coupling of sex and violence. In the *Hostel* films, for instance, the relationship between sex and violence is more implicit—narrative correlations between paying for sex and paying to torture. In *Saw*, which so strictly adheres to the code of libertinage, sex is almost non-existent, because what is eroticized is the execution of the rules of the games, not the body *per se*. Spasojevic does not turn away from graphic violence, but his presentation is different from that of American torture porn. At the end of the day, the filmmakers of the *Saw* franchise, like Sade, when read from a particular perspective, have faith in humanity, calling attention to the foibles of the ideological project that evacuates ethics from the execution of law.[57] Spasojevic appears to see things differently: he only sees the animalistic character of the human species.

And it is no wonder that Serbs who did not buy into the nationalist rhetoric (and perhaps even those who did) found themselves at the mercy of corrupt officials and cast as the pariahs of Europe. Out from under the Soviet thumb, the Yugoslavian federation fell apart and nationalists, like Slobodan Milošević, took advantage of the situation, fermenting unrest with Serbian minorities in Kosovo, leading to ethnic cleansing, armed conflict, and eventually NATO intervention (in March 1999) to stop Serbian aggression. While the bloodletting has stopped, there is still no clear mandate on the Kosovo region, and normalized relations between Serbia and the international community are tepid at best. The instability of the political and economic environment hurts ordinary Serbians—nationalists or not. No matter where one falls on the ethnic/ideological spectrum, the erosion of social/economic exchange bred an environment of brutality.

Conventional social mores cloak what lies beneath the surface, and *A Serbian Film* exhibits the human species laid bare. Stripped of his humanity, Milos becomes an animal—he is compelled to sign away his agency out of economic necessity, he is corralled like an animal, and finally given a "cattle aphrodisiac," all but completely evacuating any scrap of humanity. "Now that's our stud," Vukmir smirks. But more than this, because this amounts

Figure 3.2 *A Serbian Film*, Srdjan Spasojevic, 2010

to little more than plot—narrative content—the animalistic nature of our species is exhibited in form as well. What Spasojevic makes particular use of is Srdjan Todorovic's face (the actor who plays Milos), and, more specifically, his mouth. In the grips of sexual frenzy Todorovic bares his teeth—frequently clenched in a bestial grimace. Spasojevic, like Francis Bacon, dismantles "*the face*," as Gilles Deleuze notes, "to rediscover the head or make it emerge from beneath the face."[58]

What is revealed is the "zone of indiscernibility," the territory between animal and human, between body and flesh/meat, and finally "to becoming," that liminal zone between categories. Spasojevic's framing of Todorovic's face emphasizes not emotion (socially coded expressions) as such, but a Kristevan semiotic (un-socialized expressions) eruption through musculature, the blood vessels that bulge from his neck, the grizzled features of an unshaved face bathed in sweat, and most especially his tightly clenched teeth—in short, the meat-animal.

"The head-meat is a becoming-animal of man,"[59] Deleuze says of Bacon's paintings that rend the body open, specifically in the depiction of mouths caught screaming, gaping open, voids of black and crimson. Spasojevic does this too, but not by literally splitting open the head, but in his editing and sound design. At moments of narrative collapse—when for instance Milos is drugged, and the subjective perspective is torn from him (the film up to this point has been largely seen through his eyes)—Spasojevic introduces lightning-fast editing. This obliterates spatial and temporal continuity, making the geography of the body incoherent. Unbound by organizing principles (that is to say, socialization), the body in Spasojevic's film reveals "the Figure [which] is the body without organs," that Deleuze characterizes not as a body that "lacks organs," but rather as one that "simply lacks the organism," or an organizing system.[60] And this appears to correspond to the experience of "autoscopia" as described by Deleuze: "it is no longer *my* head, but I feel myself inside *a* head, I see and I see myself inside a head; or else I do not see myself in this naked body when I am dressed . . . and so forth."[61] Milos "loses" himself, untethered from the moorings of social mores.

And it is precisely in his frenzied states that the animalistic character emerges, subsuming his humanity—and it is not his unyielding stallion's member, or the violence that he perpetrates, but rather his mouth that expresses this. "Meat is the state of the body in which flesh and bone confront each other locally rather than being composed structurally," Deleuze observes. "The same is true of the mouth and the teeth," he continues, "which are little bones. In meat, the flesh seems to *descend* from the bones, while the bones rise up from the flesh."[62] The terror in Spasojevic's film is located in what humanity disavows: the animalistic nature of our species that shadows our every gesture, lurking behind the veneer of social mores. As Deleuze observes, Bacon does not pity animals sent to the slaughter—the butcher's shop was little more than a church for him—"but rather . . . every man who suffers is a piece of meat."[63]

Bacon worships meat. Spasojevic is different in this respect; he uses it as a figure—we are nothing more than cows sent to the slaughter. Spasojevic, nevertheless, in his depiction of convulsing bodies, particularly in Milos's body and his violently clenched teeth, finds affinities with Bacon's passion. "I've always been very moved by pictures about slaughterhouses and meat, and to me they belong very much to the whole thing of the Crucifixion," Bacon explains.[64] The painter continues, acknowledging, "Of course, we are meat, we are potential carcasses. If I go into a butcher shop I always think it's surprising that I wasn't there instead of the animal."[65] And is this not what torture porn is largely about—where we find ourselves hung up in the butcher's shop instead of an animal? (Middleton makes an analogous argument.) Relative to films like *Hostel*, or *Saw III*, there is little rending of bodies in Spasojevic's film; there is violence to be sure, and certainly violence that is coupled with sexual abuse, making it hard to stomach. So while American films graphically exhibit bodies being ripped asunder (think of the surgery in *Saw III*)—and *Martyrs* depicts the body enduring pain as a means of spiritual transcendence—*A Serbian Film* exposes the meat of the body in the spirit of Bacon's paintings.

The collection of images in the lightning-fast editing—like Bacon's superimpositions, photographic and cinematic appropriations, and distortions of the human form—exposes the meat-animal lurking within the human species. In his first instance of using this technique, Spasojevic assembles a series of images that have happened and are (in the chronology of the film) going to happen, along with images of body parts in close up and still others in extreme close ups—particularly Milos's bloodshot eye, tinted with a putrid yellow. The assemblage and fragmentation of bodies rends the coherent body apart, making it difficult to distinguish male from female, one character from another, and in some cases what one is even seeing.[66] For instance, as the cattle aphrodisiac begins to take effect, Milos's vision blurs, and he appears to be overwhelmed by the sensual—specifically, intense sexual arousal. The complete break from the sentient is marked with a sharp ratcheting up of the (non-)diegetic drone, peaking with a violent static roar. The audio elements straddle the boundaries between diegetic and non-diegetic registers as the soundscape expresses the internal subjective experience of our character, who is encountering a loss of sentient-self as he surrenders to the chaos of the animalistic. Accompanying this abrasive (non-)diegetic audio design are lightning-fast takes, illustrating various bodies sometimes in bits and pieces—Milos's frenzied face in the ecstasy of sex, the fucking of a baby, fellatio, a "beaver shot," a facial cum shot, the naked and battered corpse of a woman, a girl's eyes, Milos's bloodshot eye (in extreme close-up). The rapidity of the sequence, which is only visually intelligible going frame by frame, renders Milos's body indiscernible, fragmented, diffuse.

The sound design accompanying this montage, as already mentioned, also straddles the diegetic and non-diegetic. It is similar to the scraping metal sounds found in Charlie Clouser's audio design for the *Saw* franchise, and in this case it approaches the cadence of a human scream. Somewhere between the organic and non-organic register, the sound design straddles the bounds between what is human and what is not. The images and the sound design work together to elicit the abject, where borders are fragile and "identities (subject/object, etc.) do not exist or only barely so—double, fuzzy, hetero-geneous, animal, metamorphosed, altered, abject."[67] There is no "meaning" here. Spasojevic takes us to the point where meaning collapses—this is the cinema of sensations.[68] It is possible that we might be too generous with our observations, but the point of Spasojevic's film is not to explain the experience of two decades of war, but rather to make the spectator *feel* it. (And whether he succeeds or not is a different matter.)[69]

Furthermore, one might conclude that comparing Spasojevic's film with the great modern painter Francis Bacon is incongruous until you inspect Vukmir's conference room. The set is dressed in a high modernist aesthetic. The conference table at the center of the room is striking in its long uninter-rupted lines, the armoire and matching liquor cabinet are somewhere between art deco and Arts and Crafts, the bar with its imposing curved wood structure supporting a thick glass top; the lighting fixtures also have the qualities of high modernism, and walls are adorned with none other than Bacon paintings (or at least they are intended to look like Bacon paintings). There are two paintings in Vukmir's conference room that are clearly derived from Bacon. One shows the back of a muscular male figure—running, leaning forward, or struggling to push something. One might find affinities with Bacon's paintings that draw from Muybridge's studies of human locomotion—wrestlers, boxers, deformed figures. The large painting against the back wall, above the bar, is particularly characteristic of Bacon's portraits.

The flat charcoal background isolates the head in Vukmir's painting. More spherical than Bacon's heads—his tend to be elongated, vertical—the painting in Vukmir's conference room appears to explode outward. Where Bacon seems to dissect the head (or butcher it—slice it up), rending the flesh open with strokes of white, pink, or crimson paint, in this case (although done in the manner of Bacon) the flesh appears to exceed its bounds, more explosive than Bacon, as if the skin fails to contain the musculature beneath. At the bottom left of the painting, an arched arrow (also an attribute associated with the English painter)—sloping upward in the counterclockwise direction, like the marks depicting the flows of weather on a meteorological map—gestures toward forces beyond anyone's control. Subject to the laws of nature, despite the veneer of "Culture," all of us are nothing but flesh and bone. The painting, done in the spirit of Bacon's work, corresponds to the themes found in *A Serbian Film*—where everyone is rendered a supple thing, little more than meat, which "is the common zone of man and the beast, their zone of indiscernibility."[70]

The furniture, the high modernist décor, and the collection of artworks also share affinities with the design of *Salò*, which takes place in a secluded chateau. While the exterior of the libertine's estate, with its imposing columns and palatial greens, is neo-classical, the interior is definitively modern. Mirrors, light fixtures, floor patterns, and wall murals are characteristically art deco. In addition, the walls, and most especially the lounge, where the libertines take turns watching the final orgiastic display of torture and debauchery, are lined with modern paintings—many in the manner of Futurism. Pasolini's intention here was to suggest that the fascist libertines had confiscated the palatial estate from a rich Jewish family, deported during the war. Furthermore, the coupling of high modernism with horror itself embodies the dialectic of Enlightenment— where the progress of modernity is shadowed by its animalistic other, the very thesis of Max Horkheimer and Theodor Adorno in *Dialectic of Enlightenment*. Spasojevic's film adopts an analogous strategy—no matter what normative human mores demand of us, the semiotic animal is always already present, and given the opportunity channeled into violent eruptions.

NOTES

1. Georges Bataille, *Erotism: Death and Sensuality*, trans. Mary Dalwood (San Francisco: City Lights Books, 1986), 81.

2. Michel Foucault, "Of Other Spaces," trans. Jay Miskowiec, *Diacritics* 16, no. 1 (Spring 1986): 24.

3. Carol Clover, *Men, Women, and Chain Saws: Gender in the Modern Horror Film* (Princeton: Princeton University Press, 1992), 30–1.

4. Evangelos Tziallas, "Torture Porn and Surveillance Culture," *Jump Cut: A Review of*

Contemporary Media 52 (Summer 2010). Available at <http://www.ejumpcut.org/archive/jc52.2010/evangelosTorturePorn/> (last accessed November 25, 2015).

5. Barbara Creed, *The Monstrous-Feminine: Film, Feminism, Psychoanalysis* (New York: Routledge, 1993), 27.

6. Elaine Scarry actually argues that regimes that utilize torture tend to refer to it as a sort of staging: the "blue-lit stage" (Chile), the "production room" (Philippines), and the "cinema room" (South Vietnam). See Elaine Scarry, *The Body in Pain: The Making and Unmaking of the World* (New York: Oxford University Press, 1987). Note also the staging found in *The Act of Killing* (Joshua Oppenheimer, 2012). In addition, Sade's novel *The 120 Days of Sodom* features storytellers, placed as if on a stage, who detail gruesome stories of torture and degradation.

7. Matt Hills, "Cutting into Concepts of 'Reflectionist' Cinema? The *Saw* Franchise and Puzzles of Post-9/11 Horror," in *Horror After 9/11: World of Fear, Cinema of Terror*, eds. Aviva Briefel and Sam J. Miller (Austin: University of Texas, 2011), 119.

8. Linda Williams, "Film Bodies: Gender, Genre, and Excess," *Film Quarterly* 44, no. 4 (Summer 1991): 9.

9. Ibid.

10. Ibid., 10.

11. Ibid.

12. Ibid., 10–11.

13. Ibid., 4. For more on the visceral reception of the cinematic text see Jennifer Barker's *The Tactile Eye: Touch and the Cinema Experience* (Berkeley: University of California Press, 2009).

14. Jeffrey Bullins, "Hearing the Game: Sound Design," in *To See the "Saw" Movies: Essays on Torture Porn and Post-9/11 Horror*, eds. James Aston and John Walliss (Jefferson, NC: McFarland, 2013), 185.

15. Williams, 11.

16. Jean Baudrillard, *The Spirit of Terrorism and Other Essays*, trans. Chris Turner (New York: Verso, 2003), 4.

17. Ibid., 7.

18. Slavoj Žižek, *Welcome to the Desert of the Real!: Five Essays on September 11 and Related Dates* (New York: Verso, 2002), 11.

19. Ibid., 10

20. It is worth noting here that the *Saw* character Amanda, one of Jigsaw's protégés, is coded as a cutter.

21. Catherine Zimmer, "Caught on Tape? The Politics of Video in the New Torture Film," in *Horror after 9/11: World of Fear, Cinema of Terror*, eds. Aviva Briefel and Sam Miller (Austin: University of Texas Press, 2011), 83–106.

22. Ibid., 98–9.

23. Žižek, 10.

24. Ibid., 6.

25. This might also play into Mikhail Bakhtin's reading of the carnivalesque, in which he envisions a world of eternal return, regeneration, and where destruction (of the body) is not an end, but pregnant with the potential for new life. Bakhtin cites a grisly passage from Rabelais's *Gargantua*: "He brained some, smashed the legs and arms of others, broke a neck here, cracked a rib there. He flattened a nose or knocked an eye out, crushed a jaw or sent thirty-two teeth rattling down a bloody gullet. Some had their shoulderblades dislocated, others their thighs lammed to pulp, others their hips wrenched, others their arms battered beyond recognition (Book 1, Chapter 27)." Bakhtin observes, "This long

enumeration is typical of Rabelais' anatomization and dismemberment of the human body." At the end of the day, such bloody destruction relates "to the world's gay matter, which is born, dies and gives birth, is devoured and devours; this is the world which continually grows and multiplies, becomes ever greater and better, ever more abundant. Gay matter is ambivalent, it is the grave and the generating womb, the receding past and the advancing future, the becoming." Mikhail Bakhtin, *Rabelais and His World*, trans. Helene Iswolsky (Bloomington: Indiana University Press, 1984), 194-5.

26. According to Hills, torture porn films are "structured through thoroughgoing political incoherence, being open to a multiplicity of different politicized anxieties." See Hills, 117.

27. Jason Middleton, "The Subject of Torture: Regarding the Pain of Americans in *Hostel*," *Cinema Journal* 49, no. 4 (Summer 2010): 9.

28. Ibid.

29. Ibid.

30. See Middleton, 9, n.20.

31. Hills, 114.

32. For a discussion of the concept of the pro(an)tagonist, see Aaron Kerner, *Torture Porn in the Wake of 9/11* (New Brunswick, NJ: Rutgers University Press, 2015).

33. Gilles Deleuze, *Francis Bacon: The Logic of Sensation*, trans. Daniel W. Smith (Minneapolis: University of Minnesota Press, 2004).

34. Žižek, 9.

35. Julia Kristeva, *Powers of Horror: An Essay on Abjection*, trans. Leon S. Roudiez (New York: Columbia University Press, 1982), 140.

36. Ibid., 141.

37. Amy M. Green sees it differently. She views the film "in its totality" in this way: "the violence in *Martyrs* pales in comparison to mainstream and popular horror offerings like the *Hostel* (2005) and *Saw* (2004) films, to name only a couple." Amy M. Green, "The French Horror Film *Martyrs* and the Destruction, Defilement, and Neutering of the Female Form," *Journal of Popular Film and Television* 39, no. 1 (2011): 21.

38. Kristeva, 101.

39. Ibid., 102.

40. This revelation also seems to destroy Lucie herself, as she abruptly flees the house and commits suicide, slitting her throat.

41. Georges Bataille, *The Tears of Eros*, trans. Peter Connor (San Francisco: City Lights Books, 1989), 207.

42. Ibid., 206. John Taylor and Kate Millett are quite critical of Bataille's eroticization of real world torture. Taylor, commenting on Millett's critique, argues that she "claims, strangely, that the 'slender Chinese figure' is 'not even a woman,' so how then (she asks) can it be 'an erotic object'? . . . Ultimately, she asserts, the torture turns the condemned man into a woman, or a child. Furthermore, the eroticism of his death for Bataille is tied to his being Chinese, or what she calls 'exotic'" (Taylor, 31). What is overlooked in Millett's reading is that the image is not the thing that it depicts; rather, it is a fetish. The subject of the image (and the way in which Bataille sees it) is not the existential realities of torture *per se*, but rather, an embodiment of Bataille's own research on the strange coexistence of pleasure and pain, the profane and the sacred. Situating the image in the paradigm of photojournalism, Millett approaches it as an artifact of an historical event. Bataille, on the other hand, working within the framework of the College of Sociology, questions how the image circulates in our visual culture. "Millett interprets the photographs as if they were windows that open directly onto the scene," Taylor observes, adding that Bataille never confused "the original scene with its image." John Taylor, *Body*

Horror: Photojournalism, Catastrophe and War (Washington Square, NY: New York University Press, 1998), 32.

43. Creed, 81.

44. Regarding the photograph Mademoiselle says, "Long Sheng Province. 1912. This woman didn't believe in God. She tried to steal a hen. It cost her dearly. When this photograph was taken she was still alive. Look at her eyes." There appears to be a willful distortion of history here—the account given is radically different from the historical record, and moreover Mademoiselle gives the condemned's sex as female so that it might conform to *Martyrs*'s narrative. De-sexing Fou-Tchou-Li was part of his torture, but "re-sexing" him as female serves the fictional narrative. Kate Millett would be horrified at this distortion of historical facts, and would probably lay the blame for this squarely at Bataille's feet—see Taylor, 33–4.

45. For more on the affective in *Irreversible* see Timothy Nicodemo, "Cinematography and Sensorial Assault in Gaspar Noé's *Irreversible*," *Cinephile* 8, no. 2 (Fall 2012): 33–9.

46. Susan Sontag, *Regarding the Pain of Others* (New York: Farrar, Straus, & Giroux, 2003), 99.

47. For a discussion of (human) suffering, sacrifice, violence and the sacred see René Girard, *Violence and the Sacred*, trans. Patrick Gregory (Baltimore: Johns Hopkins University Press, 1989).

48. My students (Kerner) Megan Payne and Ashley Nunes were instrumental in working out some of the gender politics associated with *Martyrs*.

49. Amy Green also sees the womb-imagery in the film: "Laugier employs imagery related to the womb and to childbirth and turns them monstrous. He distorts the female body itself, hacking away at it until it loses all hint of sexual identity, all hint of the feminine and its connotations of compassion and its ability to give life." Green, 23.

50. Ibid., 25. Katherine Henry, "Life-in-Death: The Monstrous Female and the Gothic Labyrinth in *Aliens* and 'Ligeia'," in *Horrifying Sex*, ed. Ruth Bienstock Anolik (Jefferson: McFarland, 2007), 29.

51. This characterization of Anna finds affinities with our introduction to Lucie in the opening of the film, whom Amy Green describes as follows: "Her shaven head, pre-adolescent form, and bruised face render her identity neutral rather than overtly and explicitly female." (Green, 20.) The matriarch of the narrative is given no proper name, and is simply known as "Mademoiselle," this term suggests that the character has never married, which potentially makes her (despite her advanced years) virginal, and in that respect relatable to the tortured victims who correspond to the conventions of virgin sacrifice. She too also "de-sexes" herself in the closing moments of the film while in the bathroom she takes off her make-up and fake eyelashes.

52. Green, 25.

53. See Slavoj Žižek, "Kant with (or against) Sade," in *The Žižek Reader*, eds. Elizabeth Wright and Edmond Wright (Oxford: Blackwell, 1999), 287. Also see "Much Ado about a Thing," in Slavoj Žižek, *For They Know Not What They Do: Enjoyment as a Political Factor* (London: Verso, 1991).

54. Baudrillard, 13.

55. Srdjan Spasojevic in the DVD extra for *A Serbian Film*.

56. Mark Featherstone and Beth Johnson, "'Ovo Je Srbija': The Horror of the National Thing in *A Serbian Film*," *Journal for Cultural Research* 16, no. 1 (January 2012): 66.

57. See "The *Saw* Franchise: Videogames and the Sadistic Pro(an)tagonist Jigsaw," in Aaron Kerner, *Torture Porn in the Wake of 9/11: Horror, Exploitation, and the Cinema of Sensation* (New Brunswick, NJ: Rutgers University Press, 2015).

58. Deleuze, 19.

59. Ibid., 25.

60. Ibid., 40, 41.

61. Ibid., 43.

62. Ibid., 20–1.

63. Ibid., 21.

64. Francis Bacon interview by David Sylvester, *The Brutality of Fact: Interviews with Francis Bacon*, 3rd enlarged edition (Oxford: Thames & Hudson, 1987), 23.

65. Ibid., 46.

66. Hélène Cattet and Bruno Forzani's 2013 film *L'étrange couleur des larmes de ton corps* (*The Strange Color of Your Body's Tears*) uses an abundance of extreme close-ups to much the same effect.

67. Kristeva, 207.

68. We suspect that Deleuze would actually see *A Serbian Film* as sensational, as opposed to a film that elicits sensation: "Sensation is the opposite of the facile and the ready-made, the cliché, but also of the 'sensational,' the spontaneous, etc." Deleuze, 31.

69. An interesting debate materialized in my (Kerner) graduate seminar on the cinema of sensation: non-American-born students were fully prepared to accept Spasojevic's film as an expression from a war-torn region, while American-born students were deeply cynical and suspicious of Spasojevic's agenda. Those students originally from outside the USA pointed out that the American-born students were prepared to accept the *Saw* films or the *Hostel* films as "legitimate" expressions of post-9/11 anxiety, but unwilling or unable to make allowances for Spasojevic's film.

70. Deleuze, 21.

CHAPTER 4

Laughter: Belly-aching Laughter

The laugh being one of the few uncensored channels of affective expression may become the prime vehicle of the expression of any and all affects which suffer inhibition. Thus there is the frightened nervous laugh, the dirty laugh of contempt or hostility, the ashamed laugh, the surprised laugh, the laugh of enjoyment, the laugh of excitement and the laugh of distress, the substitute cry.[1]

— Silvan Tomkins

INTRODUCTION: "WHAT'S SO FUNNY?" IS PROBABLY THE WRONG QUESTION ...

As Linda Williams argues in *Hard Core*, cinematic hardcore showcases the quest to document proof of the female orgasm.[2] Complicated by the fact that the female orgasm is generally invisible to the unaided eye, the pornographic genre displaces the female orgasm onto the visual choreography of the money shot. At least for one, the male orgasm is impossible to fake—ejaculation is a confession of the male body, proof of sexual excitation and climactic release. The pornographic genre anticipates a spectator's mutual arousal; the comic genre, or comedic numbers in a film, also anticipates an affective response from the spectator, but in the form of laughter. "True laughter cannot be forced or faked,"[3] Tarja Laine observes, and, like pornography's "money shot," laughter manifests itself as a confession of the body. Pornography invites its spectators to mimic, or perhaps even in a sense to participate in, the arousing experience. What sets pornography and the cinematic numbers that elicit laughter in the viewing body apart is that within the story-world things might be horrifying, dreadful, or deadly serious, but nonetheless cause the spectator to erupt hysterically. There is, then, with laughter the possibility for dissonance between the diegetic narrative and how the spectator responds to it. This is precisely why Williams does not count comedy as part of the body genres; "the reaction of the audience does not mimic the sensations experienced" by the character(s) onscreen.[4] She also notes that in the genre we are generally encouraged to laugh *at*, not *with* the character onscreen.

Be that as it may, laughter nonetheless is an involuntary response to a wide range of experiences, and not simply things that we might find humorous. Rather, laughter (particularly in the communal setting of a theater, or among friends)[5] might follow jump-out-of-your-seat frights in a horror film, giddiness in response to sex, perhaps a nervous response to things that disgust. Whatever it might be, we want to consider here laughter spawned by something other than jokes—in the most generic sense. Jokes necessitate narrative contextualization, and we want to look beyond that.

Umberto Eco suggests that the comic is in some sense always bound to narrative—insofar as the comic gesture involves the violation of some rule. Eco recalls a comic strip series entitled "The movies we would like to see," published in *Mad* magazine. He cites as an example a scene where outlaws tie a beautiful woman to railroad tracks. The good guys rush to save the woman, but are too late and the train runs the woman over. "In order to enjoy this piece of chicanery," Eco says one must know the rules of the genre (in this case that of the Western), and it is the violation that "produces the comic pleasure. But the rule must be *presupposed* and taken for granted."[6] Eco is certainly correct that laughter is almost invariably the product of some sort of infraction. And this is particularly true in the case of the discourse of jokes, but we might add to this in order to account for "baser" rules of the semiotic body (in Kristevan terms)—the violation of bodily boundaries, eruptions (vomit, snot, farts) that violate the integrity of the clean and proper body. Our term "laugh" is itself laden with the corporal: "The verb 'laugh', from the Old English *hliehhan*, is of onomatopoeic (sound-imitating) origin," Robert Provine reminds us. He continues, "Laughter is instinctive behavior programmed by our genes, not by the vocal community in which we grow up."[7]

Laughter, indeed, is a universal human experience, and it has been thought to be unique to our species. Aristotle claimed that laughter is what sets humans apart from animals, "for no animal but man ever laughs."[8] On the fortieth day of life, Aristotle insisted, the new-born human child laughs and at such time the infant's soul is sparked by the air of laughter—transforming the infant from a mere human (animal), into a human being. "For Aristotle," Barry Sanders adds, the occurrence of a child's laugh on the fortieth day "so radically separated humans from all the other animals that he used it to define human essence: *animal ridens*, the 'creature who laughs.'"[9] Neurologists and others have since proven that other animals do in fact laugh, though the vocalization of laughter is different. While human laughter is a product of "outward breath," and the chopping up of the "ha" sound, with chimpanzees, laughter, as Provine observes, "resembles panting, with a single breathy vocalization being produced during each exhalation and inhalation."[10]

There are instances when laughter is spurned by something more "immediate"—something outside the discourse of jokes. Jokes invite us to ask, "What's so funny?" Henri Bergson asks a similar question at the beginning of his own inquiry on comedy: "What does laughter mean?"[11] To our minds, these are not exactly the right questions to ask; instead, we probably should be asking, "*How* is that funny?" Or perhaps even, "What does laughter reveal about the language of the body?"[12] These questions, however, also approach two separate, though intertwined, issues: (1) a referent that invites laughter, and (2) a subject that laughs.[13]

Understanding that narrative is never that far removed from anything that we might consider here, we nevertheless want to train our attention on laughter generated relatively independent of narrative context—grotesque body humor for instance. Moreover, as already indicated, comedy is not the sole progenitor of laughter, as laughter might erupt at some of the most solemn, disgusting, or even most "inappropriate" times (e.g. a funeral, or the sight of some grievous mishaps such as those featured on Comedy Central's *Tosh.O*). Hajooj Kuka's 2014 documentary *Beats of the Antonov* catches a peculiar example of laughter—immediately following a bombing raid in South Sudan, children emerge from their makeshift subterranean bomb-shelters laughing. The film explains that they laugh at the fact that they escaped death, and enter the world newly (re)born. Laughter clearly is not (solely) synonymous with humor, the comic—it is an affective utterance prompted by any number of possible referents.

Laughter in the philosophical tradition is invariably the antidote to disgust. "All theoreticians of disgust are, at the same time," Winfried Menninghaus insists,

> theoreticians of laughter. The "vital sensation" of disgust might well be considered a property no less characteristic of humanity than the capacity to laugh—a property, in fact, that represents the negative complement of laughter. The sudden discharge of tension achieves in laughter, as in vomiting, an overcoming of disgust, a contact with the "abject" that does not lead to lasting contamination of defilement.[14]

There is, then, a certain catharsis found in laughter, but it can also be "protective"—warding off an abject referent. Menninghaus adds: "laughing *at* something, as an act of expulsion, resembles in itself the act of rejecting, of vomiting in disgust. Disgust, which undergoes a countercathexis (or a sublimation), and laughter are complementary ways of admitting an alterity that otherwise would overpower our system of perception and consciousness."[15]

This might share certain affinities with the phobic who is never at a loss for words. Julia Kristeva posits that "any verbalizing activity, whether or not it names a phobic object related to orality, is an attempt to introject the incorporated items. In that sense, verbalization has always been confronted with the 'ab-ject' that the phobic object is."[16] The gift of verbosity, in other words, is fueled by an effort to name the phobic referent, and thus by naming it assuages the fear associated with it. As a non-object, though, the phobic referent can never be "named." Nonetheless, the effort is not a lost cause because verbosity itself very well might offer a provisional framing of the phobic referent, allowing the subject to negotiate his/her fear:

> The speech of the phobic adult is also characterized by extreme nimbleness. But that vertiginous skill is as if void of meaning, traveling at top speed over an untouched and untouchable abyss, of which, on occasion, only the affect shows up, giving not a sign but a signal. It happens because language has then become a counterphobic object; it no longer plays the role of an element of miscarried introjection, capable, in the child's phobia, of revealing the anguish of original want.[17]

The utterances of laughter, too, like the verbosity of the phobic that speeds "over an untouched and untouchable abyss," might negotiate the exhibition of defilement, that thing that elicits disgust; as Kristeva argues, "laughing is a way of placing or displacing abjection."[18]

KITTY PORN: INTERNET AFFECT

Whiling away time watching cute kitty videos on YouTube—in terms of viewing practices—is not far removed from the consumption of internet pornography. Funny cat videos (or whatever it might be) usually have no narrative to speak of, but rather capture some irresistibly cute incident—a short snippet of a cat at play, misadventure, or some such thing. (In addition to pornography, the affinities with early film are also abundantly evident.) One funny video might beget another, allowing the user to surf through the rabbit hole that YouTube can be—more or less allowing the user to curate their own program of short amusing videos that suits their unique interests. Bemused viewers might erupt in laughter, crack a grin, croon, or utter some sort of "aww!" at the sight of something adorable.

In 2013, a study of the site YouPorn determined that the largest percentage of videos were five to six minutes in length and lacked any sort of narrative contextualization (likely extracted from a longer original source). In practical terms, because of the interface and selection of relatively short videos, as one study on viewing habits indicates, it "appears very much like a convenient 'pick and mix' repository where users can select snippets of videos that suit their interests rather than watching entire films."[19] Alexa, a firm that measures internet traffic, "reports the average viewing time on YouPorn as only ≈ 9 minutes. With such time limitations, uploaders (particularly commercial ones) must ensure that only the most interesting elements of their films are seen by viewers."[20] The short nature of the videos and the self-curated "pick and mix" menu, like the funny cat videos, facilitate an affective release. In both cases, whether it's cute bemusing videos or pornography, a cohesive narrative is hardly the point.

And then there are reaction videos. Usually posted to a video hosting service such as YouTube, these videos document viewers' affective responses to something emotionally moving, shocking, or horrifying. In some cases, reaction videos are made by the very subject documented—with a webcam mounted above or adjacent to their computer monitor. In some instances, the individual documenting the reaction surreptitiously records his/her subject to capture an "authentic" reaction. More often than not the affecting referent remains out of view because the camera position intends to capture the viewer and their reactions, and consequently the perspective usually means that the camera is placed behind the screen. Because reaction videos are once-removed from the referent that elicits sensation, this makes for a rather strange encounter. Those watching a reaction video then are responding (at least in the first instance) to the verbal and bodily utterances of the documented viewer, not necessarily the affecting referent. In most cases, though, those watching reaction videos at the very least know the gist of the original referent, even if they have not seen it themselves.

Perhaps the most notable of reaction videos are those in response to *2 Girls 1 Cup*, which in actual fact is a trailer for the full-length pornographic film *Hungry Bitches* (Marco Fiorito, 2007). The *2 Girls 1 Cup* video, which went "viral," features two women eating feces and vomit. Oddly, the short video is set to a saccharine score: Hervé Roy's "Lover's Theme," which Susanna Paasonen reminds us evokes Roy's score for "the theme song for the softcore film *Emmanuelle* from 1974."[21] By most standards the video is disgusting and, predictably, reaction videos feature subjects that avert their eyes, wrench themselves away from the screen, their mouths agape, their hands thrown up in a defensive posture (over the eyes, over the mouth, or outward as if to push the offending sight away), while some viewers retreat altogether, cry, or blurt out expletives or other expressive linguistic utterances. Non- (or pre-) linguistic utterances are common: "ew!," "oh!," or gagging, heaving, or actual vomiting. What is perhaps less predictable is the abundance of laughter, be it that of the prankster holding the camera, or that of the subject who, only moments earlier, had shrieked in disgust.[22] Those watching the reaction video perhaps laugh along with the prankster and/or subjects having "survived" the ordeal.[23] If we are familiar with the affecting referent we might be able to trace the contour of events on the basis of the affective response of the subjects—"reading" the referent through the affectations of the documented viewing body.

There are countless examples of *2 Girls 1 Cup* reaction videos.[24] The comedian Robert Kelly, making an appearance on *The Opie and Anthony Show* (which airs on Sirius XM Satellite Radio) in 2007, was subjected to *2 Girls 1 Cup*. He is incapable of watching the short video all the way through, despite multiple attempts. He goes flush (literally turning red) and beads of sweat appear on his bald head; he coughs, turns away, heaves, vomits, and walks out of the studio to throw up in the bathroom (the camera follows him). The hosts of the radio program repeatedly subject Kelly to the experience, walking him through the video (cheering him on, "Come on Bobby!"). Holding a wastepaper basket to his mouth following multiple attempts to watch the video all the way through, Kelly vomits and, relenting, shakes his head. "I can't do it," he says, as one of the radio hosts offscreen, rolling with laughter, says, "I don't know why that's so fuckin' funny to me?" The entire studio—the radio hosts, and all the staffers in the background—are in fits of laughter. Louis CK, on the same radio program, is subjected to the same routine and has a similar reaction. Eventually he gets up angry, kicks over an office chair, sits on a couch at the far end of the studio in seeming defeat while appearing to wipe away tears, and says with resentment, "I can't unwatch that." Clearly Kelly and Louis CK are performing to one degree or another—they are on a radio program, which will be broadcast, and are videotaped as well. But for whatever performance (read: inauthenticity) there is, there are certain things (like the cum shot in porn) that cannot be faked: sweat, tears, vomit. These are the paroxysms of the body—involuntary confessions of disgust.[25]

The sight (and sound) of the subject of the reaction video gagging, vomiting, heaving, or perhaps even laughing becomes "the pinnacle of authenticity."[26] Jason Middleton argues that reaction videos might find certain affinities with Linda Williams's body genres—insofar as the subject exhibits an affective response to the referent, which follows the faint contours of what is being enacted in the originating referent. The subject(s) of a *2 Girls 1 Cup* reaction video might turn away, vomit, heave, "because on some level they can almost feel themselves doing the things the women in the video are doing."[27] We potentially take their reactions to be funny, but we also "read" the affective utterances of the body as an index of reality. The authentic symptomatic reactions are proof that the content of what they are watching is extreme, whether or not we are familiar with the stimulating referent ourselves.

What is really at stake here, though, is the body of the subject that watches a reaction video responding to the (involuntary) affectations of the documented subject. In this instance, Helen Hester's expanded notion of the pornographic is quite useful. Hester argues for "the conceptualization of the pornographic as a realm of representation that not only sporadically eschews or displaces sex, but that *need not be sexually explicit at all*."[28] Rather, Hester's notion of the expanded pornographic is something that elicits an intense affective charge in the subject. It is important to carefully differentiate the originating referent from the reaction video. On the one hand, *2 Girls 1 Cup* is a trailer for a pornographic film, and by most standards *documents disgusting acts*, whereas on the other hand, the reaction videos spawned by it document subjects that *are disgusted*. And as a record of an intense affective response, Hester argues, "the reaction videos *do* fit into a certain radically expanded notion of the pornographic." She continues:

> That is to say, these reaction videos might themselves be seen to possess pornographic qualities, despite the obvious de-emphasizing of sexual arousal that occurs within them. Certainly, these texts demonstrated an abiding preoccupation with involuntary bodily responses. We witness flinches and facial contortions, and hear exclamations of shock and horror. The most spectacular corporeal reaction to feelings of disgust— the gag or the dry heave—seems to be particularly cherished in these videos; in fartenewt's "*2 Girls 1 Cup* Reaction #1," the camera operator leaves his or her position behind the computer monitor in order to pursue one loudly gagging viewer in his hurry to leave the room.[29]

Pornography largely relies on the indexical exhibition of bodies engaged in sexual activity—offering incontrovertible evidence of penetration (meat shot) and authentic sexual excitation/climax (the money shot). Hester rehearses Williams's argument continuing by noting that the pornographic genre "displaces its interest in the supposedly invisible female orgasm onto the fetishized representation of external ejaculation."[30] Hester stipulates, however, that

> the pornographic frenzy of the visible is transferred from the paroxysms of the male body at the moment of ejaculation onto the paroxysms induced by nausea and disgust. In this sense, it is doubly displaced, shifted as it is from the obscure spasms of the female orgasm onto the more visible penile ejaculation, and then from this male cum shot onto the state of involuntary corporeal convulsion triggered by the experience of disgust. These reaction videos represent what one might call the pornography of the gag reflex.[31]

While gagging and heaving are to one degree or another fetishized in (*2 Girl 1 Cup*) reaction videos, what is perhaps most significant and signaling the climax of reaction videos is more often than not raucous laughter. Hester similarly observes:

> Perhaps the most frequently bodily paroxysm evident in the *YouTube* [reaction] videos is the shudder of laughter; involuntary convulsions of gaiety can be detected in numerous online examples. Pornography's bodily contagion of arousal—the way in which its scenes of sex try to beget sensations of sex—is reproduced in these texts via the infectious laugh, which spreads among the on-screen participants and which pierces the screen to contaminate the viewer.[32]

And in this case, the reaction video finds affinities with the body genres precisely because of the invitation to mimic, or to share in the affective spasms of laughter.

Like the joke, which in many instances trades in the currency of violation (be that the violation of social codes/mores, or even something as benign as a play on words), laughter within the diegetic space of the reaction video—such as we find in response to *2 Girls 1 Cup*—is elicited from a communion with an abject referent. What elicits such an intense affective response from *2 Girls 1 Cup*—whether it is heaving, laughing, or some combination of these—is the explicit violation of the clean and proper body, and the traversal of borders. "Food loathing is perhaps the most elementary and most archaic form of abjection," Kristeva posits:

> When the eyes see or the lips touch that skin on the surface of milk— harmless, thin as a sheet of cigarette paper, pitiful as a nail paring—I experience a gagging sensation and, still farther down, spasms in the stomach, the belly; and all the organs shrivel up the body, provoke tears and bile, increase heartbeat, cause forehead and hands to perspire. Along with sight-clouding dizziness, nausea makes me balk at that milk cream, separates me from the mother and father who proffer it.[33]

The clean and proper body dispenses with excrement; maternal authority maps the terrain of the body, polices its orifices and establishes the foundation on which the Symbolic rests.[34] The video *2 Girls 1 Cup* exhibits the willful abandon of maternal authority and returns to that most "archaic form of abjection." Furthermore, if it were not obvious, the other "corrupting" element here is that the pornographic spectacle is being shared in public spaces (with grandparents, co-workers, groups of friends)—violating the basic prohibition against the exhibition of sex in the public sphere.[35]

Within the diegetic space of a *2 Girls 1 Cup*, reaction video subjects are confronted with what amounts to prelinguistic (erotic) play; it seems only fitting that the subject respond with a prelinguistic utterance in turn—heaving, gagging, and/or laughter. The sputtering convulsive utterances, in their spastic rhythm, appear (like a stutterer trying to get the right word out) to negotiate the gross prohibitions on display. Laughter allays fears, soothes an uneasy subject.[36] Viewed through the lens of grotesque realism, as posited by Mikhail Bakhtin, laughter in response to *2 Girls 1 Cup* might be read as a "corrective" to the exhibition of degradation:

> To degrade also means to concern oneself with the lower stratum of the body, the life of the belly and the reproductive organs; it therefore relates to acts of defecation and copulation, conception, pregnancy, and birth. Degradation digs a bodily grave for a new birth; it has not only a destructive, negative aspect, but also a regenerating one. To degrade an object does not imply merely hurling it into the void of nonexistence, into absolute destruction, but to hurl it down to the reproductive lower stratum, the zone in which conception and a new birth take place. Grotesque realism knows no other lower level; it is the fruitful earth and the womb. It is always conceiving.[37]

As much as *2 Girls 1 Cup* wallows in the abject, it potentially reaffirms the bounds of the clean and proper subject. While *2 Girls 1 Cup* is vile by most standards, it nonetheless depicts a radical form of "freedom" in the wanton disregard of conventional social/sexual mores. Simply viewing these acts of degradation invites the viewer to participate (even if only to acknowledge the gross violation of prohibitions).[38] In laughter we discover the potential for rejuvenation, or perhaps the reaffirmation of proper Symbolic order—what is good and proper in contrast with what should be rejected and pushed away. Pushed away with that forceful guttural rolling "ha, ha, ha!"

BUMPS, BRUISES, AND ERUPTING BODIES

The "8 Simple Rules for Buying My Teenage Daughter" episode of the animated series *Family Guy* (season 4) includes a sequence of vomiting that lasts over a minute. Stewie, Brian, Chris, and Peter drink ipecac to see who can hold off the longest before vomiting—the winner gets the last piece of pie in the refrigerator.[39] What follows is nearly non-stop retching as each character repeatedly vomits; in short order the characters and the living-room are lathered in greenish-brown vomit. A couple of times removed—mediated through animation, as well as the screen—the scene might still elicit nausea from the spectator. At the same time, it wields the potential to invite raucous laughter. Clearly, the program aims more for the latter than for the former. This prompts a question: Why do we find vomiting so funny? There is in fact a long tradition of rendering vomiting characters to stoke laughter—in some cases to ridicule the gluttony of the privileged caste.

Though generally associated with the crasser stratum of culture, the "sport" of speed eating is gluttonous, and is featured prominently in the plot of *Taxidermia* (György Pálfi, 2006). Set in Hungary, this film is perhaps one of the most representative films of extreme cinema—it is episodic (told in three parts), includes highly stylized editing and cinematography, makes use of extreme close-ups (particularly of viscera), and is incredibly "fleshy." It emphasizes grotesque bodies: from anorexic rail-thin, to rotund and the morbidly obese; it exhibits sex not in its romanticized form, but in its sweaty and its viscous sense; it features the messy business of birthing and dying; it mixes, dismembers and reassembles bodies.[40] "*Taxidermia* does not tell a story," Steven Shaviro observes, "so much as it dramatizes a series of attractions and repulsions among grotesquely deformed bodies."[41] Shaviro also recognizes the affective charge of the film, and views it (at least in part) through Linda Williams's body genres: "The film, like other works in so-called 'body genres,' operates by a sort of affective contagion. It *forces us to feel*, arousing the audience with 'a sense of over-involvement in sensation and emotion,' that implies 'an apparent lack of proper esthetic distance.'"[42]

While some of the cinematography and compositions (e.g. extreme close-ups of viscera) are affecting, Balatony Kálmán's competitive eating sequence celebrates the consuming and erupting body. Kálmán, the protagonist of the median narrative of the tripartite story, is a rotund competitive eater. Of dubious origins, Kálmán is born with a pigtail, which his father at first sight summarily snips off. As a youngster, the roly-poly Kálmán demonstrated his potential to be a great competitive eater (suggesting that there was more to his birth anomaly—inheriting the qualities of a hog). We are introduced to Kálmán as an adult in a mesmerizing shot which twirls between Kálmán as an infant and his adulthood without any perceptible cut. The camera work fluidly glides past and around a row of competitive eaters hastily slurping a bowl of soup. The competitors represent their respective Eastern Bloc countries, as the scene takes place at the height of the Communist era in Hungary. Following this round of eating, the competitors retreat to the back of the stage where they all hurl into a large cauldron. The fluid camera, spinning 360° around at the center of the cauldron, witnesses spewing jets of vomit. The successive brownish columns of puke might well provoke disgust, but perhaps this reaction might be most related to the sound—the heaving and the viscous slush of chunky vomit gushing into the cauldron.

The second round features a solid block of food (perhaps frozen, or encased in gelatin). As the men greedily dig, in the blocks become mushy brownish clumps and take on the appearance of feces. The slippage of visual (and auditory) signifiers wields the power to disgust precisely because of its transitional condition—no longer a definable object (e.g. soup, meat, sausage) but something in-between, in a state of becoming (destined to be incorporated into the subject). The sounds of chewing, which strangely could be confused for the slurpy/sucking sounds of sex, have the potential to elicit the sensation of disgust. William Ian Miller, in his *Anatomy of Disgust*, discusses a similar phenomenon:

> Although saliva is clearly contaminating and disgust-evoking, chewed food owes its contaminating power to more than just contact with saliva. The chewing itself, the reduction of formed things into gooey things, also plays into it, but it is the simple fact of entry into the mouth that transforms the substance. That which is spit out can never be the same again. The true rule seems to be that once food enters the mouth it can only properly exit in the form of feces. This helps account for why vomit may be more disgusting than feces (only feces is playing by the rules).[43]

In *Taxidermia* we find a multiplication of disgust-provoking elements. Beyond the sheer gluttony of the scene, what elicits disgust in the second stage of the competitive eating contest is the slippage of visual signification between food and feces, where (what looks like) feces is food—another instance of not playing by the rules. (This certainly applies to *2 Girls 1 Cup* as well.)

The use of slippery signifiers (and this term seems particularly fitting here in its suggestive "wetness") fuels the affective charge likely to trigger disgust. It is the process of becoming that elicits affect, which in simpler terms we simply refer to as "the cycle of life." A number of scholars have commented on this. Mikhail Bakhtin, for instance, observes:

> The body discloses its essence as a principle of growth which exceeds its own limits only in copulation, pregnancy, childbirth, the throes of death, eating, drinking, or defecation. This is the ever unfinished, ever creating body, the link in the chain of genetic development, or more correctly speaking, two links shown at the point where they enter into each other.[44]

And this "linking" of two or more entities precisely points to the grotesque. Bakhtin continues:

> One of the fundamental tendencies of the grotesque image of the body is to show two bodies in one: the one giving birth and dying, the other conceived, generated, and born. This is the pregnant and begetting body, or

at least a body ready for conception and fertilization, the stress being laid on the phallus or the genital organs. From one body a new body always emerges in some form or other.[45]

Similarly, Miller observes that one of the most potent disgust-provoking referents is that which demonstrates the capacity to create life:

Images of decay imperceptibly slide into images of fertility and out again. Death thus horrifies and disgusts not just because it smells revoltingly bad, but because it is not an end to the process of living but part of a cycle of eternal recurrence. The having lived and the living unite to make up the organic world of generative rot—rank, smelling, and upsetting to the touch. The gooey mud, the scummy pond are life soup, fecundity itself: slimy, slippery, wiggling, teeming animal life generating spontaneously from putrefying vegetation.[46]

The slushy fecal-colored mass that the speed-eating competitors shovel into their mouths is perhaps amplified in its affecting potential, because at least in appearance it seems that the generative cycle of rot has been prematurely intercepted—the consumption of putrefaction *before* it has been assimilated into something wholesome.

What is surprising about this disgusting spectacle, and most particularly the chorus of vomiting, is its anticipation of our laughter. As with the ipecac sequence in the *Family Guy*, one might recoil at the repulsive sight but this is just as likely to be coupled with chuckles if not full-out belly laughter. The competitive eating sequence is quite absurd, even carnivalesque. It recalls the carnival sequence in *Stand By Me* (Rob Reiner, 1986), where "Lardass" barfs during a blueberry-pie-eating contest, an action which spreads like a contagion among the participants and the county fair spectators. And indeed, the exhibition of gluttony, vomit, and excrement in *Taxidermia* appears to play on medieval and ancient festivals. The mobilization of ambivalent signifiers and the topsy-turvy logic of the carnivalesque celebrate the "images of the material bodily lower stratum; they debase, destroy, regenerate, and renew simultaneously," Bakhtin notes. But these scenes of ambivalence are also "closely linked to laughter. When death and birth are shown in their comic aspect, scatological images in various forms nearly always accompany the gay monsters created by laughter in order to replace the terror that has been defeated."[47] *Taxidermia* invites us to view grotesque bodies through the carnivalesque lens, where laughter defuses what otherwise might be overwhelmingly disgusting.

The *Jackass* films (and the MTV series where the films originate) are not extreme in the same sense that *Taxidermia* is. The latter includes highly stylized treatments of the cinematic form. The *Jackass* films are for all intents and purposes documentaries in the observational mode—documenting the outlandish stunts performed by Johnny Knoxville and his crew. In terms of documentary form, the *Jackass* franchise is highly conventional—long takes, handheld camera, diegetic sound. *Jackass* narratives, however, are almost entirely episodic; there is in fact no narrative through-line to speak of. Rather, like the pornographic genre, *Jackass* is a string of stunts (usually quite juvenile in nature) that place one or more characters in a situation that causes the body onscreen to writhe in pain, in many cases culminating (again like porn) in the expulsion of some bodily fluid—blood, tears, vomit.[48] Jeff Tremaine, who directed the feature films in collaboration with Spike Jonze, is cognizant of this episodic structure of the films and its relationship to film history. The grand finale of *Jackass Number Two* (2006), for instance, features a series of set pieces referencing American musicals, Busby Berkeley choreography, Bollywood dance numbers, and Buster Keaton.[49]

Like the Rabelaisian themes found in *Taxidermia*, the *Jackass* films celebrate grotesque realism—emphasizing bodies scarred, tattooed, bloodied, bruised, haggard, leaking, or somehow atypical ("Wee Man" is a dwarf, Preston is obese); in general, the films display a propensity to focus on the lower strata of the body. Whether as part of a set piece or a surreptitious prank, members of the *Jackass* crew routinely get pummeled in the ass, or testicles. Crew member Chris Pontius regularly "dresses up" his penis for various stunts—it is made to look like a mouse for a snake to bite or to spring a mousetrap, encased in wood for a woodpecker to peck at, or left to simply dangle about. Cast members urinate in public or on one another, smear feces on one another, give themselves enemas, turn dildos into projectiles which are by various means shot at someone's ass. The *Jackass* crew clown around, pull pranks, violate social mores—invariably scenes are punctured by exuberant diegetic laughter (the films anticipate our participation in the chorus of laughter).

"Potty humor," like the tendency to lapse into pre-linguistic utterances such as groans, grunts, laughing, "is to witness the destruction of language," but Elaine Scarry adds to this that "conversely, to be present when a person moves up out of that pre-language and projects the facts of a sentience into speech is almost to have been permitted to be present at the birth of language itself."[50] There is a constant rehearsal of this in the *Jackass* films, and this move from pre-linguistic utterances to language—from "Ugh!" to "Oh fuck, that hurt"—is to also witness affect: pain, nausea, the light-headed symptoms of a blow to the head. Even as these films exhibit a great deal of "raw" content, as in pornography, we expect verification. "To have pain is to have *certainty*," Scarry notes, "but to hear about [and even to see, we would contend] pain is to have *doubt*."[51] The *Jackass* films verify pain (in particular) by displaying post-stunt bruises, close-ups of wounds, gashes, and darts penetrating the skin, and sequences of trips to the emergency room to get stitches.

While pain (like the female orgasm) might be generally invisible, revulsion and disgust are perhaps easier to verify in the paroxysms of vomit (like male ejaculation).[52] Steve O. in particular has a propensity to do things that make him vomit—eating animal dung or exotic delicacies, drinking urine. In one of his many vomit-inducing stunts, while touring Japan, Steve O. snorts wasabi (up his nose), which causes him to vomit over a plate of sushi. In *Jackass Number Two* (2006) Steve O. dons what looks like a space helmet attached to a beer funnel. Preston Lacy (the rotund *Jackass* crew member) farts into the funnel, which causes Steve O. to vomit in the helmet—jets of brownish puke splash against the spherical plexiglass helmet, and seep out around the collar. While clearly done for the sake of the film, and undoubtedly a performance, just like that of the porn actor who performs for the camera with exaggerated "uhs" and "ohs," vomiting, like male ejaculation, cannot be faked and registers an "authentic" affective experience.

And again, in a manner similar to pornography's investment in disclosing the secrets of the (female) body, the *Jackass* films make use of technology to render the body visible, to make it give up its secrets. In *Jackass 3.5* (Jeff Tremaine, 2011) Knoxville and Tremaine specifically praise the Phantom camera, which has the capacity to shoot at an incredibly high speed in high definition and to capture the minutiae of the body—for instance, Preston's rolling body fat after his body has been struck or gyrates, or Wee Man's pendulating scrotum struck with a tennis ball at high velocity. The emphasis on new digital technology as a means of capturing high-definition images in extreme slow motion shares certain affinities with the cinema of attractions and even proto-cinematic images—think Marey and Muybridge and their studies of movement.[53]

Others have associated the *Jackass* films with pornography, specifically the genre of gonzo or other forms of extreme pornography. The pornographic *Cocktails* series, produced by Extreme Associates, as Helen Hester observes,

> depicts porn actresses drinking abject bodily substances such as semen, saliva, and vomit, in a manner that recalls famous affecting moments from the *Jackass* franchise, such as cast member Ehren McGhehey eating urine-doused snow in 2002's *Jackass: The Movie* or Dave England consuming a regurgitated omelet during a scene from 2009's *Jackass: The Lost Tapes*. Interest in the body is, in the case of *Cocktails*, seemingly displaced from the realm of the arousing to the realm of the repulsive, as reflected by the elements of apparent generic slippage.[54]

This generic slippage (in the genre of extreme pornography) potentially displaces sexual arousal for disgust. We find a similar slippage in the *Jackass* films from dread (at witnessing some grievous bodily injury) or disgust into laughter. Regardless of whether we are speaking of pornography, extreme pornography, or the *Jackass* franchise, all of these intend to elicit bodily sensations in the viewer.

CORPULENCE AND LAUGHTER

> The comic performers of the marketplace were an important source of the grotesque image of the body . . . All these jugglers, acrobats, vendors of panaceas, magicians, clowns, trainers of monkeys, had a sharply expressed grotesque bodily character. Even today this character has been most fully preserved in marketplace shows and in the circus.[55]

Extreme cinema, as we have posited it, shares particular affinities with the cinema of attractions, which Tom Gunning, in turn, situates in relation to the fairground and its promise to deliver thrills. The visceral experience is not necessarily unique to extreme cinema; the attraction, which very well might be affecting, as Gunning suggests, is part of cinema's DNA, so to speak. Robert Stam similarly observes that the carnival spirit of the (American) cinema

> is both metonymic and metaphoric: metonymic in that cinema grew up, as it were, in the shadow of the side show, as an entertainment quite literally situated near the fairground and the penny arcade; and metaphoric in the sense that countless films cite the regressive pleasures of commercial carnivals—roller coasters, carousels, Ferris wheels—to analogize those of the cinema itself (e.g., the fairground sequence of [Alfred Hitchcock's 1951 film] *Strangers on a Train*).[56]

Indeed, from some of the earliest cinematic attractions (Georges Méliès's camera tricks, devils, and clowning characters) to Tod Browning's 1932 *Freaks*, and to the *Jackass* crew (who are just a stone's throw from circus performers), the cinema has never been that far removed from the traditions of the circus, the sideshow, the freak-show, the carnival. The cinematic attraction, of which extreme cinema is but a part, can thus be placed in a long continuum of the carnivalesque spirit of the cinema.

The tradition of the clown rests in a grotesque distortion of the body—over-sized feet, poorly-fitting clothing (that either causes the body to bulge at the seams or that is far too large and falls slack), a bulbous red nose, a gruesomely exaggerated grimace. Clothing that is mismatched, patched up, worn backwards, or turned inside out, and the exaggerated gestures of the clown (walking on one's hands, somersaults, and such), are rooted in the clown's role in the carnivalesque spirit of overturning conventional social mores.

Furthermore, this carnival spirit also corresponds to the cycles of life—of death and rejuvenation. This overturning is mapped onto the geography of the clown's body and his or her actions. "The entire logic of the grotesque movements of the body (still to be seen in shows and circus performances) is of a topographical nature," Bakhtin reminds us:

> The system of these movements is oriented in relation to the upper and lower stratum; it is a system of flights and descents into the lower depths. Their simplest expression is the primeval phenomenon of popular humor, the cartwheel, which by the continual rotation of the upper and lower parts suggests the rotation of earth and sky. This is manifested in other movements of the clown: the buttocks persistently trying to take the place of the head and the head that of the buttocks.[57]

The clown's logic is deeply indebted to grotesque realism—where the body is intimately connected to the world, a body that is open and always in a state of becoming. The clown repeatedly falls down, trips, stumbles, gets pummeled; but the clown almost always stages a miraculous recovery (think of the ways in which Tom and Jerry are minced into tiny pieces, but recover without so much as a scratch).[58] In this cyclical gesture Bakhtin sees the mimicry "of death-resurrection; the same body that tumbles into the grave rises again, incessantly moving from the lower to the upper level (the usual trick of the clown simulating death and revival)."[59]

We might read the wrestling match in Larry Charles's 2006 film *Borat: Cultural Learnings of America for Make Benefit Glorious Nation of Kazakhstan* through the lens of the clown's logic. A correspondent for Kazakh Television, Borat (a fictional character played by Sacha Baron Cohen), is reporting on his tour through the USA, but determines along the way to go on a quest to marry Pamela Anderson. In a hotel room Borat discovers Azamat, the obese Kazakh Television producer, completely naked, having, as he says, "a hand-party" (masturbating)—apparently aroused by the image of Pamela Anderson. Borat, who has just gotten out of a bath, upon this discovery becomes incensed. The ensuing brawl unfolds like a pro-wrestling match—each character grabs the other's genitals; Azamat breaks a lamp over Borat's head; Azamat hurls Borat into a wall (causing a mirror to shatter); they tussle on the queen-sized bed in sexually suggestive postures including the 69-position; and the pair eventually exit the hotel room (still naked), run through a hotel corridor, enter a crowded elevator, run through the hotel lobby, and barge in on a large professional conference. Azamat's body, like the clown's clothing, bulges and falls slack, and in its particularly rotund form is bulbous and exaggerated. The rough and tumble encounter finds certain affinities with the cyclical gestures of the clown, and the movement between upper and lower strata. An exceptionally

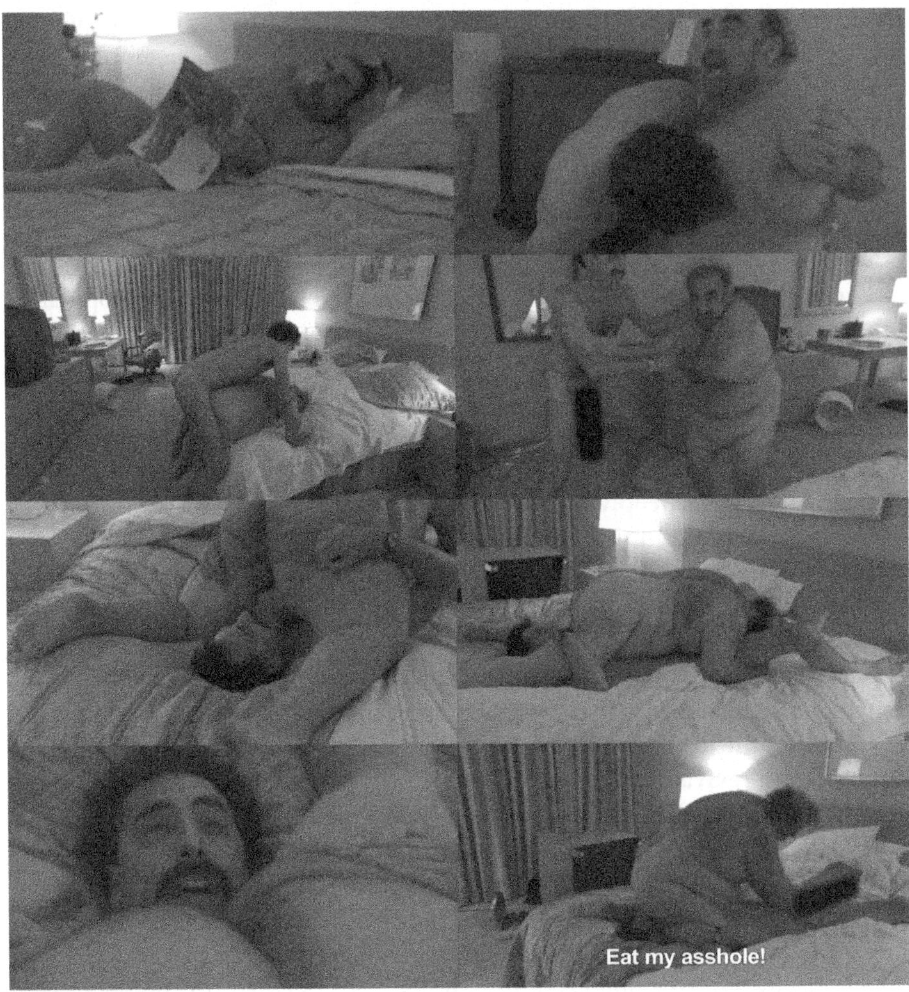

Figure 4.1 *Borat: Cultural Learnings of America for Make Benefit Glorious Nation of Kazakhstan*, Larry Charles, 2006

long black bar masks Borat's genitalia (yet another case of exaggeration), while Azamat's sagging belly largely conceals his penis. The bodily exaggerations (including the masking) find clear heredity in the carnivalesque.[60] The images of the characters in the 69-position (with Borat on the bottom) suggest the carnivalesque trading of the buttocks for the face and vice versa. The fusion between mouth and anus is made particularly evident when Azamat sits up (on Borat's face) and exclaims, "Eat my asshole!"

These very same gestures in pornography (or in real sex for that matter) might be read very differently. Pornography encourages a fetishistic disavowal and allows the subject (the spectator/individual engaged in sex) to invest erotic energy in a site generally regarded as filthy. Sexual situations invite (if not necessitate) a temporary lowering of prohibitions, and, in fact, the greater the prohibitive charge associated with a region, the greater the potential thrill in the licensed transgression. Such license is even acknowledged in colloquial speech—erotic ideation might be referred to as "dirty thoughts." "There exists no prohibition that cannot be transgressed," Bataille insists. He adds, "Often the transgression is permitted, often it is even prescribed."[61] (Overcoming disgust in the context of the sexual encounter is discussed further in Chapter 5.) Anal eroticism—even oral–anal contact—in the context of a sexual situation very well might be "permitted," and even within certain pornographic genres not only "prescribed," but demanded or expected. (There are general limits to this, though, as the *2 Girls 1 Cup* reaction videos seem to indicate.) The "problem," if we care to call it that, in *Borat* is that it is *not* framed in the conventions of the pornographic regime, or a sexual encounter as such. Thus, viewing outside the regime of sexuality, and without any clear channel toward erotic arousal, the spectator is then likely to experience a degree of unease, which might prompt disgust and/or laughter. The premise of *The Human Centipede* might very well be thought through these terms as well, particularly given that the human centipede is a grotesque figure—a chain of three people fused together in an anus-to-mouth surgical procedure. And while it is conceivable that some might find the grotesque entity laughable, it is more likely to incite disgust.

Where the sexual regime would invite a fetishistic disavowal, the carnivalesque in effect highlights the transgression in order to signify an inversion—to flout social mores. Both Bakhtin and Bataille recognize that the festival, the carnival, celebrates the overturning of social systems. Menninghaus (drawing from Roger Caillois) observes that it is "no coincidence that both authors [Bakhtin and Bataille] place laughter at the center of their social theory."[62] Furthermore, Menninghaus adds that "disgust, more specifically its relation to laughter, is what allows" us to differentiate between the two. Where Bakhtin recognizes the possibility for acts of

> degradation and exaltation, of foolish license for freedom and unofficial truth, Bakhtin's carnivalesque laughter does consistently recall the taboo to which it owes its existence. But only Bataille's laughter is in itself defined as excretion—as an analogon of anal-sadistic-excremental lust and thus as a performative traversing of a disgust taboo.[63]

Bataille positions laughter as analogous to the spasmodic releases of the sphincter when voiding the bowels—both involve a spastic expulsion from the body. And in its "expulsive" capacity laughter potentially negotiates, or even neutralizes, that which might otherwise cause us to recoil in disgust.

Though it very well might go against our moral sensibility, Azamat's fat naked body might be a source of laughter. Laughter is viewed by some as an expression of superiority,[64] the subject's effort to transfigure something that is threatening or frightening into an object of ridicule; this approach, Katariina Kyrölä insists, only works when fatness

> is understood as a butt of jokes, someone to be laughed at, and when the viewers are assumed to automatically put themselves in a superior position in relation to the body they look at. This is undoubtedly a significant part of the laughter and pleasure potential of comedy employing fat bodies, but by no means the whole story.[65]

While we agree that there is "more to this story," Kyrölä takes a different approach, locating the source of laughter in the reception of narrative content and the viewer's (presumed) subscription to normative patriarchal values. Kyrölä, who is largely concerned with the representation of (fat) women, recognizes that fat men have also been a source of laughter, but this might also be viewed through the anxieties stemming from "fear of femininity."[66] Kyrölä observes that numerous feminist theorists have linked the protrusions of the fat male body to the anxiety around feminine sexuality and the "uncontrollable maternal body." She continues, "A fat male body is therefore coded as dangerously bordering on femininity with visible breasts and protruding belly: the loss of rigid bodily boundaries would mean the loss of rigid, naturalized gender differences—in other words, the fat male body represents in some ways gender incongruity."[67] We concur with Kyrölä's assessment, but there is probably yet still more to this story. With the example of *Borat* we do in fact find the erasure of clear gender difference: Azamat's penis is largely concealed by his enormous girth, his chest follows the contours of female breasts (emphasized further by Borat's biting of Azamat's left nipple—a gesture somewhere between sex-play and a baby suckling), and in the sexually suggestive wrestling poses, Azamat appears to inhabit the conventional role of "woman." The incongruity of gender roles for the fat character very well might be a source of laughter.

The fat body, and particularly the morbidly obese, is grotesque (in the Bakhtinian sense)—a body that is not separate from the world, but is inextricably connected to the cosmic universe, which runs completely contrary to our modern conception of a self-contained Symbolic subject independent from its environment.[68] The grotesque body is potentially abject precisely because it demonstrates that it "is not a closed, completed unit; it is unfinished, outgrows itself, transgresses its own limits."[69] Bakhtin continues:

> The stress is laid on those parts of the body that are open to the outside world, that is, the parts through which the world enters the body or

emerges from it, or through which the body itself goes out to meet the world. This means that the emphasis is on the apertures or the convexities, or on various ramifications and offshoots: the open mouth, the genital organs, the breasts, the phallus, the potbelly, the nose. The body discloses its essence as a principle of growth which exceeds its own limits only in copulation, pregnancy, childbirth, the throes of death, eating, drinking, or defecation.[70]

In reality there is absolutely no difference in body types—all are grotesque, that is to say connected to the world. What perhaps sets the obese body apart, however, is its deviation from "normative" human geography. And in its "extra" convexities and protuberances the lines between inside and outside are more difficult to discern. The obese body is no less "open" than any other body; however, in its "expanses" and folds it is potentially viewed as an

unfinished and open body (dying, bringing forth and being born) . . . not separated from the world by clearly defined boundaries; it is blended with the world, with animals, with objects. It is cosmic, it represents the entire material bodily world in all its elements. It is an incarnation of this world at the absolute lower stratum, as the swallowing up and generating principle, as the bodily grave and bosom, as a field which has been sown and in which new shoots are preparing to sprout.[71]

Furthermore, as Miller indicates (cited above), echoing Bakhtin, softness potentially elicits disgust because it signifies fecundity—a body that has yet to become.[72] Fat, after all, is little more than stored energy, and the spectator's disgusted response to its display can easily slip, as we have seen, into laughter.

Azamat's body is open, not only in its "raw" corpulence, but in its gestures. First, the scene begins with another sign of fecundity—Azamat is masturbating.[73] The male genitals (which interestingly are always hidden in the film) bear the seeds of becoming: "This is why the essential role belongs to those parts of the grotesque body in which it outgrows its own self, transgressing its own body, in which it conceives a new, second body: the bowels and the phallus."[74] Excretion (which exits the anus) is not an end, but part of the rejuvenation of life; while the phallus harbors the germ of life itself. Bakhtin explains that bowels, genitals, mouths, and anuses are the sites "where the confines between bodies and between the body and the world are overcome: there is an interchange and an interorientation." The world enters and exits the body through these orifices:

Eating, drinking, defecation and other elimination (sweating, blowing of the nose, sneezing), as well as copulation, pregnancy, dismemberment, swallowing up by another body—all these acts are performed on the confines of the body and the outer world, or on the confines of the old and new body. In all these events the beginning and end of life are closely linked and interwoven.[75]

The image of the fecund body is further emphasized when Borat bites Azamat's left nipple—as already mentioned, having the connotation of a suckling baby, but there is also the suggestion of cannibalism. Furthermore, the "openness" of Azamat's body is perhaps nowhere more self-evident then when he sits on Borat's face and says, "Eat my asshole!" The connotations of this point to the unending process of becoming—incorporation/excretion, inside/outside, impure/clean and proper body. Such unsettling of the conception of the coherent and contained body, introducing the abject open body, a body in a state of constant becoming, might invite the spectator—out of disgust or out of disbelief—to laugh.

CONCLUSION: THE LAST LAUGH

Every study of disgust, in fact, runs the danger of disclosing as much about the author as about his subject.[76]

— Winfried Menninghaus

Recall the plot of *Monsters Inc.* (Pete Docter et al., 2001) where, in a parallel universe, monsters generate power with the screams of children. Monsters are sent through secret portals into children's rooms to scare them, and to elicit screams. What Sully, the big blue monster and top-scarer, and his sidekick Mike discover, though, is that a child's laugh is in fact far more powerful. In the pantheon of affective responses, laughter perhaps deserves to be placed at the top of the hierarchy. No other affective experience is as malleable—capable of responding to humor, to what disgusts, to what is sexually arousing, to the exhibition of pain and horror.[77] The only affective response that seems to come close to laughter is crying (the subject of Chapter 6). We can laugh so hard that it makes us cry. Tears, though, in many instances are bound up with emotions and narrative investment. Laughter, as we have illustrated here, is perhaps "more immediate," and can erupt outside of any narrative contextualization, and independent of the economy of emotion.

In many instances it appears that some sort of violation spawns laughter—whether it is the violation of social mores in a joke, or the exhibition of a body that falls outside "proper" socialization, the corruption of the clean and proper body. Bakhtin noted that, following the Renaissance, (Western) culture viewed the body as a complete and unified entity. "Furthermore," Bakhtin adds, "it was isolated, alone, fenced off from all other bodies. All signs of its unfinished character, of its growth and proliferation were eliminated." What is essential, Bakhtin concludes, is that "The inner processes of absorbing and ejecting were not revealed."[78] But in some instances, this shroud of fetishistic disavowal can no longer disguise the porous body, the incomplete body, the eternal cycle of becoming that is filled with affective potential. When the inner processes are revealed, when they eject from the body (e.g. vomiting), the subject might recoil in disgust and/or erupt in laughter.

Laughter demonstrates the potential to heal, to negotiate the presence of the abject, to intercept the non-object or something in the state of becoming, and thus to outline the boundaries of culture, social mores, the clean and proper body. Laughing is universal to the human subject, a semiotic (Kristeva) utterance that ruptures Symbolic discourse. Neurologists studying individuals who have suffered from hemiparalysis (paralysis on one side of the face) have observed that neural pathways remain intact

between the brain and face. When asked to grin, these patients produce crooked smiles—only one side of their face responds. However, they produce a normal, symmetrical smile if tickled or amused by a joke—the ongoing social stimuli activate intact neuronal pathways that are beyond conscious control. Here we glimpse the otherwise invisible hand of the ancient neurological puppeteer that controls spontaneous laughter and smiling.[79]

Indeed, we are the "creature who laughs," as Aristotle posited.

We are neurologically equipped with laughter, we might say hardwired for it, and we can only presume that there is an evolutionary purpose for it. Beyond comedy, we have constructed rituals, theater, festivals and other activities (including film) that facilitate the expenditure of laughter. Bakhtin celebrates the spirit of the carnival as a form of radical freedom; however, most transgressions that invite laughter are sanctioned, and in the end reaffirm "proper" order. This perhaps speaks to the sheer volume of reaction videos, exemplary of which are the responses to *2 Girls 1 Cup* (a Google video search on "2 Girls 1 Cup reaction video" brings up over 5 million hits). These reaction videos do not signify the weakness of culture, but its insistence on proper order, a self-policing mechanism.[80]

Eco is critical of Bakhtin's celebration of the carnivalesque as a discourse of liberation.[81] Raucous though the carnivalesque might be, at the same time participants must be aware of the rules they are transgressing. "One must know to what degree certain behaviors are forbidden, and must feel the majesty of the forbidding norm, to appreciate their transgression. Without a valid law to break, carnival is impossible."[82] There is nothing revolutionary about the carnival; in fact it "can exist only as an *authorized* transgression . . . If the ancient, religious carnival was limited in time, the modern mass-carnival is limited in space: it is reserved for certain places [e.g. Las Vegas], certain streets, or framed by the television screen."[83] YouTube reaction videos are the latest iteration of modern mass-carnival, sequestered from the broadcast airwaves, but immediately locatable with an internet search. Eco adds that "comedy and carnival are not instances of real transgressions: on the contrary, they represent paramount examples of law reinforcement. They remind us of the existence of the rule."[84] Sometimes the rules that are broken, as we have illustrated here, fall outside the bounds of the Symbolic realm, the world of cognition, and are rooted in a more archaic (maternal/semiotic) experience. Furthermore, this is not to suggest that laughter represents a completely vacuous "false" liberation, and we would posit that we need not surrender to Eco's wholesale dismissal. While we might certainly agree with Eco's general critique (there is nothing truly transgressive here), nonetheless, by most measures, laughter *feels* good and we would not presume to rob the viewing body of that pleasure.

NOTES

1. Silvan S. Tomkins, *Affect Imagery Consciousness: The Complete Edition* (New York: Springer, 2008), 320.
2. Linda Williams, *Hard Core: Power, Pleasure, and the "Frenzy of the Visible"* (Berkeley: University of California Press, 1989), 49, 194.
3. Tarja Laine, *Feeling Cinema: Emotional Dynamics in Film Studies* (New York: Bloomsbury, 2013), 97. Katariina Kyrölä situates laughter in a slightly different paradigm; she positions laughter as a physical reaction to any number of possible stimuli, arguing that "it is not a feeling, an emotion, or an affect in itself." See Katariina Kyrölä, *The Weight of Images: Affect, Body Image and Fat in the Media* (Farnham: Ashgate, 2014), 93.
4. Linda Williams, "Film Bodies: Gender, Genre, and Excess," *Film Quarterly* 44, no. 4 (Summer 1991): 4.
5. Robert R. Provine views laughing as inherently social: "laughter is the quintessential human social signal. Laughter is about relationships." Robert R. Provine, *Laughter: A Scientific Investigation* (New York: Viking, 2000), 44.
6. Umberto Eco, "The Frames of Comic 'Freedom,'" in *Carnival!*, ed. Thomas Sebeok (New York: Mouton, 1984), 5.
7. Provine, 1.
8. Aristotle, *On the Parts of the Animal*, trans. William Ogle (South Bend, IN: Infomotions, 2001), 58.
9. Barry Sanders, *Sudden Glory: Laughter as Subversive History* (Boston: Beacon Press, 1995), 5.
10. Provine, 81. Also see the "Laughter" episode on *Radiolab* (season 4, episode 1) podcast: <https://www.wnyc.org/radio/#/ondemand/91588> (last accessed June 27, 2015).
11. Henri Bergson, "Laughter," in *Comedy: An Essay on Comedy* (Baltimore: Johns Hopkins University Press, 1980), 61.
12. Laughter might be considered an utterance of the body, along the lines of Teresa

Brennan's ideas regarding "fleshly knowledge or codes of the body." Teresa Brennan, *The Transmission of Affect* (Ithaca: Cornell University Press, 2004), 136. Or in another theoretical register we might think of the ways in which Kristeva speaks about semiotized utterances. Robert Provine asks what laughing signifies, probably a more productive question than "What does laughter mean?" He writes, "In laughter we emit sounds and express emotions that come from deep within our biological being—grunts and cackles from our animal unconscious. But what do these vocalizations signify? . . . Our brain has a masterful appreciation of the lawful relations between cues and response, but these rules are hidden from our conscious awareness." Provine, 2.

13. "It turns out, for example, that speakers laugh more than their audiences, that women laugh at men more than men laugh at women, and that laughter has more to do with relationships than with jokes." Provine, 3.

14. Winfried Menninghaus, *Disgust: The Theory and History of a Strong Sensation*, trans. Howard Eiland and Joel Golb (New York: SUNY Press, 2003), 10–11.

15. Ibid., 11. Also see Kyrölä, 83. Silvan S. Tomkins associates disgust with our evolutionary inheritance, protecting our species from what might threaten our survival: "Disgust and nausea therefore have some of the characteristics of the other human affects, but are more similar to the more specific linkages of affect and drive found in the lower animals." (Tomkins, 358.) Later Tomkins writes, "Disgust and dissmell are drive-auxiliary responses, in my view, evolved to protect us against bad smells at a distance and bad taste if such a distance early warning system (dissmell) has been penetrated. Nausea and vomiting are the ultimate disgust response if all else fails." Tomkins, 716.

16. Julia Kristeva, *Powers of Horror: An Essay on Abjection*, trans. Leon S. Roudiez (New York: Columbia University Press, 1982), 41.

17. Ibid.

18. Ibid., 8.

19. Gareth Tyson et al., "Demystifying Porn 2.0: A Look into a Major Adult Video Streaming Website" (paper presented at the Internet Measure Conference, Barcelona, October 23–5, 2013), 419.

20. Ibid.

21. Susanna Paasonen, *Carnal Resonance: Affect and Online Pornography* (Cambridge, MA: MIT Press, 2011), 210.

22. While *2 Girls 1 Cup* intends to arouse (catering to very specific sexual tastes), for the vast majority of viewers it is most likely to elicit disgust and/or laughter. Fiorito was investigated for a US federal indictment, but he was never charged. See Carmen Cusack, *Pornography and The Criminal Justice System* (Boca Raton, FL: CRC Press, 2015), 192. For more on reaction videos see Julia Kennedy and Clarissa Smith, "His Soul Shatters at About 0:23: *Spankwire*, Self-Scaring and Hyperbolic Shock," in *Controversial Images: Media Representations on the Edge*, ed. Feona Attwood et al. (New York: Palgrave Macmillan, 2012), 239–53.

23. Jason Middleton's chapter on reaction videos in his *Documentary's Awkward Turn: Cringe Comedy and Media* similarly notes that "we laugh *with* the prankster as both of us laugh *at* the victim. But these three positions are fungible . . . As in the *Jackass* film and television franchise—which presents the performance of dangerous and stupid stunts as simultaneously ridiculous *and* admirable—the viewer and the social actors laugh with *and* at each other and themselves." Jason Middleton, *Documentary's Awkward Turn: Cringe Comedy and Media* (New York: Routledge, 2014), 124.

24. A Google video search for "*2 Girls 1 Cup* reaction videos" yields 5,450,000 hits (August 12, 2015).

25. Middleton cites a *2 Girls 1 Cup* reaction video featuring the comedian Joe Rogan, host of
    the television program *Fear Factor* (where contestants compete by doing dangerous stunts,
    or consuming what by our standards might be considered disgusting—bugs for instance).
    The Rogan reaction video "is clearly intended to demonstrate that '2 Girls 1 Cup' can be
    shocking even to someone who has 'seen it all.'" (Middleton, 129.) Rogan says as a preface
    that "I've seen all the threads about it on the Internet . . . nothing's going to shock me,
    I've seen a guy get fucked to death by a horse, I've seen people eat diarrhea, . . . I've seen
    it all . . ." Despite his jaded disposition Rogan is clearly affected by *2 Girls 1 Cup*—he
    moves away from the computer monitor, utters "ohs," pinches up his face, averts his eyes,
    at one point dry heaves, and declares, "I can't watch that. That's insane!"
26. Middleton, 126. On the subject of "authenticity" also see Helen Hester, *Beyond Explicit:
    Pornography and the Displacement of Sex* (New York: SUNY Press, 2014), 60.
27. Middleton, 127.
28. Hester, 15.
29. Ibid., 50–1.
30. Ibid., 50.
31. Ibid., 51–2.
32. Ibid., 55.
33. Kristeva, 2–3.
34. Ibid., 73.
35. Paasonen, 210–11.
36. Addressing medieval laughter Mikhail Bakhtin notes: "The acute awareness of victory
    over fear is an essential element of medieval laughter. This feeling is expressed in a
    number of characteristic medieval comic images. We always find in them the defeat of fear
    presented in a droll and monstrous form, the symbols of power and violence turned inside
    out, the comic images of death and bodies gaily rent asunder. All that was terrifying
    becomes grotesque. We have already mentioned that one of the indispensable accessories
    of carnival was the set called 'hell.' This 'hell' was solemnly burned at the peak of the
    festivities. This grotesque image cannot be understood without appreciating the defeat of
    fear. The people play with terror and laugh at it; the awesome becomes a 'comic
    monster.'" Mikhail Bakhtin, *Rabelais and His World*, trans. Helene Iswolsky
    (Bloomington: Indiana University Press, 1984), 91.
37. Ibid., 21.
38. We might view *2 Girls 1 Cup* through the spirit of the carnival: "In fact, carnival does not
    know footlights, in the sense that it does not acknowledge any distinction between actors
    and spectators . . . Carnival is not a spectacle seen by the people; they live in it, and
    everyone participates because its very idea embraces all the people . . . During carnival
    time life is subject only to its laws, that is, the laws of its own freedom." Bakhtin, 7.
39. The writers of the program were inspired by a YouTube reality-show-type clip where the
    host offers a stranger on the street $200 initially to drink ipecac and to puke on the street.
    Eventually the host ups the offer to $500, and then after he vomits numerous times, the
    host offers him another $500 to lick up one of the puddles of puke (see <https://www.
    youtube.com/watch?v=dvQ9dQPGRUo>, last accessed November 25, 2015). Also see
    "neknomination" videos, where in many instances a group of young men videotape a
    subject drinking to incredible excess in a short period of time (e.g. downing a pint of
    vodka in a single gulp). The subject, after performing the feat, then nominates someone
    else to top them. In some cases the video also documents the results of binge-drinking:
    vomiting and/or bodily injury.
40. *Taxidermia* could be read through the Rabelaisian lens, particularly in its mobilization of

grotesque and gluttonous bodies, but also in its penetrating medical gaze, peering into the body itself—namely, in the practice of taxidermy. Rabelais studied medicine and his literature frequently details the processes of the body (e.g. urination, reproduction), and long atomized lists of body parts. See Bakhtin, 194.

41. Steven Shaviro, "Body Horror and Post-Socialist Cinema: Györgi Pálfi's *Taxidermia*," *Film-Philosophy* 15, no. 2 (2011): 96.

42. Ibid., 100. Shaviro cites Williams, "Film Bodies," 5.

43. William Ian Miller, *Anatomy of Disgust* (Cambridge, MA: Harvard University Press, 1997), 96.

44. Bakhtin, 26.

45. Ibid. Later Bakhtin discusses "mudslinging" and the throwing of excrement at medieval and ancient festivals: "But such debasing gestures and expressions are ambivalent, since the lower stratum is not only a bodily grave but also the area of the genital organs, the fertilizing and generating stratum. Therefore, in the images of urine and excrement is preserved the essential link with birth, fertility, renewal, welfare. This positive element was still fully alive and clearly realized in the time of Rabelais." Bakhtin, 148.

46. Miller, 40–1.

47. Bakhtin, 151.

48. The zealous revelry with which the Jackass crew approaches their masochistic stunts bears certain affinities with Rabelais's Catchpoles. As recounted by Mikhail Bakhtin, the Catchpoles, found in the Pantagruel narrative, were "inhabitants [that] earn their living by letting themselves be thrashed. Friar John selects a 'red-snouted' catchpole (Rouge museau) and pays him twenty gold crowns: 'Friar John swung his staff manfully, thwacking and cracking Redsnout so lustily on belly and back, on head and legs that, as he fell to earth, a battered pulp, I feared for the Catchpole's death' (Book 4, Chapter 16). We see that the anatomic enumeration of the parts of the body has not been neglected. Rabelais goes on to relate: 'Then he gave him his twenty crowns. But the churl rose, happy as a king—or a pair of kings, for that matter.' . . . This image of a 'king' and 'two kings' is here directly introduced in order to describe the highest degree of happiness reached by the Catchpole who has received his reward. But the image is essentially related to the gay thrashings and abuse as well as to the red snout of the Catchpole, to his apparent death, sudden return to life, and jumping up like a clown who has received a beating. Here is a dimension in which thrashing and abuse are not a personal chastisement but are symbolic actions directed at something on a higher level, at the king. This is the popular-festive system of images, which is most clearly expressed in carnival (but, of course, not in carnival alone)." Bakhtin, 197–8.

49. In *Jackass 3.5* (Jeff Tremaine, 2011) Knoxville even notes that he had seen a Buster Keaton film with a mini-cannon, and so he had one built which he uses to surreptitiously shoot his unsuspecting crew.

50. Elaine Scarry, *The Body in Pain: The Making and Unmaking of the World* (New York: Oxford University Press, 1987), 6.

51. Ibid., 13. See Michael Richardson's chapter, "Torturous Affect: Writing and the Problem of Pain," in *Traumatic Affect*, eds. Meera Atkinson and Michael Richardson, 148–70 (Newcastle upon Tyne: Cambridge Scholars Publishing, 2013) for the difficulties in representing pain.

52. Eugenie Brinkema similarly observes, "Vomit, as a privileged confession of the materiality of the body becomes, in Freud's comparison, a privileged confession of the non-materiality of the body in that inward turn." Eugenie Brinkema, "Laura Dern's Vomit, or, Kant and Derrida in Oz," *Film-Philosophy* 15, no. 2 (2011): 51.

53. For more on Muybridge and his photographic experiments to render the confessions of the body see Williams, *Hard Core*, 37–48.

54. Hester, 67–8. Stephen Maddison similarly observes: "Extreme Associates' output represents one of the newly emerging porn genres, derived from the low-budget gonzo conventions established by John Stagliano in his *Buttman* series (1990–2005). Extreme Associates' films combine gonzo hand-held camera work and low tech style with conventions derived from slasher movies, the reality TV genres of *Jackass* stunts and gross-out and fly-on-the-wall documentaries." Stephen Maddison, "'Choke on it, Bitch!': Porn Studies, Extreme Gonzo and the Mainstreaming of Hardcore," in *Mainstreaming Sex: The Sexualization of Western Culture*, ed. Feona Attwood (New York: I. B. Tauris, 2009), 38.

55. Bakhtin, 352–3.

56. Robert Stam, *Subversive Pleasures: Bakhtin, Cultural Criticism, and Film* (Baltimore: Johns Hopkins University Press, 1989), 113. Although Stam does not offer any names, we presume that the implicit reference here is to Tom Gunning, and perhaps Sergei Eisenstein. Gunning (and his colleague André Gaudreault) appropriated the term "attraction" from Eisenstein. "The term attractions refers backwards to a popular tradition and forwards to an avant-garde subversion. The tradition is that of the fairground and carnival, and particularly its development during the turn of the century in such modern amusement parks as Coney Island. The avant-garde radicalisation of this term comes in the theoretical and practical work in theatre and film of Sergei Eisenstein, whose theory of the montage of attractions intensified this popular energy into an aesthetic subversion, through a radical theoreticisation of the power of attractions to undermine the conventions of bourgeois realism." Tom Gunning, "An Aesthetic of Astonishment: Early Film and the (In)credulous Spectator," in *Critical Concepts in Media and Cultural Studies*, ed. Philip Simpson et al. (New York: Routledge, 2004), 93, n.13.

57. Bakhtin, 353.

58. Slavoj Žižek writes, "Recall a standard Tom and Jerry cartoon: Jerry is run over by a heavy truck, dynamite explodes in his mouth, he is cut to slices, yet in the next scene he's back again with no traces of the previous disasters. The stuff of comedy is precisely this repetitive, resourceful popping-up of life—no matter how dark the predicament, we can be sure the small fellow will find a way out." Slavoj Žižek, "Camp Comedy," *Sight and Sound* 10, no. 4 (2000), 29.

59. Bakhtin, 354.

60. Bakhtin observes: "Rabelais presents a number of typical grotesque forms of exaggerated body parts that completely hide the normal members of the body. This is actually a picture of dismemberment, of separate areas of the body enlarged to gigantic dimensions. First of all, we see men with monstrous bellies (a typical grotesque hyperbola); Saint Pansard (St. Paunchman) and Mardi Gras belong to this gay race. Saint Pansard's ironic name was associated with carnival, and King Carnival, himself, is related to the family of fat paunches. Next, Rabelais depicts hunchbacks with humps of huge proportions, or monstrous noses, abnormally long legs, gigantic ears. There are men with disproportionate phalli (wound six times around their waists) and others with unusually large testes. We have a picture of a giant grotesque body and at the same time an array of carnival figures." Bakhtin, 327–8.

61. Georges Bataille, *Erotism: Death and Sensuality*, trans. Mary Dalwood (San Francisco: City Lights Books, 1986), 63. Paasonen also discusses anal eroticism in almost Bakhtinian terms—a turning over. See Paasonen, 213–14.

62. Winfried Menninghaus, *Disgust: The Theory and History of a Strong Sensation*, trans. Howard Eiland and Joel Golb (New York: SUNY Press, 2003), 355.

63. Ibid.
64. See Michael Billig, *Laughter and Ridicule: Towards a Social Critique of Humour* (Thousand Oaks, CA: SAGE, 2005).
65. Kyrölä, 104.
66. Ibid., 103.
67. Ibid., 103–4.
68. This of course is set against our conceptions of what a "beautiful" body is: "The ideal of the beautiful—the classical statue and the human body in general—is subject, from head to toe, to a topography and chronography of 'disgust.' Disgusting zones, disgusting moments are the strategic entry points of the beautiful body's construction. Folds, wrinkles, warts, 'excessive softness,' visible or overly large bodily openings, discharge of bodily fluids (nasal mucous, pus, blood), and old age are registered, on the criminal index of aesthetics, as 'disgusting.' The positive requirements of the aesthetically pleasing body—elastic and slender contour without incursions of fat, flawless youthful firmness and unbroken skin without folds or openings, removal of bodily hair and plucked eyebrows forming a fine line, flat belly and 'trim' behind, and so on—are at the same time prescriptions for the avoidance of disgust." Menninghaus, 7.
69. Bakhtin, 26.
70. Ibid.
71. Ibid., 26–7.
72. Miller, 40–1. Aurel Kolnai also argues that "the tactile impression of flabbiness, sliminess, pastiness, and indeed of everything soft, should count among the disgusting. Or rather, these exhibit a predisposition for becoming disgusting." Aurel Kolnai, *On Disgust*, eds. Barry Smith and Carolyn Korsmeyer (Chicago: Open Court, 2004), 50.
73. Although there is no excessive exhibition of fecundity here, disgust might be "aroused by exuberant, exaggerated fertility." Kolnai, 61.
74. Bakhtin, 317.
75. Ibid.
76. Menninghaus, 20.
77. Barry Sanders notes of the historical significance of laughter: "Surely the sound of laughter has always been heard as humankind's *Ursprache*, the Ur-expression of human beings unabashedly, unashamedly sounding themselves—as persons. Even grunts and groans require some pointing to convey meaning, but without a single word or gesture, laughter assures us that hopefully, playfully—at times even mildly aggressive—human activity is taking place. It requires no training and little experience to understand. It is the prelinguistic tag that we cannot shake, following us into adulthood and beyond. In its ability to make contact, it simply has no rivals. It trammels all barriers. Laughter loosens its transcendental meaning in a medieval Latin *hahahae*, or in modern English *ha ha ha*, or in a Joycean *ha he hi ho hu*." Sanders, 32–3.
78. Bakhtin, 29.
79. Provine, 52–3.
80. Plato recognized the power of laughter, and argued that laughter should be tempered otherwise it might undermine the authority of the state. Barry Sanders notes about Plato on the subject: "We don't think of Plato as the father of laughter. But in fact he devotes an awful lot of attention to laughter. He comes to the subject, not out of veneration for its origins, or out of appreciation for its beauty, but out of respect for its power. He respects its ability to subvert so effectively the status quo, its Herculean strength to twist the taut lines of power into mere haywire. He, too, smells something wrong: He knows that laughter can dig in its heels as a most awesome foe to authority, and he recognizes that

with a single laugh each and every citizen, regardless of rank, carries an incipient power to blow things apart. Moreover, derisive laughter takes over the role of a court of law, meting out its own brand of justice immediately and decisively. Indeed, it rewrites laws on the spot. The Republic cannot tolerate such a threat to its authority. People do not need to be governed so much as they need their passions controlled. So, as a leader—a philosopher in the grandest sense—Plato must make certain that laughter does not run wild." (Sanders, 88–9.) The disgust that the *2 Girls 1 Cup* video tends to elicit is perhaps an illustration of the policing of social norms such as Tomkins views it. See Tomkins, 414.

81. Robert Stam offers a forceful rebuttal of Eco's dismissal of the Bakhtinian carnival, observing that, among other things, Eco's reading is "ultimately elitist" and "Eurocentric." Stam, 91–2.

82. Eco, 6.

83. Ibid.

84. Ibid.

CHAPTER 5

Arousal: Graphic Encounters

Understanding fleshly languages as languages—structured systems of intelligent communication whose matter is intrinsic to their form—enhances the likelihood that science will identify more of them.[1]

INTRODUCTION: SEDUCTION

Taken on their own, sounds such as grunts, sighs, heavy breathing, or screaming might just as easily signify pain as sexual excitation. Similarly, divorced of any establishing shot, a tight close-up of a face forcefully pinched up, mouth agape, might very well be difficult to read. Recall, for instance, Stan Brakhage's silent short film *Window Water Baby Moving* (1959), which documents Jane Brakhage's birthing of the couple's first daughter. Individual shots, particularly close-ups of Jane's face, are easily confused for ecstatic frenzy, but given the situation clearly register the pain of childbirth. And it is precisely this confusion, which Brakhage obviously "plays with," that prompted Carolee Schneemann to make her frank erotic experimental film *Fuses* (1965).

Tsai Ming-liang's 2005 film *The Wayward Cloud* is not an extreme film in the way that *Hostel* is, for example. Nonetheless, these films are comparable in their manipulation of (aural) signifiers of pain and ecstasy (recall Josh's misrecognition of the sounds of a consensual BDSM encounter as those of violation).[2] Structurally, though, *The Wayward Cloud* approaches extreme cinema, as its conventional dramatic narrative hosts ruptures—seemingly LSD-inspired Busby Berkeley song-and-dance numbers as well as fairly frank sex scenes. Like *Window Water Baby Moving*, Tsai's film conflates sexual ecstasy with childbirth. Shiang-chyi, the central female character, mounts the stairs of her apartment block with a large watermelon under her shirt, making it appear she is pregnant. Suddenly she collapses, evidently overwhelmed with contractions. She pants and grunts, and as much as the act reflects the birthing process, it is mildly erotic insofar as the semiotic utterances, the supposed paroxysmal collapse due to pain (or is it ecstasy?), the splaying of her legs, her prone posture, her pursed lips, heavy breathing which climaxes with orgasmic wailing as the melon emerges from under her shirt—all these bodily expressions might be confused with signifiers of arousal. The slippage of signifiers is not an accident; clearly this is what Tsai intends, because the very next shot cuts to a Japanese porn actress—completely naked—masturbating on a kitchen counter with a water-bottle. Within the diegetic narrative a pornographic film is being shot, and Tsai immediately cuts to the film-within-the-film—a meta-cinematic gesture that acknowledges the slippage of audio/visual signifiers in the cinema.[3]

Whether it is pain, or orgasmic pleasure, affective "discourse" wields the potential to overwhelm the channels of the Symbolic. And while there are affinities between pain and pleasure, Elaine Scarry insists that whereas "intense physical" pain might overcome the subject and their capacity for speech, conversely pleasure is "language building." Scarry concedes that the lover's discourse might regress, reverting to baby-talk or resorting "to monosyllables, so one might say that language is backing up, the way it does when one is suddenly put in pain: language not only disappears, but you can actually chart its disappearance across the sudden reaching for monosyllables or for the kinds of cries and whispers that one made before one learned language." Love, Scarry concludes, constructs narratives.[4] But what of the carnal experience, erotic frenzy? This seems to us wholly different. Love is a narrative that contextualizes—analogous to the cinema of attractions, the erotic encounter is a "tamed attraction" in the lover's discourse.

While it is possible to confuse the aural and visual signifiers of sex, reading the signifiers of sexual excitation for pain (or vice versa), in extreme cinema the exhibition of sexually explicit content might elicit from the spectator something other than arousal. Strangely, perhaps, sexually explicit content in extreme cinema might be more likely to elicit disgust than spawn erotic feelings (as one might initially expect). What at first might seem like a strange vacillation between arousal and disgust is not so strange after all, when one realizes that both sensations are the product of a negotiated closeness.

William Ian Miller's *Anatomy of Disgust* observes that bodily transgressions in one context might register disgust, while in another (amorous) context they might be arousing:

Generally in sex the boundary crossing and permission granting are mutual, so both partners get the same disgust-related thrills and offend the gods of purity equally—a pure feast of misrule. We simply will do things or let things be done to ourselves in love and sex that violate all the norms the violation of which would trigger disgust if unprivileged, if coerced, or even if witnessed. And to do such and to have such done to us is much of what sexual intimacy is.[5]

Miller, nonetheless, is careful not to make this negotiation simply a matter of sex; rather, for him love plays a vital role in suspending the rules governing disgust. He insists that sex "does not quite suspend disgust; it indulges it. Love is something less dramatic. When I say love means the suspension of disgust rules I am speaking about much more mundane intimacies that really mark out the terrain of familiarity and the occasional contempts that it can breed."[6] What this reveals is the contingent nature of erotic arousal, and the affecting experience in general. The affecting experience is not "purely" physiological; rather, it is negotiated through overdetermined systems—neurological, subjective, linguistic, cultural systems to name a few—that mediate it. And precisely because affect is subject to negotiation this allows for a more fluid understanding of what is arousing.

Helen Hester's notion of the expanded pornographic is exceptionally productive here. In her book *Beyond Explicit*, she untethers "sexual explicitness or genital activity" from the pornographic, precisely because the terrain of material—from novels and memoirs to television and content distributed via the Web—that elicits an intense affective response displaces sexual material "as the primary locus of transgression."[7] Porn, or the pornographic, in Hester's view should not be limited to sexually explicit material, but rather, this expanded understanding of the pornographic opens up to a wider affective spectrum, "provoking more general forms of queasy *jouissance*—horror, anger, sorrow, and a certain nauseated fascination."[8] Perhaps not in the realm of the pornographic, but the erotic rather, Park Chan-wook's *Stoker* (2013) includes a sex scene for which there is no sex. The Reverend joins the young India Stoker at the piano; during a series of fetishistic shots of India's curling feet/legs, and her ecstatic face, the playing of the piano works up to an orgasmic pitch. The cinematography, the music, the fetishistic exhibition of (clothed) bodies is not so much arousing as it is sublime (this author, for one [Kerner], had hairs standing on end).

As we have seen in previous chapters (particularly Chapter 4)—and this seems to contradict Linda Williams's idea about the mimicry inherent in the body genres—there is the potential for "affective dissonance": where the stimulating referent might invite the seemingly opposite visceral response (e.g. vomiting eliciting laughter, a sexual encounter that disgusts). While a film might host sexually explicit content, this does not necessarily make it pornographic, or for that matter an example of extreme cinema. Virginie Despentes and Coralie Trinh Thi's co-directed 2000 feature *Baise-Moi*, for instance, includes graphic sexual content, but by our measure is not representative of extreme cinema. Its treatment of sex, though in most cases emotionally disturbing, is more in keeping with pornography's documentary function—the film records (read: documents) genuine sex, that is to say, penetration and ejaculation. The quality of the image, which is indicative of the video format on which it was shot, exhibits the texture of pornographic and documentary films of that period. The digital video format lends *Baise-Moi* a general gritty "realism"[9]—the grain of the image adds to the reality effect, and the supposed "authenticity" of the sex acts performed in the film.

Baise-Moi (sometimes given as *Rape Me*, or *Fuck Me*) spurned some critical attention following its release. And although the film includes graphic scenes of menstrual blood and brutal violence, what most critics focused on is the inclusion of unsimulated sex. *Baise-Moi* is effectively a rape revenge film, often compared to *Thelma and Louise* (Ridley Scott, 1991), but with graphic sex, and amplified violence. What is particularly fascinating about *Baise-moi*, though, is its relative lack of affective resonance stemming from graphic sexual content. This is due, in large part, to the way in which sexual encounters are presented. Sex in *Baise-moi* is *a part* of the narrative; it is situated within (frequently violent) cause and effect relationships, and is shot more or less in the conventions of dramatic narrative, rather than adopting the choreography of the pornographic regime. Furthermore, the sexual encounters in *Baise-moi* are for the most part not predicated on a mutual negotiation of closeness, and thus as Miller identified are more likely to "trigger disgust."[10] If, and that is a qualified "if," there are affective moments in *Baise-moi*, it is unlikely to sexually arouse; rather, it is far more likely to elicit other sensations, such as disgust—turning away at the sight of menstrual blood perhaps, or sexual violation. Catherine Zuromskis observes that *Baise-moi* might be considered pornographic because it "brings the viewer as close as possible to the sexual act on-screen." But Zuromskis similarly qualifies her position:

> Cinematically, *Baise-moi* has far more in common with the road movie genre or the thriller or even the horror film. Thus the affective pleasures taken from a film like *Baise-moi*, such as they are, stem from shock, horror, and perhaps anger but not from the pornographic titillation and gratification of sexual voyeurism.[11]

Despite the fact that the film offers occasional meat shots, full-frontal views of male and female bodies, and ejaculate (proof of (male) gratification), these elements are still nevertheless nested within the narrative—in effect utterly "tamed attractions"—and therefore outside the realm of extreme cinema. Moreover, the presentation of sexual situations is relatively flat, what we might call "style-less," neutralizing their potential to arouse. Attenuating the channels of affect, the graphic images instead serve an emotive function that details the characters' motivation. In the same way that the repeated rape of Jennifer in *I Spit on Your Grave* (Meir Zarchi, 1978; Steven R. Monroe, 2010) is rendered unarousing—or, that is to say, disturbing rather than arousing—the violent treatment of these characters offers narrative motivation (if not justification) for their ferocious revenge. Whether it is *Baise-moi* or *I Spit on Your Grave*, the sex in these films is hardly (intended to be) arousing.

There is very little, if anything, arousing in Catherine Breillat's 1999 film *Romance*. The film is highly novelistic—that is to say it is laced with extensive poetic dialogue and the lament-filled introspection of Marie, the film's sex-deprived female protagonist. In her *Feeling Cinema*, Tarja Laine describes the sex in *Romance* as "non-affective," and indeed, there is hardly anything erotic about the sex in the film.[12] "*Romance* creates a discrepancy between content and form, enunciation and reception, even between affectivity and emotion,"[13] Laine notes. Marie, who finds herself in a sex-less relationship (and perhaps loveless too) seeks satisfaction elsewhere. Her rendezvous range from blasé "vanilla sex" to BDSM, and even a random encounter on the street which begins as consensual sex but turns to rape. As in *Baise-Moi* the sexual encounters are rendered affectless, and the graphic content (meat shots, money shots, full-frontal nudity) is ultimately more likely to elicit ennui than anything else. Despite this, critics such as James Quandt count *Romance* and *Baise-Moi* among the supposedly transgressive films of the New French Extremity. Quandt laments that trends in (millennial) French cinema toward the extreme

> seem the determinants of a cinema suddenly determined to break every taboo, to wade in rivers of viscera and spumes of sperm, to fill each frame with flesh, nubile or gnarled, and subject it to all manner of penetration, mutilation, and defilement. Images and subjects once the provenance of splatter films, exploitation flicks, and porn—gang rapes, bashings and slashings and blindings, hard-ons and vulvas, cannibalism, sadomasochism and incest, fucking and fisting, sluices of cum and gore—proliferate in the high-art environs of a national cinema whose provocations have historically been formal, political, or philosophical (Godard, Clouzot, Debord) or, at their most immoderate (Franju, Bunuel, Walerian Borowczyk, Andrzej Zulawski), at least assimilable as emanations of an artistic movement (Surrealism mostly).[14]

Romance certainly includes graphic images—but on their own, they are hardly affecting. They do, however, appear to possess the power to offend, as evident in Quandt's survey of extreme French cinema. But these are not exactly of the same order—offense and affect (which we will return to shortly).

By contrast with these rather "flat" films, Michael Winterbottom's 2004 film *9 Songs* is an unabashed erotic film eliciting arousal. Of all the films discussed in this chapter, *9 Songs* is perhaps the most "straightforward" in its eroticism. From the very opening of the film it is clear that it is *about* (erotic) sensations, above and beyond any emotional (or narrative) investment. Flying over the barren landscape of Antarctica, in voiceover our primary male character, Matt, recounts, "When I remember Lisa, I don't think about her clothes, or her work, or where she was from, or what she said. I think about her smell, her taste, her skin touching mine." What Matt emphasizes is the sensations—smell, taste, touch. And with these latter phrases the film cuts to a flashback of the couple having sex. This is immediately followed by a cut to the title card *9 Songs* and to the concert venue where, Matt explains, he first met Lisa. The Manchester-inspired psychedelic-rock of Black Rebel Motorcycle Club plays with various shots of the band, and raucous spectators—the band in particular are seen in an array of colors and lighting, awash with red, caught in silhouette—as Peter Hayes the singer belts out lyrics like "Whatever happened to my rock 'n' roll?" The concert is cross-cut with Matt and Lisa in the midst of a sexual encounter, as if to answer Hayes's question. If the film has a narrative to speak of, it is scant; but that is beside the point. The film, like a song (or poetry), needs only hints of a narrative through-line; rather, it is the sensual nature of the film that shoulders the burden of carrying the spectator from start to finish. Winterbottom says as much:

> I think films that tell a love story tend to rely on a lot of narrative that doesn't have anything to do with being in love. In a way, being in love doesn't have much narrative; if you think about love poems and love songs, they're much more successful at capturing what it feels like to be in love because they're not so concerned with narrative.[15]

The ebbs and tides of *9 Songs* do in fact come closer to music than narrative (cinema).

Personal aside (Kerner): this morning, on public transport, a scent suddenly captivated me—in an instant I was suddenly transported back over two decades to when I first met my life-partner. Activating my "sense memory," the scent triggered associations with the earliest moments of our relationship—awash in euphoric elation and erotic pleasures. The *form* and the content of *9 Songs* corresponds to this idea of "sense memory," which is presented in fragmentary bursts, snippets of sensual encounters, rather than a coherent narrative as such. In sum, affect comes first, what the affective encounter "means" is imposed later—if at all. Melanie Williams's review of the film similarly adds that the jettisoning of narrative gets "to the heart of what we really remember about a past love affair: the rush of physical intimacy and the music that we were listening to at the time—the melodies that 'haunt our reverie' and transport us back to the past." What is emphasized is the affective charge associated with the memories of an erotic relationship. It makes perfect sense, then, for Winterbottom to frame the film around erotic encounters and music "as a means of getting to the quintessence of love."[16] And moreover, it is not the *meaning of the relationship* that is at stake, but Matt's feelings, or his "sense memory"—the nostalgic recollection of passionate sex.

Although the sex is unsimulated, even including one instance of (male) ejaculation, it really shares only one thing in common with conventional mainstream heterosexual pornography—it is episodic. The film is punctuated, not surprisingly, with 9 songs, and (depending on how one counts) at least nine erotic encounters. In between these elements—concerts and sex—snippets of daily life offer a small glimpse into the arc of the couple's relationship. Sex is depicted unadulterated without using familiar pornographic choreography. Erotic encounters in *9 Songs* do not necessarily work through the typical pornographic routine climaxing with the money shot, which usually signals the conclusion of a sexual episode, nor are there an abundance of meat shots. Rather, Winterbottom emphasizes fetishistic images, of mouths in particular. Probing tongues in near extreme close-ups during passionate kissing; cunnilingus; fellatio; mouths, lips and tongues following the contours of the respective partner's body; mouths agape in ecstasy. The erotic charge of the compositions is amplified by the audio—heaving breath, moans, moist lapping.

We might consider Lars Von Trier's *Nymphomaniac Volume I* and *Volume II* (2013) in a similar light. A man named Seligman finds the female protagonist, Joe, an unabashed nymphomaniac, beaten unconscious in an alley. The gentle asexual Seligman nurses Joe in his drab flat, and patiently listens to Joe recount her sexual encounters leading up to this point. The very structure of the two films is, like *9 Songs*, episodic. Joe's recollections of her sexual escapades unfold in flashbacks, and in many instances include explicit sex scenes. As with pornography, which partitions its sexual episodes with scraps of narrative, *Nymphomaniac* buffers Joe's many sexual encounters with philosophical exchanges between Joe and Seligman—the monastic bookworm, for instance, compares Joe's sexual guile with the art of fly-fishing. Joe recounts a wide range of experiences—everything from fellatio, double penetration (anal/vaginal), through BDSM—but in some cases sex is displaced for other highly charged encounters. Mrs. H. with her two young boys confronts Joe and Mr. H., with whom Joe is having an affair. Uma Thurman plays Mrs. H. and the scene (following the arc of a conventional sexual number) builds to a fevered melodramatic pitch, in the end culminating with her screams and cries, which find affinities with the orgasmic utterances and fluid emissions at the climax of a pornographic episode.

In addition to its refusal to adhere to dramatic narrative conventions in favor of the episodic, *9 Songs* has also been criticized for its rendering of the female character. In her review of *9 Songs* Williams is highly critical of

Winterbottom's fetishistic motifs, observing that "Lisa is remembered by Matt not as a complete person with any kind of cerebral life, but as a near silent sexual cipher, and a clichéd one to boot."[17] Sadly, this is true, but the story (such as it is) is Matt's, and it is told from his perspective. But, and this is critical, it *is not a story* so much as it is a reflection on sensations, the sensual experience divorced of meaning *per se*. We should not dismiss Williams's criticism that *9 Songs* denies Lisa (sexual) agency. She is categorically correct in terms of the film's narrative content. However, the *form* of Winterbottom's film nonetheless elicits erotic arousal in the viewer and is exemplary of extreme cinema.

And this brings us to an uneasy juncture. Let us be utterly frank: our body has the potential to betray our most vigilant moral position.[18] What might offend our moral disposition might nonetheless be affecting—acts of vigilante violence eliciting giddy euphoria including sweaty palms, acts of vicious humiliation that cause us to curl over laughing. As much as we would care to deny the fact, non-consensual sex acts or other depravities wield the potential to arouse. There is very much the possibility for moral dissonance in the affective realm. One of the sub-genres in Japanese pornography is "rape," while in the USA, Extreme Associates produces a line of, as Stephen Maddison calls it, "extreme (post-)gonzo" pornography, which often showcases violent sexual scenarios.[19] Regardless of the historical/cultural context, clearly there is an audience for sexual violence, and it would be naive to imagine that some do not find it arousing. We by no means want to suggest that we should surrender to a hyper-radical relativism; rather, what we intend to illustrate is that the affecting experience is highly elastic in nature—specifically what a spectator might take as arousing—and that it might run counter to our own moral disposition.[20]

THE (NASTY) TASTE AND SCENT OF SEDUCTION IN *WETLANDS*

> This book shouldn't be read or adapted to film. It's nothing more than a mirror of our sad society. Life has so much more to offer than the disgusting perversity of the human heart. We need God.
> — Comment on *Bild.de* online[21]

Adapted from Charlotte Roche's best-selling novel *Feuchtgebiete*, David Wnendt's 2013 film *Wetlands* caused something of a stir at the 2014 Sundance Film Festival—eliciting audible groans, and collective wincing, but all at the same time fostering a strange euphoric response to Helen, our 18-year-old central character, and her quest to locate authentic human intimacy.[22] Where real-world and narrative conventions dictate that subjects submit to particular mores (regarding gender roles, hygiene), Helen goes about everything "ass-backward," so to speak. Much of the film's provocative content originates in its literary source. Roche's novel sparked a storm of controversy, compelling critics to weigh in on whether her book is pornography or genuine literature—a tired and well-worn debate, rehearsed many times over. Roche views her novel as a feminist manifesto, railing against the social expectations levied on women, specifically in the social regimes that police the female body, insisting that it appear "beautiful" or not at all. "I wanted to write about the ugly parts of the human body," Roche insists. "The smelly bits. The juices of the female body . . . I created a heroine that has a totally creative attitude towards her body—someone who has never even heard that women are supposedly smelly between their legs. A real free spirit."[23] Roche's stated objective is not lost on Wnendt.

Traumatized by an authoritarian and psychologically unstable mother, as well as by her parent's divorce, Helen as an adolescent seeks pleasure in all manner of filth. Roche strove to write a funny and approachable character, and Wnendt follows her lead, offering a playfully charming aesthetic, and an affable central character even when she openly flouts social mores, or is ruthlessly cruel to others. The very first shot of the film is a tight close-up of Helen's thigh and calf pinched together. The composition of the shot makes it look like a human buttocks, though, and the truth of what we see is only disclosed when the camera pulls back to reveal our central character crouched down as she rides her skateboard barefoot. This is coupled with a punk-rock song, "You Love It," forcefully sung by Peaches (a female artist). The camera pulls back to see Helen from behind, aggressively scratching her butt with her right hand, as she skateboards down the street. In an internal monologue Helen explains that she has always suffered from hemorrhoids. In apparent desperation she looks for a public bathroom. Coming upon a subway she descends into the subterranean space and wades through the one-inch-deep pool of murky black water that covers the bathroom floor. The bathroom is dark, decrepit, and strewn with litter, soiled paper-towels and graffiti. From the first instant that Helen steps *barefoot* into the swampy water the spectator is likely to experience disgust—lurching backward away from the sight of abject filth. But it is not simply "filth" that elicits disgust; rather, it is the absence of order, the apparent abandonment of regimes of civilization.[24] In all probability, in deference to the performer (Carla Juri, the actress playing Helen), the water, the plastic bags, the rubbish, were most likely perfectly benign. However, the connotative values assigned to the bathroom—subterranean, with various elements not in their proper place (e.g. a plastic bag on the floor, standing water)—elicit disgust. On their own and in a different context, in fact, the items that litter the bathroom might be affectively neutral, or perhaps even have a positive resonance insofar as they serve a certain use-value, particularly in the operations of cleanliness (plastic wrapper), or nourishment (paper cup, water). In sum, rubbish is not *inherently* filthy; it is the context within which it is found that makes it so.

The color and lighting scheme also amplify the abject qualities of the space. Similar to the torture chambers found in torture porn, the bathroom exhibits the symptoms of abjection: dampness, seeping fixtures, indiscernibility (is it water? urine? excrement? or a mixture), surfaces that are discolored or stained, colored in the various shades of fecal matter. Suffused in a fecal palette, the torture chamber in torture porn (and this is particularly true of the *Hostel* films) approaches the conceptualization of the concentration camp, which some referred to as *anus mundi*—the asshole of the world.[25] Notably too, most of James Wan's 2004 film *Saw* takes place in a bathroom, and in terms of color scheme shares much in common with Helen's little oasis—bathed in shades of sickly greenish-blue. In addition to this comparison to torture porn, Wnendt explicitly stated that he strove to create a film somewhere between *Trainspotting* and *9 Songs*. The bathroom in the Berlin subway finds closest affinities with Renton's urgent need to use the "worst toilet in Scotland," as it is given in *Trainspotting*.

While the spectator initially perceives Helen's retreat into the public restroom as an act of utter desperation, in a frantic effort to alleviate the burning itch of hemorrhoids, Helen instead treats it as an erotic encounter. Presented in extreme close-up, Helen squeezes a bead of white hemorrhoid cream from the vaguely phallic-shaped applicator onto her index finger. The cream, Helen adds through her internal monologue, "can also be injected to pacify the inner-anal itch." Having applied the milky white cream with her finger, Helen heaves a nearly orgasmic sigh of relief. Sating her immediate corporeal needs, Helen inspects the fecal-stained toilet bowl and seat; from Helen's perspective the camera moves into an extreme close-up of a pubic hair encrusted in dried yellowish phlegm (or is it urine?). Without ever breaking from Helen's perspective, the camera, impossibly, explores the microscopic details of the single pubic hair and phlegm; the germs inhabiting the phlegm snap and growl at the embodied subjective camera flying through the infected landscape embellished with squishy sloppy audio elements.

Transitioning from the animated germ-infested landscape to Helen at the age of eight, our protagonist recounts that her mother cautioned, "It's hard to keep a pussy really clean. A pussy gets sick way easier than a penis does. That's why hygiene in the bathroom is of paramount importance!"[26] Helen as a youngster is positioned over the toilet bowl, wearing rubber gloves scouring with a toilet scrubber—the toilet is immaculate, glistening white porcelain, and purged with antiseptic blue water. Helen's bathroom is lined with all manner of cleaning products, white walls and tiles glimmer in the well-lit bathroom, the glass door to the shower is spotless, and, finally finished with the task of cleaning the toilet, Helen "freshens" the air with an "air freshener" to ensure the complete erasure of bodily emissions. Where a punk-rock audio track accompanies the public toilet—the site of rebellious transgressive eroticism—the scoring that embosses the sanitized domestic scene, like the glistening surfaces, sparkles with the twanging of an angelic harp and chimes. The scoring here suggests any number of things, including "cleanliness is next to Godliness," and even a certain angelic quality associated with the "innocent" eight-year-old Helen. The contrast between the sterilized domestic bathroom and the public toilet locates the libidinal charge associated with a rejection of Helen's mother's compulsion for cleanliness. While the spectator still recoils at the exhibition of an abject eroticism, we might at the same time appreciate the thrill that Helen finds by turning herself, as she says, "into a living pussy-hygiene-experiment." She freely sits on the filthiest toilet seats with erotic zeal, whereas her mother, as she reports, "hovers when peeing into public toilets." Not only does Helen relish sitting on filthy toilet seats, but the filthier they are the better: "With my pussy," Helen explains, "I wipe a circle all the way around!" Helen continues to declare that she has been experimenting for years and has yet to experience an infection, entrusting to us, "I have very healthy pussy flora." As she recounts the exploits of her hygiene experiments, she inserts her right index finger into her vagina; she inspects the slippery fluid, rubbing her lubricated finger and thumb together.

The ambivalent sentiments aroused in the spectator—first and foremost, in all likelihood disgust, but on the other hand an empathetic response to the character's apparent pleasure—find affinities with Julian Hanich's reading of Michael Haneke's 2001 film *The Piano Teacher*. Erika Kohut, the central female character, goes to a sex shop to visit a private viewing booth. There Kohut fishes a sperm-filled tissue out from the garbage bin, inspects it with some reservations, before finally sniffing it—the scent apparently delivering pleasure and erotic arousal. Hanich reports that he "found the scene rather repulsive," but that others reported "no sense of disgust at all. In their case empathy with the relishing protagonist prevailed."[27] While we might presume that disgust and sensual pleasure rest at polar ends of the sensorial spectrum, the vacillation between what we might conventionally think of as "negative" and "positive" affect such as we find in *The Piano Teacher* and *Wetlands* suggests a greater degree of fluidity between these affective experiences. This opens the possibility for the displacement of affect—disgust supplanting sexual arousal for instance. In her expanded understanding of the pornographic, Helen Hester argues that the novel *Wetlands* elicits an intense affective charge and prompts us to experience it in pornographic terms.[28]

The film cuts to a beachside resort, presumably during a family vacation, as Helen stands at a bar, beside her a shirtless fit young man. Helen in a continued interior monologue announces that she refrains from cleaning herself too often, cultivating a ripe vaginal aroma. "My goal is that it [her vagina] emits a lightly bewitching odor that you can smell coming from my pants." The young man inspects his pickled herring, giving it a whiff—trying to locate the source of the wafting "fishy" smell. In close-up, Helen wags her hips, as if to cast her scent toward the young man. The camera assumes the subjective perspective of the wafting odor, coupled with a diegetic whooshing. The subjective shot associated with Helen's fermented odor lends her acrid scent materiality.

Scent has mass, a particulate that emits from a referent, and carries *into* the body of another (like sexual penetration), and this is the wellspring of disgust—in the violation of boundaries, the very breakdown of civilized/ uncivilized, healthy/unhealthy, clean/unclean, proper/improper, animal/ human, me/you.[29] Lending Helen's vaginal scent agency through the subjective camera movement toward the young man's nose emphasizes the transgression of borders. Scent (and especially those characterized as foul) violates the bounds between the clean and proper subject and its other, penetrating the other's body through the olfactory cavity. Aurel Kolnai similarly argues that "through the organ of smell small particles of the alien object become incorporated into the subject, which makes an intimate grasping of the alien object possible." Kolnai continues to note that it is through its very intimacy that scent shares some affinities with "the experience of eating,"[30] where an external object is incorporated into the subject. Smelling, then, bears similarities to the sexual act—a traversal of boundaries, penetration, the exchange of molecules.

Cultivating a heady vaginal scent, Helen hopes that "Men perceive it without realizing," and that, as with sexual pheromones in the animal kingdom, she will attract a sexual partner, because as she insists, "we're all animals looking to mate with each other." Helen's aversion to social mores, particularly around hygiene, places her in the company of the natural world, with the animalistic, the non-human, the uncivilized, and this is further emphasized in the appearance of animals throughout the film: Helen's T-shirt features a chimpanzee with a gaping mouth; she witnesses an intimate moment between her father and mother as they pack the car for a family trip—beside them a boogie-board with a shark also with its mouth gaping open; a turkey (consecutively stuffed with a goose, a chicken, and finally a quail) is served at a dinner party; Helen scoops a rat out of a nightclub toilet. Animals with gaping mouths signify an uncoded body, and this perhaps paradoxically figures Helen as domesticated in the concluding shot: Helen, in pouring rain, leans out of a Volkswagen van and lets out a (*silenced*) feral scream. (The gaping mouths, of Helen and beasts alike, also display some affinities with *A Serbian Film* discussed in Chapter 3.) The purging rain, a washing away of what is impure, is coupled with the heteronormative conclusion, where Helen, having been released from a hospital, finally couples with her "proper" long-chased male love interest, Robin (at least in name another animal). The scene is clearly derived from (perhaps even a parody of) the conventions of romantic comedy. The couple, before going to Robin's flat, acknowledge that they are likely going to have sex, "But not in the ass right away," Robin contends (Helen is recovering from anal surgery). Helen's (*silenced*) feral scream—in the context of cleansing rain and the normative sexual coupling (i.e. not anal)—suggests the *proper* channeling of unbridled libidinal energies into an appropriate object and normative sex through the reconfiguration of erogenous zones (i.e. the primacy of vaginal sex). This is not to suggest that *Wetlands* necessarily denies Helen's voice (read: sexual agency), but that the central character finds a "proper" outlet for it.

In the end, despite Helen's many encounters with the abject, she appropriately directs her energies, leading to a conventional "happy ending." But before Helen channels her libidinal energy into a "proper" love-object, she explores various avenues of sexual deviance—in many instances intermingling sexual encounters with food, or eating. Seducing the young man at the bar with her light-bewitching vaginal odor, for example, she compares her vaginal secretion during heightened sexual excitation to the consistency of olive oil, or on other occasions cottage cheese. The young man "eats out" the well-fermented Helen, who observes that her vaginal secretion on this occasion is more viscous, adding, "Lots of people get off on cottage cheese surprisingly." The chunky slurp of the audio design emphasizes the thick viscosity of Helen's oozing fluids. Reaching orgasm, Helen asks her partner, "Tasty?" Helen returns the favor, and gives her partner a hand-job, allowing the ejaculate to gel to her hand. Returning home and opening the refrigerator, she says in an interior monologue, "My sex-souvenir chewing gum," beading the coagulated ejaculate into a tiny ball. She admonishes the spectator, "If you think penises, sperm and other bodily fluids are gross," placing the beaded ejaculate in her mouth, "you should just forget about sex altogether."[31] Helen's admonishing words cut to the quick, tearing apart the fetishistic veneer that makes sex tolerable, if not enjoyable; sexual attraction, and the sexual encounter, in fact, rely on a certain fetishistic disavowal. Sexual intimacy necessitates a movement between tightly policed regions of the body—mouths and genitals—and the logic of fetishism ("I know, but . . .") thinly veils why these regions are policed to begin with. In the "wrong" context sexual intimacy can quite easily slip into trespassing to elicit feelings of shame, disgust, or violent violation. Furthermore, disgust reveals a close correlation with its opposite, lust, love, desire, appetite, which are "forms of intercourse with a nearness that is wanted," as Winfried Menninghaus notes: "Appetite and erotic desire aim at the overcoming of distance—the establishment of a union."[32] It also speaks to the context of bodily fluids—during the sexual encounter, ejaculate, for instance, might have no affective charge as such. Helen, standing before the open refrigerator, treating the ejaculate as food, or "chewing gum," and thus outside the sexual encounter, potentially elicits disgust. Moreover, treating the other's bodily fluid as food (as opposed to a product of a sexual encounter, or in the context of sex) comes uncomfortably close to the taboo against cannibalism.[33]

Helen makes a blood-pact with her friend Corinna—each smearing her menstrual blood on the other's face. The pair are so in sync that Helen explains that they menstruate at the same time—even trading used homemade tampons. The problem with homemade tampons, though, is that they are not affixed with a string. When Corinna's tampon gets lost, Helen uses cooking tongs to remove it. Helen returns the cooking tongs to her father, who just happens to be barbecuing and picks up a piece of meat to throw on the grill with the bloodied tongs.

While in the hospital, Helen tells her nurse, Robin, a story: two women call for a pizza, but their order never arrives. They call and complain. When they finally receive their pizza, it tastes funny. By coincidence one woman's father is a food chemist; taking a sample to his lab he discovers the presence of ejaculate. Cutting to the pizza shop we find four of the pizza employees in a circle-jerk, with the pizza centrally placed. Spurts of ejaculate, in slow motion and in tight close-up, fly through the air to the sounds of Johann Strauss's "The Blue Danube" waltz. Streams of ejaculate collide in midair, mixing together. Laces of ejaculate hurl across the pizza like threads of glistening cheese. Helen (in a near-extreme close-up of her lips as she tells the story) says, "I would love to eat a pizza like that." All the while, as Helen tells this salacious tale, Robin and Helen eat pizza and drink beer; and in the context of Helen's narrative, Robin eats his pizza with palpable unease, nearly recoiling as he chews his food. Similar to the recontextualization of ejaculate as "chewing gum" while Helen is standing in front of an open refrigerator, here sperm is once again intimately associated with consuming food. And even though the offending substance (circle-jerk sperm) is absent altogether, the very account renders the beer and pizza—something good and appetizing—disgusting.

This temporal difference between when Helen and Robin eat pizza and the incident relayed in the flashback is reminiscent of Julian Hanich's ekphrastic evocation. Drawn from drama theory, an ekphrastic "episode relies on detailed descriptions of something that happened in the *past*, something absent in terms of time."[34] Helen's report is amplified further, as Hanich says, "by the viewer's aural perception of the narrating voice and its intonation. And often the character's visible facial expression and gesture play a crucial role as well."[35] It is significant that part of Helen's recitation is done in extreme close-up focusing on her mouth, and that slight recoiling gesture as Robin chews his pizza signifies Helen's evocation of disgust and Robin's experience of it.

Prompted by her attraction to Robin, Helen hides the fact that she has had a bowel movement in her bed (once she has a bowel movement she will be

Figure 5.1 *Wetlands*, David Wnendt, 2013

discharged from the hospital). Helen lands in the hospital following a "shaving accident," where in keeping with contemporary shaving practices she manicures her pubic hair, including shaving her anus. "My ass is part of my sexual equipment," Helen explains in one of her many voiceover monologues, "and thus subject to modern shaving trends. Not everyone knows what an anal fissure is. It's a tiny tear in the skin of [the] anal opening. Getting one is super easy, like when shaving." At this instant, a sound more commonly associated with striking swords, or the unsheathing of a sword (a sound effect common to Japanese animation and cinema), slashes through the audioscape, followed by a whipping camera movement, and a drop of blood falling to the white tiled floor. Following this incident we find Helen with visible unease skateboarding to school wearing a miniskirt. "My swollen hemorrhoids are pressing on my shaving injury," Helen explains, "tearing the fissure wider." The camera follows behind Helen to see a small trail of blood dripping down her left leg. Helen is kicked out of class; the suggestion of course is that the trickle of blood running down her leg is menstrual blood. "My ass injury developed a brimming blister, which is hanging out of my butthole. Like the inflated neck skin of those tropical birds." Wnendt cuts away to shots of great frigate birds, with their bellowing red pouches of skin trying to attract a mate. The visual analogy works well to visualize Helen's (unseen) anal blister, but it also serves the narrative because it is precisely Helen's anus that sets the stage for a budding relationship to develop between herself and her nurse, Robin. Professor Dr. Notz enters the room with a train of eager medical students. The sight of Helen's injury visibly strikes Notz, but he then eagerly steps in to inspect the inflamed blister, without so much as a word to Helen. The instant Notz touches the blister it bursts, ejecting fluid, causing him to lurch backward, and prompting Helen's bitter protest as she reels in pain. Notz, who Helen finds arrogant, recommends anal surgery.

Prompted by her developing crush on Robin, and a general disdain for Notz (self-assured that he has performed a flawless surgical procedure), Helen wants to stay in the hospital to remain close to Robin, and to prove Notz wrong. She tries to break open her healing anal wound by sitting heavily; when that fails to work she then proceeds to probe her anus with a metal fixture on her hospital bed. This causes her wound to break open, and she bleeds copiously. The exercise of auto-anal "eroticism" might be read as serving masochistic pleasure, a gift (potlatch) to Robin, or an effort to secure what Helen desires. "Most cultures, and surely ours," Miller states, "understand that the anus is not as contaminating as it is contaminatable. For the penetrator of the anus does not lose rank to the extent the penetrated does if he loses it at all. The penetrator is engaging in an act of domination, desecration, and humiliation of another and in doing so he remains relatively untainted."[36] In her auto-anal erotic encounter Helen enacts both roles, the penetrator and penetrated. Helen "violates" herself, for which she sacrifices her own blood (not unlike the rupturing of the hymen), ultimately to make herself available to Robin.

The anus is "the lowest-status place on the body"; it is the "bottom," the *butt* of base humor (e.g. fart jokes), and it is precisely for these reasons that "the anus is also a temptation. It can be seen as the gateway to the most private, to the most personal space of all. It signifies the removal of all barriers of otherness."[37] Prior to rupturing her wound, Helen asks Robin to take a snapshot of her healing anus, and he obliges. Even though Robin is Helen's nurse and personal healthcare provider, the intimacy of the photograph, the invitation to inspect casually (vis-à-vis the snapshot), at least in this isolated moment, pulls back the clinical veneer to allow for an intimate encounter. While the act of self-defilement and mutilation likely prompts revulsion in the spectator because Helen violates the basic tenet that the "anus is to be properly only an exit for foodstuffs,"[38] not to mention that the breaching of the anus produces injury and blood, Helen in her anal erotic gesture offers herself as a gift to Robin—one that he, as her nurse, hardly has a choice to refuse.

Freud observed that "in the ancient civilizations, in myths, fairy tales and superstitions, in unconscious thinking, in dreams and neuroses" filth, and namely feces, has been intimately associated with money, or treasure.[39] Drawing on Freud, Norman O. Brown adds that the infant trades in the only currency it has (excretion). He argues further that the "category of property is not simply transferred from feces to money; on the contrary, money is feces, because the anal erotism continues in the unconscious. The anal erotism has not been renounced or abandoned but repressed."[40] Brown adds later:

> Freud pointed out that it was an integral part of the anal symbolic complex to equate the feces with the penis. The infantile fantasy of becoming father of oneself first moves out to make magic use of objects instead of its own body when it gets attached to that object which both is and is not part of its own body, the feces. Money inherits the infantile magic of excrement and then is able to breed and have children: interest is an increment (cf. Greek *tokos*, Latin *faenus*, etc.).[41]

In complex overdetermined registers Helen delivers herself, produces herself, gives herself to Robin—Helen is a "piece of shit" that, like the infant, she gives to her care-giver.

Many of the "transgressive" moments in *Wetlands* trade in the economy of "misdirected" libidinal energy. Helen invests erotic energy in: (1) sexual discharges as food (vaginal secretion compared to cottage cheese, male ejaculate to chewing gum); (2) experiments in feminine hygiene (fermented "pussy flora," homemade tampons); and (3) her anus. In rudimentary terms, the "perversion" of libidinal energy *is* the narrative conflict, and viewed through this conventional storytelling lens a happy ending is achieved insofar as Helen redirects libidinal energy in vaginal pleasure—as embodied in the presumptive normative heterosexual union between herself and Robin. As much as Helen experiments with female sexuality, at the end it appears as though she "corrects" her transgressive behavior, and emerges as a "proper" woman.

THE FETISH OF "WOMAN" AND MISERY PORN IN *HELTER SKELTER*

Mika Ninagawa's 2012 film *Helter Skelter* is a recasting of the Pygmalion story. A fashion model, Lilico (played by Erika Sawajiri), has undergone a procedure replacing effectively all of her body parts to form "the most beautiful woman." The character's name to a degree resonates with "Licca-chan," the Japanese equivalent of Barbie—and it becomes clear that Lilico is no more "real" than a plastic doll. (Licca's wide eyes are supposedly the product of her progeny—her father is a Frenchman, and her Japanese mother is, of course, a fashion designer.[42] Sawajiri, as it happens, was born to an Algerian-French woman and a Japanese father.) In *Helter Skelter* Lilico is featured on the cover of nearly every magazine, makes countless television appearances, and is the envy of every teenage girl and twenty-something woman. Sex symbol, icon, top model, celebrity—Lilico is held to be *the* representative of "woman." For all her sex appeal and popularity, though, she is truly ugly—an empty vessel, and deeply lonely despite the constant attention heaped upon her.[43]

It is worth comparing Ninagawa's film to Cindy Sherman's *Office Killer* (1997). Like Sherman, Ninagawa is also a photographer, though the latter's work is not expressly concerned with a feminist agenda (even though Sherman would not characterize her own work in these terms either). That is not to suggest that Ninagawa is not self-aware; clearly she is. Ninagawa is a major figure in Japanese fashion photography, and her exhibition "Mika Ninagawa: Earthly Flowers, Heavenly Colors" broke all attendance records for an exhibition of photographs.[44] *Helter Skelter*, we might argue, examines the abject underbelly of the fashion industry, and the unrealistic expectations levied on (young) women. Similar to the ways in which *Office Killer* follows the contours of Sherman's career—moving from B-movie iconography, into the more grotesque—*Helter Skelter* finds affinities with Ninagawa's work in the fashion industry. Like Ninagawa's photographs, *Helter Skelter* explodes with vivid colors, amazing tableaux set against an immense collection of flowers, or baroque sets.

Ninagawa places Lilico in sexually charged environments, and trades heavily in the fetishistic economy of (young) female bodies, Lilico's in particular. Just like Sherman, Ninagawa is intimately familiar with the "glossary of pose[s], gesture[s] and facial expression[s]"[45] that constitute the currency of the representation of women. Ninagawa deftly mobilizes the codes of fetishism in a glossy finish, and turns them on their head. Regarding Sherman's work, Laura Mulvey notes that "Whereas the language of fashion photography gives a great emphasis to lightness, so that its models seem to defy gravity, Sherman's figures are heavy in the body and groundedness."[46] Ninagawa retains the "gravity defying" qualities of fashion photography as Lilico, an airy waif, seems to hover over the vibrant sets, but all at the same time, Ninagawa still manages to overturn the codes of fetishism just as Sherman does.

The general trajectory of Sherman's work from the 1970s through the mid-1990s slowly peels away the fetishistic veneer that is "woman"—during this period moving from her "movie stills," to fashion photography, through her use of prosthetics and the erasure of the female body to finally reveal the abject remnants that the fetishistic fantasy of "woman" hopes to disavow. Sherman, then, unmasks, as Mulvey contends, "the disgust of sexual detritus, decaying food, vomit, slime, menstrual blood, hair. These traces represent the end of the road," Mulvey continues, "the secret stuff of the bodily fluids that the cosmetic is designed to conceal. The topography of exterior/interior is exhausted."[47] In the latter part of the film Lilico's breakdown—as a result of the drugs she takes to preserve her grafted body parts, and the pressure of her career—culminates with a hallucinatory sequence played out in a television studio that ends with a shot with Lilico centrally framed. She lies on the

Figure 5.2 *Helter Skelter*, Mika Ninagawa, 2012

Figure 5.3 Cindy Sherman, *Untitled*, 1987
Chromogenic color print
47 1/2 × 71 1/2 inches (image size)
120.7 × 181.6 cm
(MP# CS—175)
Courtesy Metro Pictures, New York

gleaming gold floor; her eyes are crossed, her hair is splayed all about, and the floor is strewn with a crumbled cake, brightly colored candies, candy wrappers, smeared frosting—the content, if not the composition, certainly seems to derive from Sherman's more grotesque imagery (see e.g. *Untitled #175* (1987)).

Following the contours of Sherman's career, Mulvey observes that the figures in her photographs became "gradually . . . more and more grotesque."[48] And the term "grotesque" is quite appropriate, both in its colloquial usage referring to something repellent, and also in its etymological origins. "Grotesque" comes from the Italian, "grotto," referring to the "caves" found by curious Renaissance residents who found capricious designs covering the walls of ancient Roman ruins; the designs, which were copied and became wildly popular, were designated "grotesques." The Roman designs and the decorative Renaissance appropriations of them mixed elements freely: organic/inorganic, plant/animal, human/animal. The grotesques were, in a word, monstrous. Not only does Sherman's more "grotesque" work, then, evoke disgust—"some figures are horned or snouted, like horrific mythological hybrids,"[49] as Mulvey recounts—but her images also tend to feature a strange assemblage of body parts.

Lilico is grotesque; she too is an assemblage of body parts. During the film Lilico's body begins to "fall apart," and she has no other choice but to return to the clinic that *created* her. Lilico undergoes a procedure to stop her face from "falling apart"; three wires, for each side of her face, are inserted into her cheeks to buttress her youthful-looking skin.[50] The sound amplifies the gore as the wire punctures her flesh and is drawn through the meat of her cheeks. The wires are inserted into her face and the surgeon manipulates them to "fasten" her face in place; the taut skin shadows the movement of the wired undergirding. The surgical theater is sterile, bathed in hot white lights awash in blueish-green. Though *Helter Skelter* is nowhere as graphic or insistent upon the exhibition of gore, there are some affinities here with the medicalization of the horror genre, especially as found in torture porn. *Saw IV* (Darren Lynn Bousman, 2007), for instance, opens with the autopsy of Jigsaw's corpse presented in grisly forensic detail.

Lilico is conscious during the "corrective" procedure. She is strapped to a gurney with highly fetishistic white leather bindings around her neck, ankles, and wrists. The plastic surgeon notes that she has undergone a lot worse: "Remember when you first came here. No one took any notice of you. As if you didn't exist. You were just a lump of meat. The object of our treatment is happiness. The old you—is gone, right?" The fact that Lilico is conscious, the surgeon's reflections on the nature of ideal beauty (and the assigned value attributed to the female form), and the staging of the scene in a plastic surgery theater—all create resonances with Orlan, the French performance artist. No

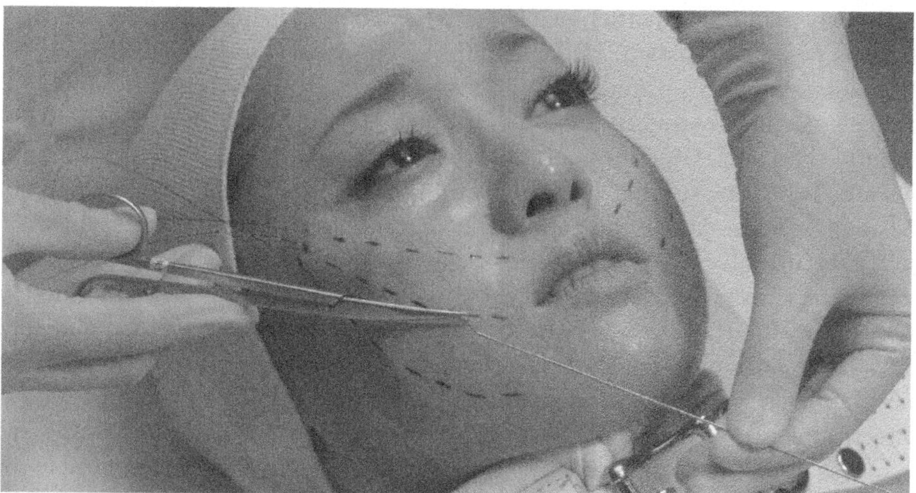

Figure 5.4 *Helter Skelter*, Mika Ninagawa, 2012

stranger to plastic surgery, and norms of feminine beauty, Orlan has undergone numerous plastic surgeries as part of her art practice. Under her direction (and while conscious), Orlan directed her plastic surgeon to "sculpt" her in the image of iconic femininity as drawn from art history: "the chin of Botticelli's *Venus*, the nose from the school of Fontainbleau's *Diana*, the mouth of Boucher's *Europa*, the eyes of Gerome's *Psyche*, and the forehead of da Vinci's *Mona Lisa*."[51] Orlan views her performances as a sort of "birthing" of herself; her performance series *The Reincarnation of Sainte Orlan* began on May 30, 1990, her forty-third birthday; she has undergone at least ten cosmetic surgeries since.

Lilico's agent, the ambassador of haute couture, bears some similarities (in appearance) to Orlan: stylish, heavily laden with make-up, wearing her hair in a bob, streaked with highlights. As the progenitor of the young model, the agent, whom Lilico calls "Mama," inhabits the position of Victor Frankenstein— Lilico is her little monster. We learn that Lilico as a youngster was ordinary in appearance, maybe even a bit plump, but under the agent's supervision she makes a Faustian bargain, surrendering her body to the beauty clinic, where she was quite literally sculpted and reconfigured from an assemblage of other body parts. The plastic surgery theater, then, like Frankenstein's lab, is an artificial womb from which the model is born. It is interesting to note that the lobby of the plastic surgery clinic is decorated with Botticelli's *Venus*, but broken into distinct (fetishistic) sections—eye, breasts, lips—once again indicating some affinities with Orlan.

Lilico is not simply a victim. The young model wears revealing clothing and lingerie, and adopts the codes of the femme fatale. A seductress, Lilico ruthlessly manipulates other characters. One lonely evening Lilico corners her frumpy personal assistant, Hada, and initiates a sexual encounter. Lilico forcefully mounts Hada's prone body and kisses her; in nearly an extreme close-up Lilico's darting tongue in a couple of quick lashes explores Hada's lips and mouth. The smacking audio emphasizes the moist exchange. Repositioning herself, Lilico insists that Hada perform cunnilingus, which she, with some hesitation, does. Above the couple is a mural with brilliant red lips, floating in a Magritte-blue sky, the image clearly taken from Man Ray's "Observatory Time, the Lovers" (1931). The play between lips and the slip into cunnilingus transfigure the Ray-inspired mural into an image of vagina dentata, and the associative links between these signifiers further suggests Lilico's monstrousness. Lilico's seduction, though, is empty of true erotic feelings, and Lilico's affectless expression as Hada performs cunnilingus emphasizes this. Hada, in acquiescing to the erotic encounter, incurs a debt that she will never be able to repay—and even though Hada is an employee, and even despite the fact that Lilico routinely insults her, as with a vampire's bite (or a really destructive relationship) Hada is forever beholden to Lilico.

The depth of Hada's loyalty to Lilico is tested in a sexual encounter between Lilico and Hada's boyfriend. Unannounced, Lilico arrives at Hada's modest apartment. She finds Hada just about to leave, and Hada's boyfriend, Shin, has just come out of the bath—his hair is wet, he has a towel draped across his neck, and he is wearing nothing more than sweatpants. Lilico wears a Flamenco-inspired dress; its v-cut collar dips very low, and her push-up bra emphasizes her figure. Lilico approaches Shin, looking him up and down with "bedroom eyes," and is startled that such a frumpy woman would be able to land such a good-looking guy. Both Hada and Shin stand dumbfounded—petrified. Lilico gets closer, inspecting Shin's body. Arms resting on Shin's shoulders, Lilico is fascinated by his lips, and ever so slightly begins to lean in for a kiss before pausing, "Can I—kiss you?" Both Hada and Shin are startled by the proposition; the dumbfounded couple exchange glances; Lilico intercepts Hada's glance and asks if she would mind if she kissed Shin. Without waiting for a response, Lilico firmly launches into a kiss. Shin cannot contain himself and succumbs to Lilico's feminine wiles. Lilico runs her hand along Shin's arm and torso before plunging below the waistband of his sweatpants, prompting Lilico to pronounce, "You're as hard as a rock." Lilico commands Hada to watch, and with a devilish grin says, "I'm going to do something bad with your boyfriend." Sullenly slumped up against the kitchen cabinets, Hada, in stunned silence, watches as Lilico straddles Hada's boyfriend and fucks him. Ninagawa steeps the scene with an erotic charge, and some viewers might find it arousing—trading heavily on fetishistic images (revealing dress, probing hands) and gestures (drooping eyelids, cocked head leaning in for a kiss) as well as the transgressive (the danger associated with Lilico as the monstrous-feminine, adultery).

While Lilico's seduction of Shin is (erotically) affecting, perhaps the most affecting scene in *Helter Skelter* comes when Lilico has her climactic breakdown. Shin and Hada—poisoned by Lilico's seductive guile—are conscripted to eliminate a rival model who is poised to unseat Lilico from her position as top model. Stalking Lilico's rival, Kozue Yoshikawa, at a fashion shoot in the Asakusa amusement park, Hada prepares to lacerate the model's face with a drawn box-cutter. This is cross-cut with Lilico's television appearance on a variety program staged on a vibrantly garish studio set (highly characteristic of popular Japanese television programs). The parallel lines of action—the Asakusa amusement park and the television studio—are set to Beethoven's Ninth Symphony. Lilico's breakdown causes her to hallucinate, as dozens of brilliantly colored butterflies assail her, and other surrealistic elements on the studio set are emphasized—a giant strawberry, for instance, grows an eye. Shot from Lilico's perspective, the set goes out of focus, colors blur (almost appearing to melt), the camera quickly zooms in and out, objects (a clock, for instance) spin at high velocity, a dwarf approaches spinning a cane and dressed as if a carnival barker. There are jarring camera movements, and frenzied editing is coupled with a screeching non-diegetic audio element—the editing, camera movement, and audio design display affinities with the stylistic treatment of terror found in the *Saw* franchise, namely, when characters awake to discover themselves in a Jigsaw trap. Recall, for example, Amanda in the reverse beartrap in *Saw* (James Wan, 2004), rendered through frenetic editing and circling camera movements, coupled with Charlie Clouser's highly embellished metallic dissonant soundscape. A number of shots during Lilico's breakdown, coupled with jarring non-diegetic audio, are quite similar to the highly stylized presentation of traps in the *Saw* franchise. Returning to Lilico's rival, Yoshikawa fearlessly and without a care in the world stares Hada down, prompting Hada to go ahead and "Do it." Lilico's rival continues, "We will be forgotten. We're machines for the processing of desires. 'Cute!' 'Cool!' 'That's what I want to be!' Desire doesn't care. It just keeps on [going] with another name and another face." Understanding that Hada cannot go through with her mission, Lilico's rival leans in staring, before casually slouching back, completely disinterested, and placing her earbuds back in her ears. As the film cuts back to Lilico's breakdown, the model collapses into a Shermanesque tableaux (discussed above)—her hair strewn about, framed by cake frosting and sweets against the golden floor, a swarm of butterflies flutter about as Lilico twitches, muttering "more beautiful."

The cross-cut sequence is deeply affecting in no small part because of Beethoven's Ninth Symphony—the rhythm of the sequence works well with the rousing choral climax of the score. While Beethoven's score is affecting in its own right—causing the hairs of this author (Kerner) to stand on end— Ninagawa's strikingly vivid colors, production design, camera and editing work embellish the affecting audioscape. What is striking is that this affecting moment is coupled with the film's most poignant critique of the fetishistic economy—laying bare in explicit terms the logic of desire. The affecting sequence, then, perhaps akin to Sherman's photographs, interrogates the (erotic) spectacle economy by invoking the very mechanisms (popular television, fashion industry) that perpetuate it.

Perhaps more shocking or startling than really affecting, the money shot of the film comes with Lilico's *mea culpa*. Once Lilico's secret is revealed—that her beauty was completely manufactured, she having undergone full-body cosmetic surgery—she is compelled to hold a press conference to presumably come clean. Clad in stark white she stands before a legion of reporters and press photographers—flashbulbs constantly going off. Barely keeping it together, Lilico stands before her audience silently and then suddenly plunges a small knife into her eye. Blood spurts violently, splashing against the white surface of the press table. The blood spatter is highly reminiscent of Majid's suicide—a gift to Georges—in Michael Haneke's 2005 film *Caché*. The shape of the spatter is similar in both of these films. The shocking scene is also clearly derived from Toshio Matsumoto's 1969 film *Bara no soretsu* (*Funeral Parade of Roses*), which is a retelling of the Oedipal drama, which climaxes with Eddie, the main character, poking out his eyes. It just so happens that Ninagawa's father, Yukio Ninagawa, is an important theater director, and Matsumoto cast him for a small part in *Bara no soretsu* as a bar patron.

Locating the money shot here in the context of Lilico's *mea culpa* resonates with Hester's observations regarding what has been dubbed "misery porn"—memoirs that typically feature traumatic accounts of abuse, addiction, or abject suffering. Misery displaces sex, Hester argues, and as a result angst-filled memoirs might be read as the "'pornography of emotional hurt' not because they court genital sexual arousal but because they facilitate a somehow unwholesome enjoyment of accounts of suffering and precarious lives."[52] A number of best-selling memoirs, though, proved to be less than truthful accounts (e.g. James Frey's *A Million Little Pieces*, and J. T. LeRoy's harrowing short stories). The revelations "and exposés are, in some sense, misery porn's money shots; they are the seemingly verifiable proof that something really happened."[53] *Helter Skelter* is no memoir, Lilico is a fictional character, and the eye-gouging is simulated, but what Ninagawa does here is to follow the contours of the expanded pornographic—as detailed by Hester—which relies on the authentication of intense affect. In other words, the *mea culpa*—in misery porn exposés, or Lilico's press conference—is the paroxysm that replaces the involuntary discharge of bodily fluids in sexual excitation.

CONCLUSION: THE CONVERGENCE OF EXTREME CINEMA AND PORNOGRAPHY?

Common to the films discussed here is the episodic, or the eruptions of spectacle in the otherwise conventional linear narrative. *Wetlands* and *Helter Skelter* host affecting spectacles; Michael Winterbottom's *9 Songs* is only cursorily concerned with narrative and is more episodic in its structure. What we have witnessed is that there is a tendency within extreme cinema *to approach* the generic patterns found in pornography. By way of a conclusion we might consider Maja Miloš's 2012 film *Clip*, which is a portrait of disaffected Serbian youth that features scenes of hardcore sex. The hardcore content consists of brief moments of female masturbation (as well as extreme close-ups of labia during a shaving scene, and a scene in which the labia are wrapped around a thong), some more extended moments of male masturbation (including ejaculation), and many instances of fellatio. Oral sex is almost always shown in extreme close-up, which is perhaps in part necessitated by the fact that the actors, who are actually teenagers and therefore underage, could not legally engage in sexual acts for the camera. Thus, the film makes use of body-doubles for the hardcore sex acts for practical purposes, as the viewer is unable to discern that different actors are being used. But there is a diegetic reason for the extreme close-ups, too: almost all of the sex scenes are recorded by the characters on camera phones. The sex acts that the audience sees are *almost* always seen through the screen of the phone. Sometimes the phone screen is a frame within the frame, while at other times the grainy low-resolution camera phone image takes up the entire frame. Thus, some of the footage in the film is POV footage—with a character doing the filming. In fact, the film opens this way, with a male offscreen voice talking to the main character Jasna, who preens for the camera. Though this particular scene is not exactly fully sexually explicit (there is no nudity), it does contain sexual behavior, with both Jasna and the unseen (except for his hand) male character touching her genitals, underneath her clothes. The film thus takes the form of "gonzo" pornography (popularized by John Stagliano's "Buttman" series), while at the same time it is meant to take the form of the YouTube videos and amateur pornography that people (and particularly teenagers) make throughout the world and upload to various tube-sites.

The director, Miloš, has said that she was primarily inspired to make this film by the innumerable videos circulating online from teenagers throughout the world who document their sexual activity, their partying, their fighting.[54] Indeed, the film could be seen as moving from one sex scene to the next, from one drunken and drug-fueled (marijuana and cocaine) party and nightclub to the next, and from one fight to the next. And the characters—particularly Jasna and her frequent sexual partner Djole—obsessively chronicle it with their phones. At points, it almost seems that they cannot do anything *without* documenting it with their phones. The most interesting example of this occurs about halfway through the film. In order to direct his attention away from videogames and toward her, Jasna shows Djole a video clip (on her phone) of an extreme close-up of her masturbating. He begins masturbating himself, and rebuffs her attempt to fellate him. Instead, he wants to film himself climaxing onto her—and, from the camera phone frame within the frame, we see his erect penis looming over her prostrate body. He says "Don't you dare touch yourself" when she attempts to begin masturbating herself. We eventually, still through the camera phone frame, see him ejaculate onto her stomach. We are meant to understand our view as his view: he is not looking directly at her as he masturbates, but at her image, mediated through the phone. It does seem that Guy Debord's worst nightmares have come to pass, where the most inti-mate of human encounters—sex—is mediated through media.

For much of the film, it seems all of the sex acts are mediated: several scenes of fellatio are shown this way—they are always shown with phone in hand, and almost all the images that we the audience see are shown through the phone, mouth wrapped around a penis in extreme close-up. As much as the explicit content in its own right might make *Clip* an example of extreme cinema, its form is perhaps even more significant. The handheld camera phone, the composition associated with intimate contact (a camera apparently held by an individual engaged in sex), the grain of the image bestowing on it the "reality effect"—not only are we given a meat shot (actual penetration/autoerotic sex), but the medium, texture and composition all lend the image "authenticity." The title of Miloš's film—*Clip*—also points us in the direction of pornogra-phy, particularly pornography found on the web, which more often than not is only *a clip* from a longer feature, excised from any narrative whatsoever.

What we are left to wonder, then, is whether pornography too will begin to converge with extreme cinema. Perhaps not—it is not likely that most pornography will begin to approach narrative. As we have already indicated, pornography, it seems, has been venturing further and further from narrative, and in many instances is organized around a particular theme. But what a film like *Clip* points to is the use of camera phones and the aesthetics associated with them as an instrument closely associated with the body. Pornographic themes such as POV films, and amateur films, will undoubtedly witness the increased use of the camera phone as image quality continues to improve. The camera phone trades in the currency of the authentic—a mimetic trace of the body and its movement. And this is something that both pornography and extreme cinema prize.

NOTES

1. Teresa Brennan, *The Transmission of Affect* (Ithaca: Cornell University Press, 2004), 141–2.
2. Another example of this—the conflation/confusion of pain and ecstasy—might be found in Kim Ki-duk's 2000 film The Isle, where the central female character inserts fishing hooks in her vagina. When the male character removes them, the woman's sighs and gasps might be confused for aural signifiers of sexual excitation.
3. The slippage of signifiers might be viewed through the Bakhtinian lens. Bakhtin intertwines the processes of life—consumption and excretion, death and birth. There is a carnivalesque element to birthing a watermelon. See Robert Stam, Subversive Pleasures: Bakhtin, Cultural Criticism, and Film (Baltimore: Johns Hopkins University Press, 1989), 157.
4. Elaine Scarry, "'The Body in Pain': An Interview with Elaine Scarry" [interview by Elizabeth Irene Smith], Concentric: Literary and Cultural Studies 32, no. 2 (September 2006): 224.
5. William Ian Miller, Anatomy of Disgust (Cambridge, MA: Harvard University Press, 1997), 138. Silvan S. Tomkins makes a similar claim, associating disgust with proximity: "Disgust is primarily . . . an act of distancing the self from an object, and it is felt primarily toward objects which are purely negative in quality. It is possible to be disgusted at attractive objects only under the condition that imitation of them, or increased closeness, or incorporation of them is also tabooed." The rituals that surround taboo objects amount to "handwashing" and aim to keep the offending object at a distance. Silvan S. Tomkins, Affect Imagery Consciousness: The Complete Edition (New York: Springer, 2008), 358–9; also see 418.
6. Miller, 138.
7. Helen Hester, Beyond Explicit: Pornography and the Displacement of Sex (New York: SUNY Press, 2014), 189.
8. Ibid., 185–6.
9. Wheeler Winston Dixon, Visions of the Apocalypse: Spectacles of Destruction in American Cinema (Columbia: Columbia University Press, 2003), 111.
10. Miller, 138.
11. Catherine Zuromskis, "Prurient Pictures and Popular Film: The Crisis of Pornographic Representation," The Velvet Light Trap 59 (2007): 13, n.2.
12. Tarja Laine, Feeling Cinema: Emotional Dynamics in Film Studies (New York: Bloomsbury, 2013), 130.
13. Ibid., 134.
14. James Quandt, "Flesh and Blood: Sex and Violence in Recent French Cinema," in The New Extremism in Cinema: From France to Europe, eds. Tanya Horeck and Tina Kendall (Edinburgh: Edinburgh University Press, 2011), 18-19.
15. Michael Winterbottom cited in Melanie Williams, review of 9 Songs, Film Quarterly 59, no. 3 (Spring 2006): 61.
16. Melanie Williams, 61.
17. Ibid., 62.
18. Commenting on photographs that record cruelty or crimes, Susan Sontag observes: "Not all reactions to these pictures are under the supervision of reason and conscious. Most depictions of tormented, mutilated bodies do arouse a prurient interest." Susan Sontag, Regarding the Pain of Others (New York: Farrar, Straus, & Giroux, 2003), 95.
19. Stephen Maddison, "'Choke on It, Bitch!' Porn Studies, Extreme Gonzo and the

Mainstreaming of Hardcore," in Mainstreaming Sex: The Sexualization of Western Culture, ed. Feona Attwood (New York: I. B. Tauris, 2009), 39.

20. See Eugenie Brinkema, "Laura Dern's Vomit, or, Kant and Derrida in Oz," Film-Philosophy 15, no. 2 (2011): 51–69.

21. This is the title card that introduces the film Wetlands.

22. See for instance Jada Yuan's report from the Sundance screening, "Wetlands Is Sundance's Crassest, Most Outrageous Movie," Vulture.com (January 24, 2014). < http://www.vulture.com/2014/01/wetlands-sundance-crass-outrageous-movie.html> For a good critical assessment of Roche's novel and its reception by the press see the second chapter, "Rethinking Transgression," in Hester, 35–47.

23. Cited in Sallie Tisdale, "Graphic Novel," New York Times (April 16, 2009), no pagination.

24. Julia Kristeva, Powers of Horror: An Essay on Abjection, trans. Leon S. Roudiez (New York: Columbia University Press, 1982), 4.

25. Aaron Kerner, Torture Porn in the Wake of 9/11 (New Brunswick, NJ: Rutgers University Press, 2015), 129.

26. See Miller's discussion of genital hygiene in his Anatomy of Disgust (Cambridge, MA: Harvard University Press, 1997), 104–5.

27. Julian Hanich, "Toward a Poetics of Cinematic Disgust," Film-Philosophy 15, no. 2 (2011), 24–5.

28. Hester, 56–7. In this specific instance Hester is discussing the novel, but we believe this equally applies to the film adaptation.

29. Winfried Menninghaus, Disgust: The Theory and History of a Strong Sensation, trans. Howard Eiland and Joel Golb (New York: SUNY Press, 2003), 190–1.

30. Aurel Kolnai, On Disgust, eds. Barry Smith and Carolyn Korsmeyer (Chicago: Open Court, 2004), 50.

31. See a discussion of semen and its capacity to elicit disgust in Miller, 103–4.

32. Menninghaus, 1–2.

33. Miller, 97.

34. Hanich, 21.

35. Ibid.

36. Miller, 100.

37. Ibid., 100–1.

38. Ibid., 100.

39. Sigmund Freud, "Character and Anal Erotism," in On Sexuality: Three Essays on the Theory of Sexuality and Other Works Volume 7, trans. James Strachey (London: Penguin Books, 1991), 214.

40. Norman O. Brown, Life Against Death: The Psychoanalytic Meaning of History (Middletown CT: Wesleyan University Press, 1985), 191.

41. Ibid., 279.

42. Motomi Kobayashi, "Licca-chan's secret—the story of Japan's Barbie," The Asahi Shimbun (December 28, 2011). Available at <http://ajw.asahi.com/article/cool_japan/style/AJ201112280042> (last accessed November 25, 2015).

43. Lilico is nothing more than spectacle; her cravings for intimacy are always frustrated by this. "To Kristeva, happiness depends on intimacy—intimacy both with oneself and with others. Intimacy with others and in turn the happiness it bestows, in fact, hinge on an initial inquiry into oneself—on the level of the unconscious. Therefore, with so much at stake, like Guy Debord in The Society of the Spectacle, Kristeva rails against our consumerist, image-obsessed, robotizing society of the spectacle—as it is anathema to

intimacy, damaging to her highly cherished 'culture of revolt,' and ultimately threatening to psychic life." Frances Restuccia, The Blue Box: Kristevan/Lacanian Readings of Contemporary Cinema (New York: Continuum, 2012), 15.

44. Mika Ninagawa website: <http://www.ninamika.com/en/profile/index.html> (last accessed November 25, 2015).

45. Laura Mulvey, Fetishism and Curiosity (Bloomington: Indiana University Press, 1996), 65.

46. Ibid., 71.

47. Ibid.

48. Ibid.

49. Ibid.

50. Regarding putrefied skin and eliciting disgust see Jennifer Barker, *The Tactile Eye: Touch and the Cinematic Experience* (Berkeley: University of California Press, 2009), 47–51.

51. Danielle Knafo, "Castration and Medusa: Orlan's Art on the Cutting Edge," *Studies in Gender and Sexuality* 10 (2009): 146.

52. Hester, 145.

53. Ibid., 177–8.

54. Taken from a video interview with the filmmaker included on the North American DVD release of the film.

CHAPTER 6

Crying: Dreadful Melodramas—Family Dramas and Home Invasions

INTRODUCTION: CRY ME A PUDDLE (OF BLOOD)

Melodramas are family affairs—usually involving the destruction of the familial unit—that typically elicit tears from the spectator. And in the genre's insistence upon the discharge of bodily fluids from the spectator, melodrama shares certain affinities with pornography. Furthermore, like horror and pornography, melodrama nests its affecting ruptures within discrete numbers framed by otherwise conventional "realistic" narrative sequences. When conversing with his composer, Marvin Hamlisch, for *Sophie's Choice* (1982), Alan Pakula told him, "The film is so emotional, the film is about such horror, that it runs the great danger of becoming emotional pornography."[1] Sophie's choice—choosing which of her two children would be sent to the gas chamber—is terribly heart-wrenching, and it verges on the pornographic precisely because of the setting (the ultimate human horror of the concentration camp) and the fact that the entirety of the film rests on this single emotive moment.

Unlike pornography, horror, or other affecting instances in extreme cinema that might on their own carry a strong charge, the emotive events in melodrama generally cannot stand on their own *and* be as affecting as when seen in the context of the whole narrative. For instance, the concluding moments of Douglas Sirk's *All That Heaven Allows* (1955), if seen on their own, might strike the spectator as utterly pat—as they would not have any emotional investment in the unconscious man (Ron) and the doting woman (Cary). This is not to suggest that this holds across the board. It is certainly possible to take melodramatic scenes in isolation and discover that they are affecting. For instance, the heart-wrenching scene in *Sophie's Choice* on its own, in isolation from the narrative, wields the potential to spawn tears in the spectator. However, what this latter example demonstrates is that it is nonetheless laden with narrative, and is *emotionally* charged. There is within this isolated scene enough of a narrative arc—we are introduced to a mother and her children; the mother is compelled to make a choice; and it resolves (unhappily) in a choice being made.[2] The "micro narrative" featuring the loss of a child offers enough narrative context for the spectator to become emotionally invested in the characters.

Melodramas play host to highly affecting material that is usually emotional in nature, rather than sensational, precisely because this material is so tightly woven into the narrative—what spawns tears is generally sadness over a loss of some kind. Furthermore, as Tarja Laine notes, "cinematic emotions regularly emerge as a result of character identification or sympathetic engagement, emotionally experienced as concern for the characters."[3] While this holds true in many cases, the redirection of our attention "from character-affinity to aesthetic elements that are less character-bound" opens a space for "feeling cinema,"[4] as Laine calls it, and what we are calling extreme cinema. And this is precisely what sets these films apart from the "run of the mill" melodramatic genre. The films discussed in this chapter very well might play on emotions and draw from the conventions of the genre, but displace emotive tropes for affecting ones. Film critics are generally dismissive of genres such as torture porn precisely because the affecting events (the torture numbers) lack narrative motivation. Hence it is deemed "porn" because the torture set pieces aim for the gut irrespective of the narrative situation. Discussing literary melodrama, Franco Moretti cites three passages where, if they are set in their respective context, "the vast majority of readers burst into tears." But if one were only to read these passages in Moretti's text—that is to say, out of their context—"not a single reader will have cried."[5] Narratives, then, are supremely important in the melodramatic genre; a spectator must be invested in the character(s) for the emotive elements to likely have any purchase.

Melodrama is marked by specific cinematic conventions and syntax. "Melodrama originally meant, literally, drama + melos (music)," Geoffrey Nowell-Smith reminds us, and this speaks to the fusion of emotive content with excesses in dramatic form.[6] What we find, then, are cinematic devices such as flashbacks, dissolves, zooms, and swelling non-diegetic scores, which tend to embellish poignant and emotive moments in melodrama. To convey a narrative of missed encounters, or characters that arrive too late, the cinematic syntax might emphasize, as Steve Neale observes, "a meeting and exchange of looks across an eyeline match"[7] that does not find its desired object. These frustrated encounters (or missed encounters) are amplified in the spectator because, as Neale notes, "melodrama involves the production of discrepancies between the knowledge and point of view of the spectator and the knowledge and points of view of the characters, such that the spectator often *knows more*."[8] And because the spectator often knows more than the characters in the diegetic narrative, we understand that a character has arrived *too late*—which is what commonly prompts tears in the character and the spectator alike. Similarly, Linda Williams observes that melodramas are "always tinged with the melancholy of loss. Origins are already lost, the encounters always take place too late, on death beds or over coffins."[9] Neale adds to this idea, or modifies this conception of "too late," writing that a specific "place is constructed for the spectator, a place from which . . . we are led to wish 'if only.'"[10]

While many of these conventions and syntactical elements of the melodrama are evident in extreme cinema's familial dramas, including tears within the diegetic universe, the spectator is more likely to experience dread, disgust, or some other affective response. Douglas Sirk's 1959 film *Imitation of Life*, emblematic of the melodramatic genre, ends with Sarah Jane flung across her mother's coffin and declaring her love for her. Sarah Jane—a young black woman who passes for white—has continually rejected her mother, who exhibits the common features of "black-ness." "But her mother will never hear the declaration of love that we, as spectators, can hear," Neale notes. "It is too late. Sarah Jane is in tears. The spectator is in tears."[11] A specific moment in Kim Jee-woon's 2010 film *I Saw the Devil* is remarkably similar to the highly emotive climax of Sirk's film; however, this recognition of being "too late" comes *too early* for us, as it is situated in the opening moments of Kim's film. The primary character, Soo-hyeon, is an agent in a Korean police service, and despite this (or maybe even because of it—he is overly consumed by his job) he cannot come to the aid of his fiancée, whose car has broken down in the middle of nowhere on a cold snowy night. Waiting for roadside service alone, she is abducted and brutally murdered. While mourners wail all around him, he says, standing before the crematory oven, "Always too late." There are tears within the diegetic world, but likely not for the spectator. It is *too soon* for us—we are not invested in their characters yet. Instead, what makes *I Saw the Devil* a possible example of (melodramatic) extreme cinema is that Soo-hyeon seeks revenge through extra-judicial means against the serial killer who murdered his fiancée—the narrative then hosts spectacles of violence. *I Saw the Devil*, like many of the films discussed in this chapter, includes tropes associated with melodrama, but replaces emotional triggers with affecting ones in highly embellished scenes of sex, intense psychic breaks, violence and gore.

FAMILY DRAMAS

With *I Saw the Devil* we find a certain strain of extreme cinema coming full circle. Korean and Japanese films were influential for filmmakers like Eli Roth—the mind behind the *Hostel* films (2005, 2007). Park Chan-wook's vengeance trilogy—*Sympathy for Mr. Vengeance* (2002), *Oldboy* (2003), and *Lady Vengeance* (2005)—proved particularly inspirational. Park's dramatic thrillers include elements of extreme violence. Addressing the role that Asian extreme cinema played in the making of *Hostel*, specifically citing Japanese filmmaker Takashi Miike and Park, Roth observed that these filmmakers are not making "exactly pure horror movies . . . there is a wave of these ultra-violent films that are much more horrific than scary . . . It's about real people, doing real things, and it's just horrifying and disturbing, and that's the type of film that I really wanted to make."[12] In one incredibly brutal scene, Dong-jin uses a scalpel to cut through Ryu's Achilles' tendon in Park's *Sympathy for Mr. Vengeance*, a device which is subsequently employed by Josh's torturer in *Hostel*. Where Roth draws from Park's work, Kim in turn appropriates elements found in the *Hostel* films.

In *I Saw the Devil*, the murder of Soo-hyeon's fiancée is brutal, and shares some of the hallmarks of American torture porn. Mercilessly beaten with a hammer and barely conscious, the woman pleads for her life, declaring that she is pregnant. But there is no reasoning with Kyung-chul, the stone-faced killer who dispatches the woman with a single blow of a meat cleaver—presumably beheading her. The mise-en-scène has a lot in common with American torture porn, particularly the *Hostel* films. The workshed that Kyung-chul uses as his kill-room (he is clearly well-rehearsed in the act of killing) is dank and dark. The uneven and cracked bare cement floor is damp—covered in water and blood. Victims are strung to large well-worn timber posts for the butchering process, and, just as in many torture porn films, Kyung-chul's worktable is cluttered with an array of instruments with which to inflict grievous bodily injury. Chains, hooks, and other instruments of torture are hung from the workshed walls. Kyung-chul fastens a heavy gauged chain to the woman's arm and yanks it into place to make a clean cut—the use of overlap editing emphasizes the yanking of her arm, repeating the jerking movement in succession from three different angles. While the mise-en-scène shares a lot in common with American torture porn, Kyung-chul does not necessarily seem interested in torturing the women that he abducts—he is a more dispassionate serial killer, like a butcher in a butcher's shop, matter-of-factly cutting meat into pieces. Kyung-chul wears heavy raingear—rubber raincoat, heavy duty rainboots—and this finds affinities with the torturers in *Hostel*, or Showtime's *Dexter*. Although the killing scene is gruesome in its own right and is likely affecting for some viewers, what amplifies the affective qualities is the steam that rises from the body, coupled with the slurpiness and the cracking sounds of Kyung-chul cutting through tissue and bone. The scene concludes with a drainpipe, apparently leading out of Kyung-chul's workshed to a drainage-ditch, as clear water pouring from the drain turns to a (dare we say, beautiful) brilliant deep crimson.

The steam rising from the partially dismembered body and the audio design emphasize that the body *is* meat. Like Kyung-chul, Francis Bacon "is certainly a butcher," Deleuze claims, but the painter "goes to the butcher shop as if it were a church, with the meat as the crucified victim. Bacon is a religious painter only in butcher shops."[13] Surely there is nothing religious in Kyung-chul's habituated act of killing, but the butchered woman is destined to be consumed—we later discover that Kyung-chul delivers dismembered corpses to his cannibal friend. Cleaning up his private abattoir, hosing down the floor and sweeping away tides of blood, he sets aside containers of body parts. The rising steam—which wafts over blood and body parts—mark the zones of indiscernibility where the body is in the state of becoming meat, and this is where affect might be located.

The main protagonist of *I Saw the Devil*, Soo-hyeon, takes a leave of absence from his job in a Korean police service, so that he might pursue the murderer on his own, and reap revenge. Soo-hyeon goes on the rampage, tracking down the four people whom the police have identified as suspects—he brutally beats the first two suspects *Dexter*-style before he determines that Kyung-chul is the killer. Soo-hyeon in his pursuit of "justice" becomes the very thing that he is fighting. He in fact captures Kyung-chul multiple times, inflicts severe injuries, and lets him go. Kyung-chul seeks refuge with his cannibal friend, Tae-joo, who notes, "He's our kind. He's enjoying the excitement of the hunt. Catching and letting go of the prey. He's playing the hunter. He relishes torturing his prey." Tae-joo continues, "You've created a monster. How interesting." Soo-hyeon possesses an uncanny ability to locate Kyung-chul, and he eventually realizes that Soo-hyeon must have implanted some sort of homing beacon on, or in, him. Robbing a pharmacy, Kyung-chul steals laxatives and takes a handful of pills. After defecating, he fishes through the loose stool to find the beacon—more than any other moment this scatological scene caused this author (Kerner) to cringe, topped only by *2 Girls 1 Cup*. With the tables turned, Kyung-chul now enjoys the thrill of the chase, and actively taunts Soo-hyeon. Knowing that Soo-hyeon is listening, Kyung-chul informs him that his fiancée begged him not to kill her, and that she was pregnant.

Soo-hyeon does in the end find Kyung-chul to mete out his revenge. Whereas much of the film appears to draw heavily from the *Hostel* films, the climax finds certain similarities with the *Saw* franchise. Back in Kyung-chul's workshed, and illustrating beyond a doubt that Soo-hyeon is no different from Kyung-chul, Soo-hyeon fashions a trap: he ties a rope between a door and a guillotine, which is perched above Kyung-chul's head, and places the end of the rope in his captive's mouth. Listening to what transpires over the homing beacon, Soo-hyeon stoically walks away. When his family arrives home, Kyung-chul makes muffled screams, but they cannot hear his warnings. When they open the door, the rope slips from Kyung-chul's mouth, causing the blade of the guillotine to drop and sending his head rolling to his mother's, father's, and adolescent son's feet. The final shot ends with Soo-hyeon walking down the middle of the street, sobbing, set to an overly saccharine sentimental piano and string score. While Soo-hyeon might have reaped his revenge, it was always already *too late*, as nothing could ever bring his fiancée back. In a conventional melodrama the spectator might be encouraged in the climactic moment to cry. In this case, though, we are unlikely to cry with Soo-hyeon, but instead experience something like dread, or disgust at the sight of the beheading.

Park's films—particularly his vengeance trilogy—end in nearly identical fashion. Where characters very well might reap revenge, it is always already *too late*; the act is never as fulfilling as it endeavors to be.[14] There is no way to make up for the loss, which drives the individual plots of Park's films. Woo-jin Lee in *Oldboy* ostensibly achieves his objective, but his vengeance is hardly satisfactory. This is further complicated by the fact that Park places our sympathies with Dae-su Oh—the target of Lee's vengeance. Similarly, in *Lady Vengeance* Geum-ja Lee successfully orchestrates an elaborate scheme to bring Baek—who kidnaps, ransoms and kills children—to "justice." Geum-ja gathers the parents of the abducted children and each is given the opportunity to torture Baek in an abandoned schoolhouse, and to finally kill him. In the end, though, sympathies, plots, and character motivations are the provenance of narrative. Park's films are much closer to the conventional melodramatic genre than Roth's *Hostel*, for example; nonetheless, Park, like his fellow countryman Kim, laces his films with violent ruptures.

Like the work of these Korean filmmakers, Shion Sono's films are not necessarily extreme through and through, but they feature episodes of exaggerated violence (often laced with vibrant colors—spewing crimson blood for instance), and multiple storylines that fracture narrative coherence. Historically, we might track some affinities between Sono and the work of Seijun Suzuki—a filmmaker known for his candid irreverence, manipulation of genres (particularly the yakuza film), meandering plots, and bold use of color. Sono's films are frequently quite difficult to negotiate, not because the content is inordinately graphic (though sometimes it is), but rather because his work is so eclectic. Sono refuses to conform to any one specific cinematic genre, or form. His 2008 film *Ai no mukidashi* (*Love Exposure*), for example, is a madcap melange of melodrama, comedy, action thriller, and a dusting of other genres that runs for nearly four hours. The length itself already verges on long-format television.

We find familial motifs in his films, specifically with characters that are *too close*. His 2005 film *Kimyo na sakasu* (*Strange Circus*) is something of a sur-realistic freakshow, as the title suggests. The film opens to a freakshow, with ghoulish Grand Guignol set pieces. The primary character Mitsuko Ozawa, who at the start of the narrative is a twelve-year-old girl, narrates in voice-over, "It's almost like I was born on the execution stand." The film cuts from the freakshow to Mitsuko's parents, in the midst of sex and bathed in red light. Mitsuko continues her narration, "If not, I was born to my mother as she awaited execution. I've been standing in for her there ever since." From the very start Mitsuko is positioned *too close* to her (standing in for her). The abject nature of this mother–daughter relationship is further colored by extreme violence (execution/freakshow) and sex with incestual connotations, which the film communicates formally through highly stylized elements such as color, gooeyness, editing, and compositions.

Mitsuko's father, Gozo, who also happens to be the principal of her school, summons the youngster to his office, where he evidently rapes the girl for the first time. After the violent sexual encounter (which takes place offscreen) Mitsuko steps into a school hall that is bathed in blood. Mitsuko cups her hands to her face, sickened by the sexual encounter; a trickle of blood drips down her hand. A non-diegetic drone fills the oneiric space, and Mitsuko's footsteps are gooey, suggesting that the architectural features have taken on fleshy qualities. In the bloody hallway Mitsuko meets herself in the form of her mother's body; she narrates, "My mother looked just like me. I was just like my mother. My mother was just like me."

The pair stand before one another, as if at a mirror, each extending out a bloody hand. Here is the return to the maternal—in a near-literal sense Mitsuko encounters her mother, Sayuri, but this is also a return to the womb. The hall is vaginal—in its deep crimson hue, the fleshy texture, the audio design that signifies a sticky wetness, its proximity to the sexual encounter, and the portal through which two return to the state of being one (fused in the mother–child bond).[15]

The soundscape of the uterine imagery is abject precisely because it threatens to swallow-up Mitsuko, to reabsorb the child into the maternal body, to fuse with the mother. The fleshy cavernous space approaches the devouring mother, a figure, as Barbara Creed observes, that is "associated with the dread of the generative mother seen only as the abyss, the all-incorporating black hole which threatens to reabsorb what it once birthed."[16] The scene itself is not overwhelmingly shocking or grotesque; nonetheless, it might elicit a degree of disgust. William Ian Miller notes that disgust is evoked surprisingly not from deathly things, but rather from what possesses the capacity to spawn life, where death and decay signify the eternal cycle of becoming.[17] What Miller identifies as spawning disgust is the erasure of clear borders, what is in the state of becoming, what is in-between or transitioning from one thing to another. Finally then, because the corridor is presented in near-comic-book red, what truly seems to elicit an affective response are the slurpy sounds that evoke the "gooey" surfaces that signify the potential to regenerate. Furthermore, the narrative content—that Mitsuko is destined to take her mother's place— suggests the endless cycle of recurrence.

Figure 6.1 *Strange Circus*, Shion Sono, 2005

This ever-recurring cycle is also replicated in the incestuous relationship. Mitsuko's father places his daughter in a cello case, fitted with a peephole. He compels his daughter to watch as he and Sayuri have sex. Mitsuko in a voiceover reflects on the experience of watching: "I felt like I was the one being made love to." Gozo alternates having sex with Sayuri and with Mitsuko, who announces that the only difference between them is that her mother seems to enjoy having sex, but "The expressions on her face slowly became mine." Lying Mitsuko on the bed she says in voiceover, "When I lay down, I became my mother." The use of match-on-action editing in this particular instance creates the seamless appearance of the two, once again becoming one. As Mitsuko's father lays her gently onto the bed, a match-on-action cut seamlessly carries the action from the child Mitsuko, in the process of being laid down, to Mitsuko as her mother, lying fully prone on the bed. The cut permits the young Mitsuko to literalize her fusion with her mother's body—perhaps even usurping her. Mitsuko's voiceover, now mixed with Sayuri's voice, informs us (while she is having sex with her father—though visualized as an embodiment of Sayuri) that "I turned into my mother as he kept loving me. I finally started to enjoy having sex with my father. That's because I have become my mother."

Suddenly it is revealed that what we have seen thus far is actually a novel that is being authored by Taeko Mitsuzawa—a famous female author who specializes in erotic-grotesque literature. The break from the Mitsuko narrative, which takes place about a third of the way through the film, is somewhat jarring. It marks a rupture in the coherent linear narrative structure, and is in keeping with the tendency in extreme cinema for more episodic storytelling. The denouement of the film unfolds largely in the expositional mode—bringing the Mitsuko narrative together with the "objective" story-world. Taeko's pretty-boy assistant, Yuji, reveals that (s)he is actually Mitsuko (having what appears to be an amateur double mastectomy to disguise his/her true sex). Taeko is so delusional that she presumed that she was Mitsuko, but she slowly comes to terms with the fact that she is Sayuri.

Interestingly, Yuji wears a shirt with multiple prints of Egon Schiele's "Self-Portrait as St. Sebastian" (1914/15), even taking on a Schiele-like posture, indicating that (s)he is in fact the genuine victim (or martyr)—not Taeko, who likes to lay claim to this. Yuji/Mitsuko, returning to the site of original trauma, has Gozo chained to the bed (where he raped Mitsuko/Yuji)—Gozo has since had all of his extremities amputated. Yuji repeatedly kicks the shackled, crippled man. The strikes precipitate a flashback to a sexual encounter—Gozo fucking Sayuri—with the rapid cross-cutting between the two scenes, present and flashback, inviting a comparison between the exhibition of extreme violence and sex. The violent jostling of Yuji's kicking (matched with the jostling of the handheld camera) and his/her guttural utterances further locate the confluence of violence and sex. When Sayuri finally realizes the truth of the situation—that she is not, in fact, Mitsuko, as she had imagined—she says, "I am sorry," but it is far *too late*; there is nothing that will undo the trauma that Mitsuko/Yuji has endured.[18]

Why don't you play in hell (2013), like many of Sono's films, cannot be situated in any one genre—yakuza/gangster film, comedy, action, horror. It is in a sense a meta-film, as part of the plot involves the making of a hyper-violent yakuza film. Like *Strange Circus* and *Love Exposure*, it is not a full-on extreme film, but rather plays host to a number of extreme ruptures. In an absolutely brilliant scene of revenge, Mitsuko gets revenge upon her two-timing boyfriend, with the help of her "pretend boyfriend," a diminutive young man infatuated with her. Barging into her cheating boyfriend's apartment, Mitsuko breaks a beer bottle, collects the shards of glass, and places them in the man's mouth, while her pretend boyfriend holds him in place. Mitsuko places a shard of glass in her mouth and gives the unfaithful boyfriend one last sensuous kiss. The kiss is deep and long—emphasized further by the smacking of saliva and the clinking of broken glass.

Blood oozes from the deep passionate kiss—eventually a shard of glass punctures the ex-boyfriend's cheek, splitting apart the taut skin. Beyond the explicit exhibition of violence is the slurpy sound (particularly at the end of the kiss), with the excess of saliva and blood oozing from Mitsuko's mouth serving as an aural signifier for the transgression of boundaries—in this specific instance a traversal that is both violent and sensual.

Sono remains fond of filling spaces with blood, as demonstrated in a scene reminiscent of the vaginal hallway sequence in *Strange Circus*. The young Mitsuko, the central female character of *Why don't you play in hell*, arrives home in the wake of a rival gang's attack. The intended target was Mitsuko's father, who was not home at the time of the attack (he was attending to his

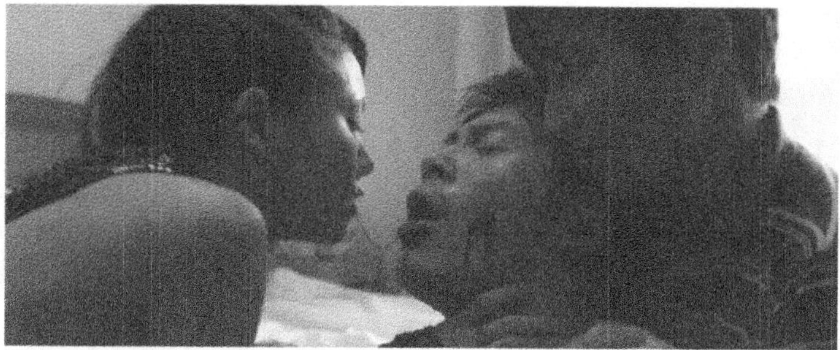

Figure 6.2 *Why don't you play in hell?*, Shion Sono, 2013

mistress). When confronted with the rival gang, Mitsuko's mother unleashes holy hell, fighting off the assailants with a kitchen knife. Unaware of what has transpired, Mitsuko swings open a door and slides forcefully (or, it would seem, is dragged) across the room, made slippery by a pool of brilliant red blood that completely fills the space. The vibrant red set, in contrast to the white furniture and Mitsuko's white dress, is awe-inspiring.

Mitsuko's exaggerated slide across the vast pool of blood is set to the swelling of a non-diegetic string score (so characteristic of melodrama) and her diegetic scream, which is processed and given a reverberant resonance. Whereas conventional melodramas use dissolves and other cinematic techniques at moments of heightened emotion, frequently set to overwrought strings in this case, we witness the use of both slow motion and overlap editing, which elongates Mitsuko's action. In addition, this overripe scene, literally "blood soaked," is set to an embellished diegetic and non-diegetic soundscape. When Mitsuko finally comes to a stop she finds herself face to face with Ikegami, the gangster leading the group of hitmen. In a tight close-up they exchange glances in a rapid shot/reverse shot, further emphasized with quick dissolves making for near-graphic matches. Adhering to the temporal formulation of "too late," melodramatic narratives frustrate diegetic gazes, where an eyeline does not locate its desired object; in this specific case, however, the eyeline gaze *is* met (again, emphasized in a near graphic match). This matching gaze approaches the *too soon* of horror—which, interestingly, Williams associates with exhibitions of violence, blood, sadomasochism, castration.[19] The exchange of glances appears to sweep across the body genres, if only cursorily: the startled expression of the characters (the *too soon* of horror), the slight erotic charge found in Ikegami's fascinated gaze (the *on time* of pornography), and finally Mitsuko's demand that Ikegami clean up the mess he has made (returning us to the domestic realm and the *too late* of melodrama).[20] And in this sweep across body genres, blood displaces tears.

Whereas Sono features maternal characters that are *too close*, Lars Von Trier's 2009 film *Antichrist* features a mother who is *too distant*—leading to

Figure 6.3 *Why don't you play in hell?*, Shion Sono, 2013

the destruction of the familial unit. The film begins with an unnamed couple
making love—the graphic exhibition of sex is shot in slow motion, rich black
and white, dramatically lit in low-key lighting, and set to a deeply embellished
operatic score ("Lascia ch'io pianga mia cruda sorte," "Let me weep over my
cruel fate," from Handel's *Rinaldo*). During the coital act, the couple's child
gets out of his crib, mounts a desk, and falls out of a window to his death.[21] It
is as tragic as it is melodramatic. As solemn as *Antichrist* is, though, its basic
plot recalls a source a bit less lofty than Handel: Sean Cunningham's 1980
classic slasher *Friday the 13th*. The motivation for Mrs. Voorhees to go on a
killing spree in *Friday the 13th* is prompted by her son's death; Jason drowns
in the lake because the camp counselors were having sex, neglecting their
duties as lifeguards. Where *Friday the 13th* is peppered with erotically charged
killing-numbers, the narrative of *Antichrist* is punctuated with moments of
intense hysteria, sadism, and masochism. Viewed through this lens, *Antichrist*
isomorphically renders the patterns of the slasher over the melodramatic
genre—the couple even retreat to a remote cabin in the woods, and rather than
being stalked by a boogieman, they face their own "inner demons"—hence the
title *Antichrist*?

   At a number of points, Von Trier, particularly when leading up to or during a psychic crisis, infuses the otherwise "realistic" narrative with highly stylized audio/visual elements that are quite indicative of the melodramatic genre. As Geoffrey Nowell-Smith observes, "music and mise-en-scene do not heighten the emotionality of an element of the action: to some extent they substitute for it." By way of comparison, Nowell-Smith notes, in the hysteric patient repressed trauma is expressed through their physiological symptoms.[22] The excessive stylized form of melodrama, then, is somatic—articulating a profound suffering that fails to find articulation in the Symbolic (or narrative content). The traumatic epicenter of *Antichrist*—the loss of a child—is coupled with the highly stylized visual and audio treatments of the sexual number, and this deeply embellished stylization serves as the vehicle for the "siphoning of the excess but where there may still be explosions of a material that is repressed rather than expressed; and in the dramas proper, where the extreme situations represented turn up material which itself cannot be represented within the convention of the plot and mise-en-scene."[23] Where there is cinematic embellishment, we find affective potential.

Oneiric interludes rupture the conventional realist narrative. These eruptions are highly stylized treatments of the mise-en-scène, particularly of the forest—shot in slow motion, desaturated while at the same time allowing certain colors (e.g. greens) to materialize in fairly vivid ways. The lighting too is dramatic, often coming from below. The stylized treatment of the forest amplifies the fairytale qualities of Von Trier's film. Regarding these stylized eruptions the cinematographer, Anthony Dod Mantle, in an interview, noted:

> In one of the "visualization sequences," as we called them, She [the unnamed female character] is traveling across the bridge in the forest. Lars and I had talked about going for the completely non-naturalistic look of a painting. I think that when you have images that last for up to 30 seconds in cinema, people start to perceive them differently, more like they would a painting. So we did many layers of high-speed photography and combined them [in post]. I'd light the scene naturalistically, and then I'd flip the lights in the other direction and shoot the water under the bridge at different frame rates, do passes for the foreground and for the background—basically anything we could do to destroy any naturalistic references. We brought in mist and fog and lit them differently for texture. It's a painting, really. For Lars and me, these were some of the most enjoyable moments on the entire film.[24]

These "visualization sequences," as Mantle and Von Trier called them, externalize the emotional friction in the characters (especially the female character). For instance, when the female character begs her partner for help, Von

Trier cuts away to a shot of trees and vines lit with a moving light that casts shadows on a forest thicket signifying overloaded neural networks. The female character is frequently struck dumb with panic attacks—quivering, unable to breathe, or unable to process the outside world. These moments of angst might be punctuated with stylistic elements, such as extreme close-ups.

The female character wallows in melancholic sadness—or is it guilt? A flashback (another melodramatic device) reveals that the female character very well might have seen her son fall out of bed, but, too enthralled by sexual frenzy, did nothing. She is, in the clearest melodramatic sense, *too late*. The male character also discovers photographs of their child, and he notices that his shoes are on the wrong feet. The autopsy report indicated that the child's feet were deformed. The implication is that the female character *consciously* bound the child's feet, and the subsequent deformation that this caused perhaps compromised his stability, and finally contributed to the fatal accident. The male character's revelation, also, comes *too late*, but also entertains Neale's "*if only*"—if only he had noticed that his partner was abusing the child things might have been different. Not only does the female character wallow in sadness/guilt, but she punishes herself, and compels her partner to engage in sadomasochistic sex—demanding that he slap her during sex. The coupling of sex and sadomasochism returns the female character to the site of trauma (linking sexual frenzy to the tragic accident) and at the same time enacts punishment.

The male character is a cognitive-behavioral therapist, and he approaches the tragedy armed with cool stoicism. The couple retreat to a family cabin in the woods to escape the weight of urban life and the traumatically charged site of the accident. At the cabin the female character begins therapy under her partner's supervision. While she does appear to make something of a breakthrough, in the end all the male character's therapeutic exercises and impermeable stoicism only stoke the female character's guilt-filled anguish, which eventually manifests as violence. The most affecting moments in *Antichrist* happen in the intersection of graphic sexual content and violence.

Helen Hester advocates for an expanded notion of the pornographic, where we locate deeply affecting non-sexual content within the pornographic paradigm. Linda Williams identifies the involuntary spasm of pleasure, a confession of the body, as central to pornography, but Hester on the other hand insists:

> This paroxysm . . . need not be sexual to solicit our prurient interest. Reactions of pain or disgust are just as capable of fascinating as those of pleasure, and the involuntary shudder induced by the gag reflex is capable of functioning for the viewer in ways reminiscent of the spasms of orgasm. Evidently sexual fluids, as well [as] sexual paroxysms, can be

displaced by various alternatives under the generalized interests of prurience and of being affected.

Hester continues by noting the affinities between pornography and horror;
citing Tanya Krzywinska: "Horror films, especially body horror films, also
use disgust as a means of blurring the distinction between authenticity and
artifice." Hester adds:

> As different as these genres are in terms of factors such as violence,
> viewing conditions, and content, there is a certain point in the Venn
> diagram where their affects and textual strategies can be seen to inter
> sect. It may be that it is the notion of intensity—as demonstrated by the
> experience of *jouissance* in the consumer-viewer which marks this point
> of intersection.[25]

With *Antichrist*, though, there is more than an intersection, more than a displacement; we witness instead a seemingly complete conflation—blood is cum,
and cum is blood. The female character, astride her male partner, forcefully
engages in sex—while the male partner professes his love for her, the female
character frantically retorts that she does not believe him. Frustrated, and
during a violent struggle, she dismounts from her partner and thrusts a log
into his groin. Once again astride him, manually stimulating his erect penis,
the female character pants slightly, flips her hair, before the unconscious male
character ejaculates—the blood-color ejaculate spurting on her blouse, and
across her hand. The choreography here (while certainly more violent than
most) finds clear affinities with pornography.

Violence escalates. Feelings of guilt overwhelm the female character—and
she lashes out against herself and her male partner. The female character, for
example, drills a hole through the male character's calf to secure a grindstone,
fashioning an impromptu ball and chain—punishing and shackling him like a
prisoner. The strong negative emotional charge associated with the woman's
anguish is evident not only in the content, but also in the cinematic form—
overlap editing (e.g. the woman's scream viewed multiple times), dramatic
lighting, flashbacks, slow motion. In other words, the character's anguish,
which exceeds the Symbolic register, finds an outlet with all the devices that we
associate with melodrama, particularly at points of heightened psychic crisis. As
Nowell-Smith observes regarding the melodramatic genre: "Often the 'hysterical' moment of the text can be identified as the point at which the realist representative convention breaks down."[26] Assailed by a flashback of the couple's
lovemaking (with the woman's eyes open, presumably noticing her child out of
the crib) the woman, asking her male partner to hold her, performs a clitoridectomy upon herself—cutting off her clitoris with scissors. To the character's

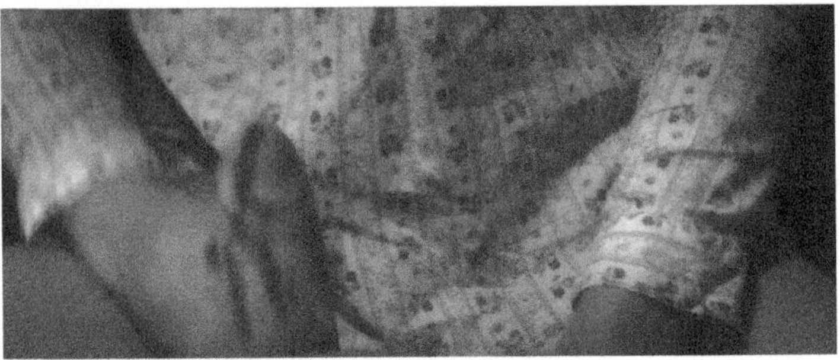

Figure 6.4 *Antichrist*, Lars Von Trier, 2009

mind, the woman directs her punishment directly at the offending site—sexual excitation and pleasure. (Little wonder why so many have characterized *Antichrist* as misogynistic.) Functioning as a narrative parallel with the bloody cum shot earlier, the clitoridectomy also corresponds to the choreography of pornography. The clitoridectomy is presented in forensic close-up, akin to the meat shot in pornography, and offers evidence of the veracity of the image. Immediately following the excision, there is a spewing of blood coupled with a scream of pain, a parallel with pornography's money shot, which is usually coupled with loud orgasmic utterances. The exhibition of sadomasochistic sexual violence—laces of blood-colored semen, clitoridectomy—is affecting, likely causing the spectator to cringe, or gasp. While some of the content in its own right is viscerally shocking, the highly stylized "visualization sequences" intend to represent the charged internal struggle of the characters and at the same time elicit an affective experience for the spectator. And these affecting eruptions find close affinities with the cinematic syntax of melodrama.

HOME INVASIONS

Alexandre Bustillo and Julien Maury's 2007 film *Inside*, like *Martyrs*, also explores the boundaries of life, and specifically the necessary cleft between mother and fetus, where one must become two. The film opens with a car accident. In the wake of the accident we find Sarah, in her second trimester, barely conscious, her face bloodied by the violent impact. Her partner, Matthieu, dies in the crash. We do not learn who is in the other car until the latter moments of the film; a woman—who is likewise pregnant—is driving the other vehicle. The woman—who is never named in the narrative—returns on the eve of Sarah's delivery (Christmas Eve), to claim Sarah's child, as hers died in the car wreck. The figure of the avenging woman is familiar from the slasher genre, as is her choice of weapons, which includes scissors, among other things. What

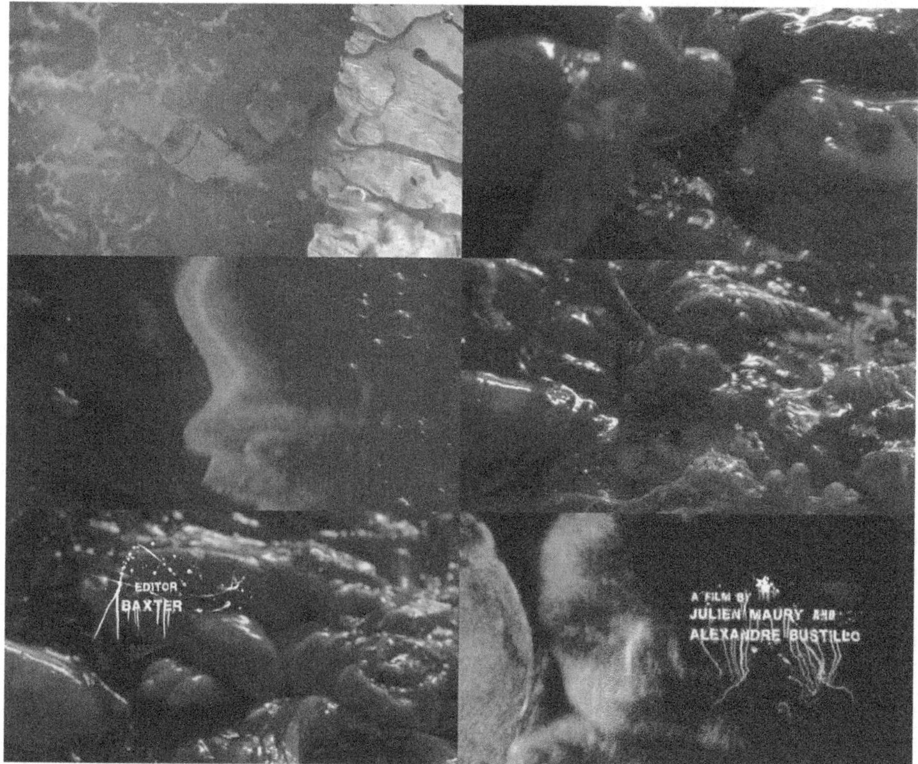

Figure 6.5 *Inside*, Alexandre Bustillo and Julien Maury, 2007

sets *Inside* apart from the slasher tradition, however, is that the unnamed woman is no boogieman.

The opening credit sequence, which features a chaotic web of blood-soaked images, wields the potential for eliciting affect. The images dissolve from definable forms—clothing, ultrasound images of a fetus, fetal hands (maybe?)—before losing form, surrendering to the indistinguishable, formlessness. As with *A Serbian Film* discussed in Chapter 3, the interconnected maternal/fetal relation is another encounter with the zone of indiscernibility. This is where the territory between animal and human collapses. In its bare biological condition, divorced from the socialized body, the human body gives way to the flesh/meat; it is the human in a state of becoming. And the encounter with maternal/fetal in-between-ness, a liminal non-category, a non-object, bears the potential to elicit affect. And these "things" (mother-fetus, abstracted bodies, borders)—and they are not really "things" properly speaking—manifest in form precisely because they do not pertain to meaning, that is to say an object as such, but to affect. The opening credits rely on dissolves, allowing fluids and forms to bleed into one another—webs of blood, fluid, partial body parts, flesh/meat.

This tactic harbors affective potential, as Martine Beugnet observes:

> Blurring or overload of photographic precision, extreme close-ups, superimpositions, under-exposure or over-exposure, variations in sound pitch and intensities: when cinema becomes a cinema of the senses it starts to generate worlds of mutating sounds and images that often ebb and flow between the figurative and the abstract, and where the human form, at least as a unified entity, easily loses its function as the main point of reference. One way or another, the cinema of sensation is always drawn towards the formless ("*l'informe*"): where background and foreground merge and the subjective body appears to melt into matter.[27]

The opening credits of *Inside* have a loose hold on identifiable imagery and the saturation of color begins to approach what Deleuze terms the Figure, and potentially elicits a sensorial experience for the viewer.

These opening credits are where *Inside* most forcefully approaches the murky terrain of the violence of sensation in visual terms. As was explored in Chapter 2, the film gets its affective charge largely from sound. In terms of narrative, with its focus on the maternal body and on the invasion of domestic space, *Inside* borrows a great deal from earlier films. This is particularly true of the horror genre. For instance, just like Adam in *Saw*, the primary female character, Sarah, is a photographer (for a newspaper), and when the avenging woman first appears at Sarah's home she uses her camera as a weapon to stun, and hopefully frighten the unwelcomed visitor away. *Saw* likewise derives this from the latter moments of *Rear Window*. Pregnant and grieving at the loss of her partner, Sarah is haunted by images of "happy families." Seeing a "properly" triangulated family unit, she snaps photographs almost out of spite, or bitterness—as seen, for example, in a sequence when she photographs a couple with their toddler at a park. When she develops photographs in her in-home darkroom, hoping to identify the strange woman who has mysteriously appeared at her door, the photographs of the family in the park reveal upon closer inspection the avenging figure lurking in the bushes in the background. This is clearly a reference to Michelangelo Antonioni's 1966 film *Blow-Up*, where the protagonist inadvertently captures a gunman lurking in the shrubs, discovering this fact only after blowing up (hence the title) the image to magnify the incriminating detail.

The graphic rending of the body (discussed in Chapter 2) is less interesting than the more abstract images found in the opening credits and a dream sequence, relatively early in the film, prior to the avenging woman's arrival. In both the opening credits and the dream sequence the film explores the limits and boundaries of life. The pregnant body is (especially in patriarchal culture) monstrous—for during pregnancy it is difficult, if not impossible, to ascertain the limits between the mother's body and the developing fetus. It represents a conceptual problematizing of the imagined single unified body—where one is two. In addition to this, it discloses the utter artifice of the division between animal and human. The activities that reveal the "animalistic," which lies just below the surface and is contained within the context of culture, harbor the potential to be affecting. Eating, for instance, is framed by the conventions of food preparation, aesthetics, regional delicacies, practices such as "the family meal." Sex is contextualized within the discourses of romance, love, or in less than flattering terms as conquest. Pregnancy and childbirth are potent qualities that threaten to reveal the naked truth that lurks behind the thin veil of culture. Modern practices attempt to throw a cultural veneer over the birthing process—at least in the so-called "developed world"—applying the discourse of science in the sterile and controlled environment of the hospital, which is not simply a matter of practicality, or medical expediency, but an effort to contain the abject. The birthing process exhibits the mixing of fluids and excretions—blood, amniotic fluid, shit, sweat, and (perhaps) tears. The female body transforms: enlarged breasts, lactation, the appearance of supernumerary nipples, swelling of the belly, and stretch marks. And finally of course there is the physical separation of effectively one entity into two—mother and child. All these "things"—and they are not really "things" so much as they are states, or mixed entities that are not exactly one or the other—are manifest as abject referents.

Viewed from a particular perspective the fetus is parasitical. The history of horror films explores the anxiety surrounding the birthing process, from *Invasion of the Body Snatchers* (Philip Kaufman, 1978) to *The Thing* (John Carpenter, 1982). In both cases, "the primal scene is . . . presented as a series of grotesque bodily invasions; here the creature is able to take over both the human and animal body and clone itself into an exact replica of the invaded being. In both these films conception and birth are presented as a form of cloning; the sexual act becomes an act of vampirism."[28] *Inside* does not depict the primal scene as such, but the dream sequence does exhibit pregnancy as a sort of "sickening" invasion.

Like these earlier horror films, *Inside* also touches on these anxieties, and it is particularly evident in the dream sequence. Sarah gently rocks in her rocking chair, clutching her heavily pregnant belly, and begins to heave. Leaning forward and falling from the chair, on all fours (like an animal), she begins to vomit copious amounts of milk. She rolls on her back, continuing to heave, with quick cuts to her snarling cat (associating Sarah not only with the animal kingdom, but also witchcraft). Her neck pulsates, milk spewing from her mouth turns to blood, and what appears to be a second-term fetus

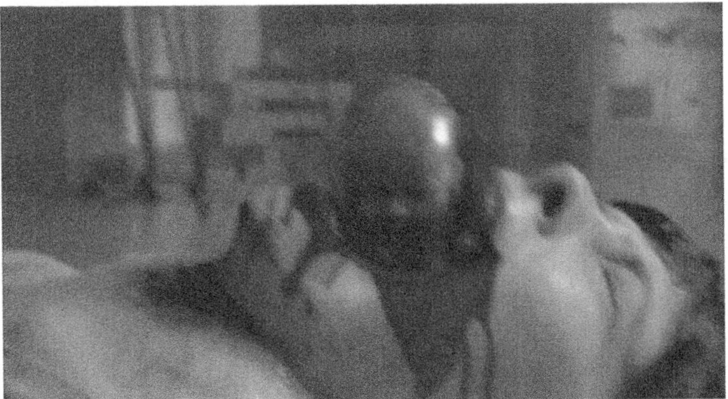

Figure 6.6 *Inside*, Alexandre Bustillo and Julien Maury, 2007

crowns, emerging from her gaping mouth. Sarah's child is full-term, so the fact that the fetus that emerges in her dream is second-term associates it with the avenging woman's child killed in the car wreck at the beginning of the film.

The emergence of the fetus from Sarah's mouth is similar to the birth of the alien that violently erupts from Kane's abdomen in Ridley Scott's 1979 classic sci-fi horror film *Alien*. The fears and anxieties surrounding the pregnant body are largely the product of a patriarchal culture that (perhaps jealously) seeks to contain the generative powers associated with the female body. Male bodies generally do not transform (and certainly not in relation to the procreative processes—save penile erection and the discharge of seminal fluid), and when male bodies do mutate in the horror genre, as Barbara Creed observes they "take on characteristics associated with female bodies; in this instance man's body [like Kane's in *Alien*] becomes grotesque because it is capable of being penetrated. From this union, the monstrous creature is born." Monstrosity materializes in an "unnatural" union, or some other violation, and the violence of the car wreck at the beginning of *Inside* is where monsters are conceived. Moreover, the monstrous fetus that births from Sarah's mouth evokes certain childhood fantasies about the primal scene and pregnancy. As Creed goes on to observe, the

> birth of the alien from Kane's stomach recalls Freud's description of a common misunderstanding that many children have about birth, that is, that the mother is somehow "impregnated" through the mouth—she may eat a special food—and the baby grows in her stomach, from which it is born. Here, we have a version of the primal scene in which the infant is conceived orally.[29]

This oral fantasy also evokes the connotations of a parasitical relation, where one body consumes another. What is not entirely clear, though, is which body consumes the other. The *Alien* narrative deploys a "mother" who refuses to give up her children and threatens to devour them, to re-incorporate them back into the maternal body, whereas *Inside* perhaps envisions the reverse—a child/parasite that consumes its host. "Fear of the uncontrollable generative mother repels me from the body; I give up cannibalism because abjection (of the mother) leads me toward respect for the body of the other, my fellow man [*sic*], my brother."[30] Indeed, *Inside* is a cannibalistic narrative, in which there is no respect for the body of the other.

Like the work of Park Chan-wook, Michael Haneke's films are not blatantly extreme; rather, Haneke uses instances of violence like an exclamation mark—"slow burns" abruptly punctuated with some violent eruption. *Benny's Video* (1992), *Funny Games* (1997, 2007), and *Caché* (2005) constitute Michael Haneke's "glaciation trilogy." Catherine Zimmer observes that Haneke's trilogy "could easily be seen as the artsy predecessors of the recent American horror market—a point driven home by the US release of the American remake of *Funny Games* in 2007, directed by Haneke himself and demonstrating that the earlier films are now retroactively inseparable from recent trends in American film."[31] The first film of the trilogy highlights the proximity of the Bosnian conflict, relative to the seemingly indifferent Austria. In *Caché* (*Hidden*), mysterious videotapes with ghastly childlike illustrations appear on the doorstep of a French family. Who and exactly why the videotapes are made is never explicitly revealed—they appear like uncanny specters. Nevertheless, the videotapes and the violence associated with them materialize like the return of the colonial repressed. As with all the films in the "glaciation trilogy," malevolence appears like a ghostly apparition in *Funny Games*; the two antagonists are even dressed in all-white tennis or golf outfits—suggesting their ghostly character.

Haneke made essentially two identical versions of *Funny Games*—first, an Austrian film in 1997, and ten years later an American version. Two young men—Peter and Paul—arrive at an exclusive summer vacation spot, a lake dotted with holiday homes. The pair skip from one house to another, holding families hostage. The film focuses on one such family, whom Peter and Paul deride, savagely and coldly killing each member. David Edelstein does not find *Funny Games* particularly amusing, because "In the end, *Funny Games* is little more than high-toned torture porn with an edge of righteousness that's not unlike Peter and Paul's. Audiences flock to nightmarish 'home invasion' thrillers because of an implicit pact with the filmmaker that the invaders will be vanquished and the family unit saved." Edelstein imagines that "Some could make the case that Haneke deserves a measure of respect for reminding us how pathetically dependent we are on that pact and its cathartic endings."[32] What Edelstein openly dismisses is the degree to which Haneke is self-aware: his use of videotapes, mediating images (frames-in-frames), and out-of-frame space.

Funny Games also features the "breaking of the fourth wall," where Paul turns to the audience to give a wink and a nod (sometimes literally), or to explicitly address the audience. Haneke refuses to bow to the virtual imperative to contain, and/or to contextualize violence within the framework of narrative/character motivation, and most importantly to restore familial units. Instead, he elicits the spectator's heuristic faculties—demanding that we contemplate the nature of representing violence, mediated through the media, from television news to the cinema. Indeed, in *Funny Games* particularly, motivations are nowhere to be found, because Haneke repeatedly directs us to interrogate cinematic form. Paul even directly tells us so, in one instance turning to the camera and quizzing the spectator about narrative expectations.

Funny Games might be read as meta-torture porn, because it precisely investigates the visual and narrative structures that elicit sadistic pleasure in the spectator. "The self-reflexivity of *Funny Games* undercuts the illusion of narrative and reminds the audience that what they are watching is an artificial construct," Kevin Wetmore observes. And this is set in stark contrast to recent trends in horror that adopt the "reality effect"—surveillance cameras, webcams, handheld amateur footage. "The false self-reflexivity of *Cloverfield* or *[REC]* is designed to enhance verisimilitude and convince the viewer what he or she is watching is genuine."[33] Where these films use the "reality effect" for narrative purposes, Haneke views *Funny Games* as a film *about* "the portrayal of violence in the media or in film."[34]

In an interview, Haneke speaks about *Caché*, saying that the film is about "how one lives with guilt."[35] (In fact, Haneke even proclaims elsewhere that the theme of all of his films is guilt.) Casting off the yoke of memory (or history) is how we generally negotiate guilt, or actually, more precisely, responsibility for the past; the primary male character, Georges, for instance, abdicates his responsibility: "I was only six, how am I supposed to remember?" The videotapes arrive on his doorstep as unwanted gifts, in the same way that a bad memory might unexpectedly return to a subject's consciousness. The videotapes from this perspective in *Caché*—as if arriving from the depths of Georges's own unconscious—find affinities with the video and audiotape messages found in the *Saw* series. Jigsaw effectively operates as the marauding superego, wagging the finger of discontent, lambasting his ensnared victims, lecturing to them about their misdeeds, or vice. Jigsaw's recorded messages demand atonement, and the trapped subject must endure some excruciating punishment to satisfy Jigsaw-cum-the-superego's demand, usually manifesting in some masochistic exercise—cutting off one's own limb, pulling out one's own teeth, impaling oneself on hooks, etc. And in this sense, violence is always rooted within instead of coming from without. The recorded messages in these films, then, are merely projections of the victim's own guilt—reaping what they sow. Viewed from this perspective, violence originates from within the subject.

The antagonists of *Funny Games* are also insiders; Catherine Zimmer observes that

> the casting of the scene of torturous violence as that of [a] highly mediated bourgeois home, and the perpetrators of the violence not as outsiders to that environment, but as themselves white, educated, 'proper' young men. The way in which even a home-invasion narrative is posited as one in which the invaders seem more like insiders than outsiders highlights how internal this violence is to that domestic space.[36]

The "safety" of the enclosed gated estate is turned on its head, and transformed into the sadist's chamber. Just as in Pier Paolo Pasolini's *Salò* (1975), where the sadistic theater plays out behind the walls of the chateau, Peter and Paul conduct their little rituals in the private homes of their victims.

Throughout *Funny Games*, Paul, the angelic torturer, peppers the Farber family with questions, riddles, and little games—one of the hallmarks of sadism. Paul in particular mobilizes his commanding intellect and verbosity to terrorize the family. Peter Brunette suggests that this inversion of intellect, which is usually associated with human progress, is

> a nod to the German theorists Max Horkheimer and Theodor Adorno's *Dialectic of Enlightenment*, which Haneke surely read as a philosophy student, we understand in the person of Paul the theory of the utterly irrational outbreak—for Horkheimer and Adorno, the Nazis and the Holocaust—not as an outgrowth or intensification of irrationality but as a product of the *ultra-rational*, inherited from the Enlightenment, that disregards all purely human, nonlogical values.[37]

At the midpoint of the film, Paul propositions the Farber family with a bet—betting when each character will die. Eventually, Paul turns to us, the viewer, and asks, "I mean, what do you think? You think they stand a chance? You're on their side, aren't you? Who are you betting on, hmm?" Toward the conclusion, after the film languishes in the suffering of the Farber family—including the execution of the Farber's young boy—Paul once again addresses the camera directly: "Do you think it's enough? I mean, you want a real ending, right? With plausible plot development, don't you?" These digressions from the narrative diegesis bother some, and they are unquestionably didactic, but nevertheless the intention obviously is to call attention to our own narrative expectations and desires; we want, we crave retribution, but Haneke refuses to give it to us. The little games that Paul (in particular) plays with the Farber family share certain affinities with Jigsaw. Paul's games, though, are never "winnable." Nevertheless, as with Jigsaw, Paul relishes the experience of delivering riddles.

In fact, during the latter part of the film Paul tauntingly asks Ann to play a game; if she "wins" she gets to choose who will die first and how—with a knife or a shotgun. The absolute callous cruelty exhibited by Peter and Paul elicits not only anger from the audience, but a desire for retribution. This desire is brought to a fevered pitch as Paul continues to taunt Ann. Frantically, Ann reaches for the shotgun on the table and shoots Peter in the abdomen; the blast is so violent that it throws him up against the wall, spraying blood across the pristine surface. But this moment of pleasure—and let there be no mistake there is a definite sense of narrative gratification at the sight of violent revenge—is taken away from us. Paul, distressed, screams out, "Where's the remote control?" Finding it, he simply puts the scene in reverse, and restarts the scene at the point where Ann reaches for the shotgun; this time, Paul stops her. Outside the frame George is then summarily shot, as he lies prone on the floor. What makes this scene stand out is not simply the cheeky cinematic conceit of rewinding the film as we watch the film unfold, but that whenever Peter or Paul kill, it always happens offscreen. *Funny Games* is not outright extreme cinema, but rather asks us to consider how violence is represented in cinema.

Melodrama frequently uses flashbacks, often accompanied by saccharine non-diegetic music—for instance, when Otto Frank, in George Stevens's 1959 film *The Diary of Anne Frank*, is presented with his daughter's diary *after* the catastrophic event: as Otto clutches the diary, the camera zooms into his hands, music swells, and, finally, a dissolve leads into a flashback where the Frank family, *alive*, go into hiding. Although the strategy of rewinding finds certain affinities with the dissolve leading to a flashback, in effect it functions as an anti-melodramatic device. Franco Moretti advances the notion of "agnition" in melodrama—the narrative trope of "too late"—and within the melodramatic text

> time does not stop, and it does not heed anyone's bidding. Still less does it turn back and allow us to use it differently. This is what the protagonist's death is for: to show that time is *irreversible*. And this irreversibility is perceived that much more clearly if there are no doubts about the *different direction* one would like to impose on the course of events.

Moretti posits that this irreversibility of time, and of being "too late," is what prompts tears, which "are always the product of *powerlessness*. They presuppose two mutually opposed facts: that it is clear how the present state of things should be changed—and that this change is impossible."[38] While Haneke traces the outlines of melodramatic syntax—the visual surface of raster lines and reverse motion corresponding to the cinematic dissolve (accentuated with a rippled surface), and finally the shift in temporal dimensions—the filmmaker baits the spectator with their own pat narrative expectations, only to deny the satisfaction that the spectator desperately craves. This might be the instance where the syntax of melodrama might prompt tears, but Haneke subverts the melodramatic. Crying, as Neale notes, is

not just an expression of pain or displeasure or non-satisfaction. As a demand *for* satisfaction, it is the vehicle of a wish—a fantasy—that satisfaction is possible, that the object can be restored, the loss eradicated. There would be no tears were there no belief that there might be an Other capable of responding to them.[39]

NOTES

1. Alan Pakula cited in Jared Brown, *Alan J. Pakula: His Films and His Life* (New York: Back Stage Books, 2005), 276.
2. One of my (Kerner) students, Derek Kanowsky, pointed out that the scene in *Sophie's Choice* could in fact work as a short film in itself.
3. Tarja Laine, *Feeling Cinema: Emotional Dynamics in Film Studies* (New York: Bloomsbury, 2013), 5.
4. Ibid. Later in her book Laine summarizes, "what triggers our emotion in melodrama is not so much empathy with the suffering cinematic characters, but our compassionate participation in their inability to cope with the rift between the conditional spheres of what-is and if-only." Laine, 64.
5. Franco Moretti, *Signs Taken for Wonders: Essays in the Sociology of Literary Forms* (New York: Verso, 1988), 159.
6. Geoffrey Nowell-Smith, "Minnelli and Melodrama," in *Home Is Where the Heart Is: Studies in Melodrama and the Women's Film*, ed. Christine Gledhill (London: BFI, 1994), 70.
7. Steve Neale, "Melodrama and Tears," *Screen* 27, no. 6 (1986): 9.
8. Ibid., 7.
9. Linda Williams, "Film Bodies: Gender, Genre, and Excess," *Film Quarterly* 44, no. 4 (Summer 1991): 11.
10. Neale, 12.
11. Ibid., 19.
12. "Eli Roth on *Hostel*," (February 2006): <http://www.youtube.com/watch?v=j5ArtKwbobY> (last accessed November 25, 2015).
13. Gilles Deleuze, *Francis Bacon: The Logic of Sensation*, trans. Daniel W. Smith (Minneapolis: University of Minnesota Press, 2004), 21–2.
14. On the theme of revenge in Park's films see Steve Choe, "Love Your Enemies: Revenge and Forgiveness in Films by Park Chan-wook," *Korean Studies* 33 (2009): 29–51.
15. The hall finally reaching the mirror might bear some similarities to the early moments of *Alien* where the camera tracks down a vaginal-like hall, through a cervix-like opening, into the incubation chamber where the crew hibernate.
16. Barbara Creed, *The Monstrous-Feminine: Film, Feminism, Psychoanalysis* (New York: Routledge, 1993), 27.
17. William Ian Miller, *The Anatomy of Disgust* (Cambridge, MA: Harvard University Press, 1997), 40–1.

18. When Yuji/Mitsuko reveals his/her double mastectomy scars, his/her disfigured body resembles the photographs taken by Georges Dumas of Fou-Tchou-Li—tortured to death by being cut into pieces. As discussed in Chapter 3, this same photograph is presented in *Martyrs*, and interestingly in the film Fou-Tchou-Li is referred to as a woman. The conscious misreading of the historical photograph in *Martyrs* is possible because the tortured man has been rendered effectively sexless, and ultimately this is what happens to one of the victims in *Martyrs*, Anna, as well: she is stripped of the markers of sexual difference.

19. Linda Williams actually uses the phrase "too early!" She writes, "In contrast to pornography, the fantasy of recent teen horror corresponds to a temporal structure which raises the anxiety of not being ready, the problem, in effect, of 'too early!' Some of the most violent and terrifying moments of the horror film genre occur in moments when the female victim meets the psycho-killer-monster unexpectedly, before she is ready." Williams, 11.

20. Ibid., 9.

21. Interestingly, in *Strange Circus* Mitsuko, in a suicide attempt, jumps from a building—the fall captured in slow motion (DVD time-code 29:39), set to Johann Sebastian Bach's "Largo from Concerto for Keyboard and Strings in F Minor," and presented in a desaturated color palette. The fall from the building recalls the opening of *Antichrist*, though Sono's film was released four years prior to Von Trier's. When Mitsuko is rushed to the hospital, *Strange Circus* begins to exhibit some similarities to torture porn— especially the trope of medicalized gore in the American genre.

22. Nowell-Smith, 73–4.

23. Ibid., 74.

24. Anthony Dod Mantle interviewed by Jon Silberg, "The Root of All Evil," *American Cinematographer* 90, no. 11 (November 2009): 72.

25. Helen Hester, *Beyond Explicit: Pornography and the Displacement of Sex* (New York: SUNY Press, 2014), 137. Tanya Krzywinska, "The Dynamics of Squirting: Female Ejaculation and Lactation in Hard-core Film," in *Unruly Pleasures: The Cult Film and its Critics*, eds. Xavier Mendik and Graeme Harper (Guildford: FAB Press, 2000), 33.

26. Nowell-Smith, 74.

27. Martine Beugnet, *Cinema of Sensation: French Film and the Art of Transgression* (Carbondale: Southern Illinois University Press, 2007), 65.

28. Creed, 17.

29. Ibid., 19.

30. Julia Kristeva, *Powers of Horror: An Essay on Abjection*, trans. Leon S. Roudiez (New York: Columbia University Press, 1982), 78–9.

31. Catherine Zimmer, "Caught on Tape? The Politics of Video in the New Torture Films," in *Horror After 9/11: World of Fear, Cinema of Terror*, eds. Aviva Briefel and Sam J. Miller (Austin: University of Texas, 2011), 94.

32. David Edelstein, "Audience is Loser in Haneke's Unfunny 'Games'," *Fresh Air*, March 14, 2008. Available at <http://www.npr.org/templates/story/story. php?storyId=88230619> (last accessed November 25, 2015).

33. Kevin J. Wetmore, *Post-9/11 Horror in American Cinema* (New York: Continuum, 2012), 65.

34. Michael Haneke, interview by Serge Toubiana, *Funny Games*, directed by Michael Haneke (1997), DVD.

35. Michael Haneke, interview by Serge Toubiana, *Caché*, directed by Michael Haneke (2005), DVD.

36. Zimmer, 101.
37. Peter Brunette, *Michael Haneke* (Urbana: University of Illinois Press, 2010), 62.
38. Moretti cited in Neale, 8. Franco Moretti, *Signs Taken for Wonder: Essays in the Sociology of Literary Forms* (New York: Verso, 1988), 162.
39. Neale, 21–2.

CHAPTER 7

The End of Extreme Cinema?

A void that is not nothing but indicates, within its discourse, a challenge to symbolization. Whether we call it an *affect* or link it with infantile semiotization—for which pre-signifying articulations are merely *equations* rather than symbolic *equivalents* for objects, we must point to a necessity within analysis. This necessity, emphasized by that type of structure, consists in not reducing analytic attention to language to that of philosophical idealism and, in its wake, to linguistics; the point is, quite to the contrary, to posit a *heterogeneity of signifiance*. It stands to reason that one can say nothing of such (effective or semiotic) heterogeneity without making it homologous with the linguistic signifier.[1]

INTRODUCTION: NOT A STYLE, BUT STYLIZED CINEMA

As we have indicated in the present volume, one of the most significant tropes of extreme cinema is its potential to elicit affect. And this enterprise is potentially frustrating, for in the very instant that we subject affecting moments in the cinema to analytic discourse we can witness them slip away—in effect trying to render the non-object (semiotic) in the realm of discourse (Symbolic).[2] And for better or for worse, submitting the affective referent to the analytic gaze wields the potential to neutralize that which spawns sensation. Furthermore, the affective experience is hardly universal, and although we have perhaps over-"idealized" the affective as pan-cultural in certain instances, it is clear that it is subject to cultural, historical, and personal mediation. While we appreciate the dangers inherent in such a project, we have nonetheless made preliminary gestures toward identifying general tendencies in extreme cinema.

Inadvertently, we admit, we might have also "fed the beast." Jinhee

Choi and Mitsuyo Wada-Marciano correctly raise concerns about the term "extreme," particularly as it has been applied to Asian films. Distributors in fact, have used "extreme," as a marketing device—promising to deliver spectacles of gore and/or salacious sexual content (almost invariably tinged with violence). "Asia Extreme" is a "DVD label launched by London-based distributor Metro Tartan," and has been used as a convenient way to package films from radically different cultural contexts. "The strategic designation 'Asia Extreme' has undoubtedly created a regional affiliation among these [Asian] directors' films, but the category itself is purposefully flexible in order to include a range of Asian cinema that seems exportable."[3] The marketing of disparate films under a recognizable heading encourages us (at the behest of a distribution company) to read these films through a particular lens. The very name "Asia Extreme," as Chi-Yun Shin observes, invites, and even relies on,

> the western audiences' perception of the East as weird and wonderful, sublime and grotesque. At the same time, the ways in which Tartan registers and navigates the vagaries of distinct national cultures and different genres gathered under the Asia Extreme banner provide a fascinating site to explore how the West consumes East Asian cinema.[4]

Such critiques are important to bear in mind—and this goes for the Western films that we have considered in this volume as well. *A Serbian Film* comes out of a historical/cultural context radically different from the context that *Hostel*, for example, comes out of.

Where Choi, Wada-Marciano and others have raised concerns regarding the profit-driven motivations for the term "extreme," as well as the ways in which it evokes the colonial gaze, Tanya Horeck and Tina Kendall's edited volume *The New Extremism in Cinema* squarely situates "the new extremism" within the tradition of European art cinema. Horeck, Kendall, and their contributors demonstrate how a number of European films self-reflexively stage scenes of spectacular violence—demanding that viewers, for instance, confront scenes of rape, animal slaughter, and other imagery that many might consider "unwatchable."[5] Their work emphasizes the use of art cinema techniques and interrogates the subsequent philosophical and ethical concerns these films raise. This is an important line of inquiry, which builds off Martine Beugnet's work on sensation and transgression in the specifically French cinematic context.[6] Horeck and Kendall continue to expand upon their work on extreme cinema, and their preface to an issue of the journal *Cinephile* devoted to "Contemporary Extremism" acknowledges both transnational trends in extremism and the ways in which techniques of extreme cinema have been absorbed into mainstream filmic practices.[7] Nevertheless, the articles contained in the *Cinephile* issue tend to remain focused on European art cinema.[8]

We have striven to locate the commonalities that these European "art" films have with works from Asia, the USA, and elsewhere, including mainstream films (like torture porn), and the comedic genre (like *Jackass*). Many of these films exhibit the human form in the throes of sex and/or a violent encounter, in many instances treated in highly embellished ways (e.g. use of extreme close-ups, manipulation of film speed, rapid-fire editing, play between diegetic and non-diegetic sound). These cinematic strategies wield the potential to elicit an affective response in the spectator, which in a number of cases aligns with Linda Williams's conception of body genres—embodied, physical responses of the audience. The notable exception is laughter, particularly in response to the comedic genre, where we might be invited to laugh at, not with, the character onscreen.

Eugenie Brinkema has argued that the "turn to affect" that has animated much humanities scholarship in recent years (not least in film and media studies) has been accompanied by a withdrawal from practices of close reading. Instead, she argues, "the defenders of affect are left with only the mild rhetorical force of summary and paraphrase, intoned synonyms, and thematic generalizations."[9] What Brinkema diagnoses, in part, is what she sees as an overemphasis on the body: bodies onscreen and, even more so, the bodies of spectators, which are vaguely moved by intensities, sensations, and difficult-to-describe feelings that emanate from the image. This frequently results, she claims, in teleological arguments, in which spectators' myriad possible reactions are instead presented as singular, uniform, predetermined. Brinkema describes her project as "a de-contribution to spectatorship studies, an attempt to dethrone the subject and the spectator."[10] She proposes instead that scholars attend to the specificities of form, by engaging in close readings of texts.

While we admire Brinkema's intervention and sympathize in particular with her call to focus on form, we hesitate to move so distinctly away from the body (indeed Brinkema anticipates such responses). We remain convinced that the body remains central to extreme cinema, and that there is more work to be done exploring how these films depict bodies onscreen and affect bodies off it. We have tried to account for the many different ways in which spectators might react to the imagery of extreme cinema—and this is perhaps particularly true of Chapters 4 and 5, where we explore "laughter" and "arousal" respectively. For instance, in the *Jackass* films, we see how images of bodies in pain do not necessarily elicit sympathetic responses in the viewer, and instead can lead to howls of laughter. This could be equally true of the horror films that we explored in Chapter 3, "Pain," where we see bodies beaten and flayed. After all, as Eli Roth has said of horror fans, some just "want to see people gettin' fucked up bad."[11] There is every reason to think that some audience members might respond to scenes of extreme carnage with cheers or guffaws. For that matter, the performers within *Jackass* demonstrate the fluidity and particularity of affect, as they sometimes end up laughing at, or perhaps with, their pain. This slippage of affect is also evident in YouTube reaction videos, whether to *2 Girls 1 Cup* or to *A Serbian Film*, where a spectator might turn away, laugh, and vomit, perhaps all in the same video and in no particular order. Furthermore, laughter can sometimes lead to tears, which would signify something quite different from the weeping traditionally associated with melodrama, a genre we explore in Chapter 6. And, to be clear, some viewers might respond with indifference to all of the violent, disgusting, and sexually charged imagery described herein.

The notion of slippage is at the core of much extreme cinema. Through scenes of explicit, unsimulated sex, moments of what could be considered real, "documentary" footage slip into what would otherwise be considered "fictional," the domain of the narrative film, where violence (and usually sex) are simulated. And, as we argue in Chapter 2, "Hearing," sound is particularly adept at slipping between registers, blurring the boundaries between diegetic and non-diegetic. Sound is sometimes used to underscore the force of the imagery, while at other times it can trouble it. As Lisa Coulthard has argued, noise can be wielded as a weapon of sorts, to physically affect the bodies of spectators, to make them uncomfortable.[12] In addition to the sonic, violence manifests itself in a variety of ways: through jagged editing, through unnaturally vibrant color, through disorienting camera work. It is through form, above all, that extreme cinema gains its power. It is not simply *what* the films represent that is extreme; it is *how* they do it. Extreme cinema is full of sounds and images that throb and shudder.

In the end, what we have outlined in this book is the existence of a trend in post-millennial international cinema toward extreme cinema, which in some cases turns away from conventional narrative structure and its appeal to our emotions, favoring instead an affecting cinema. There certainly is no cohesive extreme style as such. But because extreme cinema aims to elicit sensations, we might say that it tends to be *stylized* to "render" the non-object, the semiotic, abjection, the sublime. It is unclear to us whether we have mapped the opening to some new frontier, or have charted the ebb and tide of a waning cinematic trend we have been calling extreme cinema.

The *South Park* episode "Informative Murder Porn" (which aired October 2, 2013) parodies the crass depiction of murder mysteries on television. The parents of South Park look forward to quasi-journalistic programs like *Dateline*, which typically feature stories about spousal murder and rely on reenactments; they find pleasure in the salacious depictions of violence that are amplified further with sexual plot elements (e.g. extramarital affairs), which the children subsequently dub "murder porn." Helen Hester's notion of the expanded pornographic, which centers on intensely affecting material that is not necessarily sexual in nature, is enacted in a literal sense: Stan's parents watch murder porn as if it were sexually explicit pornography, incorporating it into part of their sex play.

What does this tell us about extreme cinema? Have the tropes of extreme cinema been appropriated by mainstream media? And thus effectively neutralized, or rendered banal? Television has assimilated some of the tropes associated with extreme cinema—for instance, the Comedy Central program *Tosh.O*, which is episodic, depicts real bodies in pain or amid some vile act (the bursting of a cyst, vomiting, leaking orifices). Hester also gives considerable attention to the British television program *Embarrassing Bodies* (2008–9, 2013), which features stories of various human ailments, delivering doses of affecting viewing. A premium is placed on "authentic" bodies that exhibit visible signs of distress, leading some to characterize the program as pornographic: "As with the genre of adult entertainment, the viewer is presented with real bodies really experiencing corporeal phenomena on screen." Hester adds: "The difference is that it is not arousal, sexual pleasure, or orgasmic climax that undergird the discourse but uncomfortable sensations, physical suffering, and bodily malfunction."[13] Thus, in Hester's expanded pornographic, bodily fluids that are traditionally associated with sickness, such as pus and mucous, can stand in for semen, offering a climax, or evidence, of a different sort. While television might grant significant allowances to depictions of violence, the same cannot be said of sexual content (particularly in the American context), although, as the expanded notion of the pornographic (as well as the *South Park* episode cited above) indicates, explicit content can easily be displaced. Although television tends to tone down cinematic trends, perhaps we have only seen the tip of the iceberg. From Asia and Europe, from "serious" art cinema to self-generated content (e.g. reaction videos), the tropes of extreme cinema can be found in nearly every corner of our global media culture.

NOTES

1. Julia Kristeva, *Powers of Horror: An Essay on Abjection*, trans. Leon S. Roudiez (New York: Columbia University Press, 1982), 51.

2. This is precisely why Susanna Paasonen uses the term "resonance" in her book *Carnal Resonance*: "Resonance is carnal by definition, and the sensations and vibrations that it entails are not necessarily easy to articulate or translate into language. The concept also points to the material factors of porn—the fleshy substance of the body; the texture of images, screens, and signals; the technologies of transmission and the materialities of hardware, cables, and modems." Susanna Paasonen, *Carnal Resonance: Affect and Online Pornography* (Cambridge, MA: MIT Press, 2011), 18.

3. Jinhee Choi and Mitsuyo Wada-Marciano, "Introduction," in *Horror to the Extreme: Changing Boundaries in Asian Cinema*, eds. Jinhee Choi and Mitsuyo Wada-Marciano (Hong Kong: Hong Kong University Press, 2009), 5. Also see Chi-Yun Shin, "Art of

Branding: Tartan 'Asia Extreme' Films," *Jump Cut* 50 (Spring 2008). Available at <http://www.ejumpcut.org/archive/jc50.2008/TartanDist/text.htm> (last accessed November 25, 2015).

4. Shin.

5. See Asbjørn Grønstad, "On the Unwatchable," in *The New Extremism in Cinema: From France to Europe*, eds. Tanya Horeck and Tina Kendall (Edinburgh: Edinburgh University Press, 2011), 192–205.

6. See Martine Beugnet, *Cinema and Sensation: French Films and the Art of Transgression* (Edinburgh: Edinburgh University Press, 2007).

7. Tanya Horeck and Tina Kendall, "The New *Extremisms*: Rethinking Extreme Cinema, *Cinephile* 8, no. 2 (Fall 2012): 6–9.

8. The most notable exception is Dave Alexander's essay on a Quebecois film. Peter Schuck's contribution looks at a work of German television.

9. Eugenie Brinkema, *The Forms of the Affects* (Durham, NC: Duke University Press, 2014), xiii.

10. Brinkema, 36.

11. Quoted from the commentary included on the US DVD release of Roth's film *Hostel: Part II*.

12. Lisa Coulthard, "Dirty Sound: Haptic Noise in New Extremism," in *The Oxford Handbook of Sound and Image in Digital Media*, eds. Carol Vernallis, Amy Herzog, and John Richardson (New York: Oxford University Press, 2013), 115–26.

13. Helen Hester, *Beyond Explicit: Pornography and the Displacement of Sex* (New York: SUNY Press, 2014), 60.

Bibliography

Abel, Marco. *Violent Affect: Literature, Cinema, and Critique After Representation*. Lincoln: University of Nebraska Press, 2007.

Aftab, Kaleem. "Drag Me to Hell—Don't Lose Your Head." *Independent*, June 5, 2009, <http://www.independent.co.uk/arts-entertainment/films/features/drag-me-to-hell—dont-lose-your-head-1697053.html>

Altman, Rick ed. *Sound Theory, Sound Practice*. New York: Routledge, 1992.

Andersen, Nathan. *Plato's Cave and Cinema*. New York: Routledge, 2014.

Aston, James, and John Walliss (eds.). *To See the "Saw" Movies: Essays on Torture Porn and Post-9/11 Horror*. Jefferson, NC: McFarland, 2013.

Aston, James, and John Walliss. "'I've Never Murdered Anyone in My Life. The Decisions Are Up to Them': Ethical Guidance and the Turn toward Cultural Pessimism." In *To See the "Saw" Movies: Essays on Torture Porn and Post-9/11 Horror*, ed. James Aston and John Walliss, 13–29. Jefferson, NC: McFarland, 2013.

Atkinson, Meera and Richardson, Michael (eds.). *Traumatic Affect*. Newcastle upon Tyne: Cambridge Scholars Publishing, 2013.

Attali, Jacques. *Noise: The Political Economy of Music*. Trans. Brian Massumi. Minneapolis: University of Minnesota Press, 1985.

Attwood, Feona (ed.). *Mainstreaming Sex: The Sexualization of Western Culture*. New York: I. B. Tauris, 2009.

Attwood, Feona, Vincent Campbell, I. Q. Hunter, and Sharon Lockyer (eds.). *Controversial Images: Media Representations on the Edge*. Basingstoke: Palgrave Macmillan, 2013.

Augé, Marc. *Non-Places: Introduction to an Anthropology of Supermodernity*. Trans. John Howe. New York: Verso, 1995.

Badt, Karin. "Family Is Hell and So Is the World." *Bright Lights Film Journal*, 50 (November 2005), <http://brightlightsfilm.com/50/hanekeiv.htm>

Bakhtin, Mikhail. *Rabelais and His World*. Trans. Hélène Iswolsky. Bloomington: Indiana University Press, 1984.

Barker, Jennifer M. *The Tactile Eye: Touch and the Cinema Experience*. Berkeley: University of California Press, 2009.

Barker, Jennifer M. "Chew on This: Disgust, Delay, and the Documentary Image in *Food, Inc.*" *Film-Philosophy*, vol. 15, no. 2 (2011): 70–89.

Barker, Martin, and Julian Petley (eds.). *Ill Effects: The Media/Violence Debate*. New York: Routledge, 1997.

Barkham, Patrick. "The Extraordinary Story Behind Danny Boyle's *127 Hours*," *Guardian*, <http://www.theguardian.com/film/2010/dec/15/story-danny-boyles-127-hours>

Bataille, Georges. *Erotism: Death and Sensuality*. Trans. Mary Dalwood. San Francisco: City Lights Books, 1986.

Bataille, Georges. *The Tears of Eros*. Trans. Peter Connor. San Francisco: City Lights Books, 1989.

Baudrillard, Jean. *The Spirit of Terrorism and Other Essays*. Trans. Chris Turner. New York: Verso, 2003.

Beeler, Stan. "From Silver Bullets to Duct Tape: Dexter versus the Traditional Vigilante Hero." In *Dexter: Investigating Cutting Edge Television*, ed. Douglas L. Howard, 221–30. London: I. B. Tauris, 2010.

Bennett, Jill. *Empathic Vision: Affect, Trauma, and Contemporary Art*. Stanford: Stanford University Press, 2005.

Bergson, Henri. "Laughter." In *Comedy: An Essay on Comedy*, introd. Wylie Sypher, 61–190. Baltimore: Johns Hopkins University Press, 1980.

Berns, Fernando G. Pagnoni, and Amy M. Davis. "From Jigsaw to Phibes: God, Free Will and Foreknowledge in Conflict." In *To See the "Saw" Movies: Essays on Torture Porn and Post-9/11 Horror*, ed. James Aston and John Walliss, 73–85. Jefferson, NC: McFarland, 2013.

Bersani, Leo. *The Freudian Body: Psychoanalysis and Art*. New York: Columbia University Press, 1986.

Beugnet, Martine. *Cinema of Sensation: French Film and the Art of Transgression*. Carbondale: Southern Illinois University Press, 2007.

Billig, Michael. *Laughter and Ridicule: Towards a Social Critique of Humour*. Thousand Oaks, CA: SAGE, 2005.

Black, Joel. *The Reality Effect: Film Culture and the Graphic Imperative*. New York: Routledge, 2002.

Blackwood, Gemma. "*Wolf Creek*: An UnAustralian Story?" *Continuum: Journal of Media and Cultural Studies*, vol. 21, no. 4 (December 2007): 489–97.

Blake, Linnie. *The Wounds of Nations: Horror Cinema, Historical Trauma and National Identity*. Manchester: Manchester University Press, 2008.

Blake, Linnie. "'I Am the Devil and I'm Here to Do the Devil's Work': Rob Zombie, George W. Bush, and the Limits of American Freedom." In *Horror after 9/11: World of Fear, Cinema of Terror*, ed. Aviva Briefel and Sam J. Miller, 186–99. Austin: University of Texas, 2011.

Braziel, Jana Evans, and Kathleen LeBesco (eds.). *Bodies Out of Bounds: Fatness and Transgression*. Berkeley: University of California Press, 2001.

Breger, Claudia. "Configuring Affect: Complex World Making in Faith Akin's *Auf der anderen Seite (The Edge of Heaven)*." *Cinema Journal*, vol. 54, no. 1 (Fall 2014): 65–87.

Brennan, Teresa. *The Transmission of Affect*. Ithaca: Cornell University Press, 2004.

Briefel, Aviva, and Sam J. Miller (eds.). *Horror after 9/11: World of Fear, Cinema of Terror*. Austin: University of Texas Press, 2011.

Brinkema, Eugenie. "Laura Dern's Vomit, or, Kant and Derrida in Oz." *Film-Philosophy*, vol. 15, no. 2 (2011): 51–69.

Brinkema, Eugenie. *The Forms of the Affects*. Durham, NC: Duke University Press, 2014.

Brooker, Will. "Camera-Eye, CG-Eye: Videogames and the 'Cinematic.'" *Cinema Journal*, vol. 48, no. 3 (Spring 2009): 122–8.

Brottman, Mikita. *Offensive Films*. Nashville, TN: Vanderbilt University Press, 2005.

Brown, Jared. *Alan J. Pakula: His Films and His Life*. New York: Back Stage Books, 2005.

Brown, Norman O. *Life Against Death: The Psychoanalytic Meaning of History*. Middletown CT: Wesleyan University Press, 1985.

Brown, Simon, and Stacey Abbott. "The Art of Sp(1)atter: Body Horror in *Dexter*." In *Dexter: Investigating Cutting Edge Television*, ed. Douglas Howard, 205–20. London: I. B. Tauris, 2010.

Brunette, Peter. *Michael Haneke*. Urbana: University of Illinois Press, 2010.

Buckland, Warren. "Video Pleasure and Narrative Cinema: Luc Besson's *The Fifth Element* and Video Game Logic." In *Moving Images: From Edison to the Webcam*, ed. John Fullerton and Astrid Söderbergh Widding, 159–64. London: John Libby, 2000.

Bullins, Jeffrey. "Hearing the Game: Sound Design." In *To See the "Saw" Movies: Essays on Torture Porn and Post-9/11 Horror*, ed. James Aston and John Walliss, 176–93. Jefferson, NC: McFarland, 2013.

Burrill, Derek A. *Die Tryin': Videogames, Masculinity, Culture*. New York: Peter Lang, 2008.

Butler, Andrea. "Sacrificing the Real: Early 20th Century Theatrics and the New Extremism in Cinema." *Cinephile*, vol. 8, no. 2 (Fall 2012): 27–31.

Caputi, Jane. "Advertising Femicide: Lethal Violence against Women in Pornography and Gorenography." In *Femicide: The Politics of Woman Killing*, ed. Jill Radford and Diana E. H. Russell, 203–21. New York: Twayne, 1992.

Chion, Michel. *Audio-vision: Sound on Screen*. Trans. Claudia Gorbman. New York: Columbia University Press, 1994.

Chion, Michel. *The Voice in Cinema*. Trans. Claudia Gorbman. New York: Columbia University Press, 1999.

Choe, Steve. "Love Your Enemies: Revenge and Forgiveness in Films by Park Chan-wook." *Korean Studies*, vol. 33 (2009): 29–51.

Choi, Jinhee, and Mitsuyo Wada-Marciano (eds.). *Horror to the Extreme: Changing Boundaries in Asian Cinema*. Hong Kong: Hong Kong University Press, 2009.

Chow, Rey, and James A. Steintrager. "In Pursuit of the Object of Sound: An Introduction." *differences*, vol. 22, nos 2 and 3 (Summer/Fall 2011): 1–9.

Clover, Carol J. *Men, Women, and Chain Saws: Gender in the Modern Horror Film*. Princeton, NJ: Princeton University Press, 1992.

Coleman, Lindsay. "'Damn You for Making Me Do This': Abu Ghraib, *24*, Torture, and Television Masochism." In *The War Body on Screen*, ed. Karen Randell and Sean Redmond, 199–214. New York: Continuum, 2008.

Collins, Brian H. "A Voice and Something More: Jigsaw as Acousmêtre and Existential Guru." In *To See the "Saw" Movies: Essays on Torture Porn and Post-9/11 Horror*, ed. James Aston and John Walliss, 86–104. Jefferson, NC: McFarland, 2013.

Collins, Jim, Hilary Radner, and Ava Preacher Collins (eds.). *Film Theory Goes to the Movies*. New York: Routledge, 1993.

Corbett, John, and Terri Kapsalis. "Aural Sex: The Female Orgasm in Popular Sound." In *Experimental Sound and Radio*, ed. Allen S. Weiss, 97–106. Cambridge, MA: MIT Press, 2001.

Coulthard, Lisa. "Dirty Sound: Haptic Noise in New Extremism." In *The Oxford Handbook of Sound and Image in Digital Media*, ed. Carol Vernallis, Amy Herzog, and John Richardson, 115–26. New York: Oxford University Press, 2013.

Cowan, Douglas E. *Sacred Terror: Religion and Horror on the Silver Screen*. Waco, TX: Baylor University Press, 2008.

Creed, Barbara. *The Monstrous-Feminine: Film, Feminism, Psychoanalysis*. New York: Routledge, 1993.

Cromb, Brenda. "Gorno: Violence, Shock and Comedy." *Cinephile*, 4 (2008), <http://cinephile.ca/archives/volume-4-post-genre/gorno-violence-shock-and-comedy/>

Cusack, Carmen. *Pornography and The Criminal Justice System*. Boca Raton, FL: CRC Press, 2015.

De Vleminck, Jens, and Eran Dorfman (eds.). *Sexuality and Psychoanalysis: Philosophical Criticisms*. Leuven: Leuven University Press, 2010.

Debord, Guy. *Society of the Spectacle*. Trans. Black and Red. Detroit: Black and Red, 1983.

Del Rio, Elena. *Deleuze and the Cinemas of Performance: Powers of Affection*. Edinburgh: Edinburgh University Press, 2008.

Deleuze, Gilles. "He Stuttered." In *Essays Critical and Clinical*. Trans. Daniel W. Smith and Michael A. Greco, 107–14. London: Verso, 1998.

Deleuze, Gilles. *Francis Bacon: The Logic of Sensation*. Trans. Daniel W. Smith. Minneapolis: University of Minnesota Press, 2004.

Dennis, Kelly. "Leave It to Beaver: The Object of Pornography." In *Strategies for Theory: From Marx to Madonna*, ed. R. L. Rutsky and Bradley Macdonald, 187–224. Albany: State University of New York Press, 2003.

Dixon, Wheeler Winston (ed.). *Film and Television after 9/11*. Carbondale: Southern Illinois University Press, 2004.

Dixon, Wheeler Winston. *Visions of the Apocalypse: Spectacles of Destruction in American Cinema*. Columbia: Columbia University Press, 2003.

Doane, Mary Ann. "The Voice in the Cinema: The Articulation of the Body and Space." *Yale French Studies*, 60 (1980): 33–50.

Donnelly, K. J. "*Saw* Heard: Musical Sound Design in Contemporary Cinema." In *Film Theory and Contemporary Hollywood Movies*, ed. Warren Buckland, 105–23. New York: Routledge, 2009.

Dyer, Richard. *Only Entertainment Second Edition*. London: Routledge, 2002.

Eco, Umberto. "The Frames of Comic 'Freedom.'" In *Carnival!*, ed. Thomas Sebeok, 1–8. New York: Mouton, 1984.

Edelstein, David. "A Threat, Hidden in Plain Sight." *Fresh Air*, NPR, January 13, 2006, <http://www.npr.org/templates/story/story.php?storyId=5156201>

Edelstein, David. "Now Playing at Your Local Multiplex: Torture Porn." *New York*, vol. 39, no. 4 (February 6, 2006): 63–4, <http://nymag.com/movies/features/15622/>

Edelstein, David. "Audience Is Loser in Haneke's Unfunny 'Games.'" *Fresh Air*, NPR, March 14, 2008, <http://www.npr.org/templates/story/story.php?storyId=88230619>

Eisenstein, Sergei. "A Dialectic Approach to Film Form." In *Film Form*, ed. and trans. Jay Leyda, 45–63. New York: Harvest, 1949.

Fahy, Thomas, ed. *The Philosophy of Horror*. Lexington: University Press of Kentucky, 2010.

Faludi, Susan. *The Terror Dream: Fear and Fantasy in Post 9/11 America*. New York: Metropolitan Books, 2007.

Featherstone, Mark and Beth Johnson. "'Ovo Je Srbija': The Horror of the National Thing in *A Serbian Film*." *Journal for Cultural Research*, vol. 16, no. 1 (January 2012): 63–79.

Foucault, Michel. "Of Other Spaces." Trans. Jay Miskowiec. *Diacritics*, vol. 16, no. 1 (Spring 1986): 22–7.

Foucault, Michel. *Discipline and Punish: The Birth of the Prison*. Trans. Alan Sheridan. New York: Vintage Books, 1995.

Freeland, Cynthia A. *The Naked and the Undead: Evil and the Appeal of Horror*. Boulder, CO: Westview, 2000.

French, Karl (ed.). *Screen Violence*. London: Bloomsbury, 1996.

Freud, Sigmund. *On Sexuality: Three Essays on The Theory of Sexuality and Other Works Volume 7*. Trans. James Strachey. London: Penguin Books, 1991.

Frost, Craig. "Regendering the Final Girl: Eli Roth's *Hostel.*" *Cinemascope*, 12 (January–June 2009): 1–10.

Galloway, Patrick. *Asia Shock: Horror and Dark Cinema from Japan, Korea, Hong Kong, and Thailand.* Berkeley: Stone Bridge, 2006.

Geyskens, Tomas. "Painting as Hysteria—Deleuze on Bacon." In *Sexuality and Psychoanalysis: Philosophical Criticisms*, ed. Jens De Vleminck and Eran Dorfman, 215–29. Leuven: Leuven University Press, 2010.

Girard, René. *Violence and the Sacred.* Trans. Patrick Gregory. Baltimore: Johns Hopkins University Press, 1989.

Gledhill, Christine (ed.). *Home Is Where the Heart Is: Studies in Melodrama and the Women's Film.* London: BFI, 1994.

Goldberg, Elizabeth Swanson. "Splitting Difference: Global Identity Politics and the Representation of Torture in the Counterhistorical Dramatic Film." In *Violence and American Cinema*, ed. David Slocum, 245–70. New York: Routledge, 2001.

Goodman, Steve. *Sonic Warfare: Sound, Affect, and the Ecology of Fear.* Cambridge, MA: MIT Press, 2010.

Grant, Barry Keith, and Christopher Sharrett (eds.). *Planks of Reason: Essays on the Horror Film.* Lanham, MD: Scarecrow, 2004.

Green, Amy M. "The French Horror Film *Martyrs* and the Destruction, Defilement, and Neutering of the Female Form." *Journal of Popular Film and Television*, vol. 39, no. 1 (2011): 20–8.

Grey, Sarah Cameron Loyd. "Dead Time: Aporias and Critical Videogaming." *Symploke*, vol. 17, nos 1–2 (2009): 231–46.

Gross, Sheryl W. "Guilt and Innocence in Marathon Man." *Literature Film Quarterly*, vol. 8, no. 1 (1980): 52–68.

Gruno, Kristina E. "*Martyrs.*" *Journal of Feminist Family Therapy*, vol. 23, no. 2 (2011): 151–8.

Guerrasio, Jason. "The Vacation Planner." *Filmmaker*, vol. 15, no. 3 (Spring 2007). Film and Television Literature Index, EBSCOhost.

Gunning, Tom. "An Aesthetic of Astonishment: Early Film and the (In)credulous Spectator." In *Critical Concepts in Media and Cultural Studies*, eds. Philip Simpson, Andrew Utterson, and K. J. Shepherdson, 78–95. New York: Routledge, 2004.

Gunning, Tom. "The Cinema of Attraction[s]: Early Film, Its Spectator and the Avant-Garde." In *The Cinema of Attractions Reloaded*, ed. Wanda Strauven, 381–8. Amsterdam: Amsterdam University Press, 2006.

Hainge, Greg. *Noise Matters: Towards an Ontology of Noise.* New York: Bloomsbury, 2013.

Haneke, Michael. Interview by Nick James, "Darkness Falls." *Sight & Sound*, vol. 13, no. 10 (October 2003): 16–18.

Hanich, Julian. *Cinematic Emotion in Horror Films and Thrillers: The Aesthetic Paradox of Pleasurable Fear.* New York: Routledge, 2010.

Hanich, Julian. "Toward a Poetics of Cinematic Disgust." *Film-Philosophy*, vol. 15, no. 2 (2011): 11–35.

Haskell, Molly. *From Revenge to Rape: The Treatment of Women in the Movies.* New York: Holt, Rinehart, & Winston, 1975.

Hawkins, Joan. *Cutting Edge: Art-Horror and the Horrific Avant-Garde.* Minneapolis: University of Minnesota Press, 2000.

Hayward, Philip (ed.). *Terror Tracks: Music, Sound, and Horror Cinema.* Oakville, CT: Equinox, 2009.

Hester, Helen. *Beyond Explicit: Pornography and the Displacement of Sex*. New York: SUNY Press, 2014.

Higgins, Scott. "Suspenseful Situations: Melodramatic Narrative and the Contemporary Action Film." *Cinema Journal*, vol. 47, no. 2 (2008): 74–96.

Hills, Matt. "Cutting into Concepts of 'Reflectionist' Cinema? The *Saw* Franchise and Puzzles of Post-9/11 Horror." In *Horror after 9/11: World of Fear, Cinema of Terror*, eds. Aviva Briefel and Sam J. Miller, 107–23. Austin: University of Texas Press, 2011.

Horeck, Tanya and Tina Kendall. "The New *Extremisms*: Rethinking Extreme Cinema. *Cinephile*, vol. 8, no. 2 (Fall 2012): 6–9.

Horeck, Tanya and Tina Kendall (eds.). *New Extremism in Cinema: From France to Europe*. Edinburgh: Edinburgh University Press, 2011.

Horkheimer, Max and Theodor Adorno. *Dialectic of Enlightenment*. Trans. John Cumming. New York: Continuum, 1996.

Horn, John. "Some Viewers Need a Hand after the Forearm Amputation in '127 Hours.'" *Los Angeles Times*, <http://articles.latimes.com/2010/oct/31/entertainment/la-et-arm-movie-20101031>.

Hosenball, Mark. "Report Reveals CIA Conducted Mock Executions." *Newsweek*, August 20, 2009, <http://www.thedailybeast.com/newsweek/2009/08/20/report-reveals-cia-conducted-mock-executions.html>

Huntley, Jacob. "The Jigsaw Assemblage." In *To See the "Saw" Movies: Essays on Torture Porn and Post-9/11 Horror*, eds. James Aston and John Walliss, 123–38. Jefferson, NC: McFarland, 2013.

Hutchings, Peter. *The Horror Film*. Harlow: Pearson Longman, 2004.

Jones, Steve. "'Time Is Wasting': Con/sequence and S/pace in the *Saw* Series." *Horror Studies*, vol. 1, no. 2 (2010): 225–39.

Jones, Steve. *Torture Porn: Popular Horror after* Saw. New York: Palgrave, 2013.

Jones, Steve. "The Lexicon of Offence: The Meanings of Torture, Porn, and 'Torture Porn.'" In *Controversial Images: Media Representations on the Edge*, eds. Feona Attwood, Vincent Campbell, I. Q. Hunter, and Sharon Lockyer, 186–200. Basingstoke: Palgrave Macmillan, 2013.

Jones, Steve. "Twisted Pictures: Morality, Nihilism and Symbolic Suicide." In *To See the "Saw" Movies: Essays on Torture Porn and Post-9/11 Horror*, eds. James Aston and John Walliss, 105–22. Jefferson, NC: McFarland, 2013.

Kahn, Douglas. *Noise, Water, Meat: A History of Sound in the Arts*. Cambridge, MA: MIT Press, 1999.

Karimova, Gulnara. "Interpretive Methodology from Literary Criticism: Carnivalesque Analysis of Popular Culture: *Jackass, South Park*, and 'Everyday' Culture." *Studies in Popular Culture*, vol. 33, no. 1 (2010): 37–51.

Kendall, Tina. "Introduction: Tarrying with Disgust." *Film-Philosophy*, vol. 15, no. 2 (2011): 1–10.

Kennedy, Julia and Smith, Clarissa. "His Soul Shatters at About 0:23: *Spankwire*, Self-Scaring and Hyperbolic Shock." In *Controversial Images: Media Representations on the Edge*, eds. Feona Attwood, Vincent Campbell, and I. Q. Hunter, 239–53. New York: Palgrave Macmillan, 2012.

Kerner, Aaron. *Torture Porn in the Wake of 9/11: Horror, Exploitation, and the Cinema of Sensation*. New Brunswick, NJ: Rutgers University Press, 2015.

Kinser, Samuel. *Rabelais's Carnival: Text, Context, Metatext*. Berkeley: University of California Press, 1990.

Klossowski, Pierre. *Sade My Neighbour*. Trans. Alphonso Lingis. London: Quartet Books, 1991.

Knafo, Danielle. "Castration and Medusa: Orlan's Art on the Cutting Edge." *Studies in Gender and Sexuality*, 10 (2009): 142–58.

Kobayashi, Motomi. "Licca-chan's Secret—The Story of Japan's Barbie." *The Asahi Shimbun* (December 28, 2011), <http://ajw.asahi.com/article/cool_japan/style/AJ201112280042>

Kolnai, Aurel. *On Disgust*, eds. Barry Smith and Carolyn Korsmeyer. Chicago: Open Court, 2004.

Kristeva, Julia. *Powers of Horror: An Essay on Abjection*. Trans. Leon S. Roudiez. New York: Columbia University, 1982.

Kristeva, Julia. *Strangers to Ourselves*. Trans. Leon S. Roudiez. New York: Columbia University Press, 1991.

Kyrölä, Katariina. *The Weight of Images: Affect, Body Image and Fat in the Media*. Farnham: Ashgate, 2014.

Krzywinska, Tanya. "The Dynamics of Squirting: Female Ejaculation and Lactation in Hardcore Film." In *Unruly Pleasures: The Cult Film and its Critics*, eds. Xavier Mendik and Graeme Harper, 30–43. Guildford: FAB Press, 2000.

Laine, Tarja. "Imprisoned in Disgust: Roman Polanski's *Repulsion*." *Film-Philosophy*, vol. 15, no. 2 (2011): 36–50.

Laine, Tarja. *Feeling Cinema: Emotional Dynamics in Film Studies*. New York: Bloomsbury, 2013.

Landay, Lori. "The Mirror of Performance: Kinaesthetics, Subjectivity, and the Body in Film, Television, and Virtual Worlds." *Cinema Journal*, vol. 51, no. 3 (2012): 129–36.

Lane, Anthony. "Recurring Nightmare." *New Yorker*, March 17, 2008, <http://www.newyorker.com/arts/critics/cinema/2008/03/17/080317crci_cinema_lane>

Lane, Anthony. "Happy Haneke." *New Yorker*, October 5, 2009, <http://www.newyorker.com/reporting/2009/10/05/091005fa_fact_lane>

Lehman, Peter. "Revelations about Pornography." *Film Criticism* (Fall/Winter 1995): 3–16.

Lockwood, Dean. "All Stripped Down: The Spectacle of 'Torture Porn.'" *Popular Communication*, vol. 7, no. 1 (2009): 40–8.

Lockwood, Dean. "Work Is Hell: Life in the Mannequin Factory." In *To See the "Saw" Movies: Essays on Torture Porn and Post-9/11 Horror*, eds. James Aston and John Walliss, 139–56. Jefferson, NC: McFarland, 2013.

Lowenstein, Adam. "Spectacle Horror and *Hostel*: Why 'Torture Porn' Does Not Exist." *Critical Quarterly*, vol. 53, no. 1 (2011): 42–60.

Maddison, Stephen. "'Choke On It Bitch!': Porn Studies, Extreme Gonzo and the Mainstreaming of Hardcore." In *Mainstreaming Sex: The Sexualization of Western Culture*, ed. Feona Attwood, 37–53. New York: I. B. Tauris, 2009.

Manning, Erin. *Politics of Touch: Sense, Movement, Sovereignty*. Minneapolis: University of Minnesota Press, 2007.

Mantle, Anthony Dod. Interview by Jon Silberg, "The Root of All Evil." *American Cinematographer*, vol. 90, issue 11 (November 2009): 66–75.

Marks, Laura. *The Skin of the Film: Intercultural Cinema, Embodiment, and the Senses*. Durham, NC: Duke University Press, 2000.

Marks, Laura. *Touch: Sensuous Theory and Multisensory Media*. Minneapolis: University of Minnesota Press, 2002.

Massumi, Brian. *Parables for the Virtual: Movement, Affect, Sensation*. Durham, NC: Duke University Press, 2002.

McCann, Ben. "Body Horror." In *To See the "Saw" Movies: Essays on Torture Porn and Post-9/11 Horror*, eds. James Aston and John Walliss, 30–44. Jefferson, NC: McFarland, 2013.

McCarthy, Todd. "Trick and Treat." *Film Comment*, 16 (1980): 17–24.

McRoy, Jay, (ed.). *Japanese Horror Cinema*. Honolulu: University of Hawai'i Press, 2005.

Menninghaus, Winfried. *Disgust: The Theory and History of a Strong Sensation*. Trans. Howard Eiland and Joel Golb. New York: SUNY Press, 2003.

Middleton, Jason. "The Subject of Torture: Regarding the Pain of Americans in *Hostel*." *Cinema Journal*, vol. 49, no. 4 (Summer 2010): 1–24.

Middleton, Jason. *Documentary's Awkward Turn: Cringe Comedy and Media*. New York: Routledge, 2014.

Miller, William Ian. *The Anatomy of Disgust*. Cambridge, MA: Harvard University Press, 1997.

Moretti, Franco. *Signs Taken for Wonders: Essays in the Sociology of Literary Forms*. New York: Verso, 1988.

Morris, Jeremy. "The Justification of Torture-Horror: Retribution and Sadism in *Saw*, *Hostel*, and *The Devil's Rejects*." In *The Philosophy of Horror*, ed. Thomas Fahy, 42–56. Lexington: University Press of Kentucky, 2010.

Mulvey, Laura. *Fetishism and Curiosity*. Bloomington: Indiana University Press, 1996.

Murray, Gabrielle. "*Hostel II*: Representations of the Body in Pain and the Cinema Experience in Torture-Porn." *Jump Cut*, 50 (Spring 2008), <http://www.ejumpcut.org/archive/jc50.2008/TortureHostel2/>

Muybridge, Eadweard. *Muybridge's Complete Human and Animal Locomotion*. New York: Dover, 1979.

Nancy, Jean-Luc. *Listening*. Trans. Charlotte Mandell. New York: Fordham University Press, 2007.

Ndalianis, Angela. *The Horror Sensorium: Media and the Senses*. Jefferson, NC: McFarland, 2012.

Neale, Steve. "Melodrama and Tears." *Screen*, vol. 27, no. 6 (1986): 6–22.

Newman, Kim. "Horror Will Eat Itself." *Sight and Sound*, 19 (May 2009): 37–8.

Nicodemo, Timothy. "Cinematography and Sensorial Assault in Gaspar Noé's *Irreversible*." *Cinephile*, vol. 8, no. 2 (Fall 2012): 33–9.

Nowell-Smith, Geoffrey. "Minnelli and Melodrama." In *Home Is Where the Heart Is: Studies in Melodrama and the Women's Film*, ed. Christine Gledhill, 70–4. London: BFI, 1994.

Paasonen, Susanna. *Carnal Resonance: Affect and Online Pornography*. Cambridge, MA: MIT Press, 2011.

Parvulescu, Anca. *Laughter: Notes on a Passion*. Cambridge, MA: MIT Press, 2010.

Paul, William. *Laughing Screaming: Modern Hollywood Horror and Comedy*. New York: Columbia University Press, 1994.

Pinedo, Isabel Cristina. *Recreational Terror: Women and the Pleasures of Horror Film Viewing*. Albany: State University of New York Press, 1997.

Plantinga, Carl. "Disgusted at the Movies." *Film Studies*, 8 (2006): 81–92.

Polan, Dana R. "Eros and Syphilization: The Contemporary Horror Film." In *Planks of Reason: Essays on the Horror Film*, eds. Barry Keith Grant and Christopher Sharrett, 142–52. Lanham, MD: Scarecrow, 2004.

Porton, Richard. "Collective Guilt and Individual Responsibility: An Interview with Michael Haneke." *Cineaste*, vol. 30, no. 1 (Winter 2005): 50–1.

Powell, Anna. *Deleuze and Horror Film*. Edinburgh: Edinburgh University Press, 2005.

Presdee, Mike. *Cultural Criminology and the Carnival of Crime*. New York: Routledge, 2000.

Provine, Robert R. *Laughter: A Scientific Investigation*. New York: Viking, 2000.

Quandt, James. "Flesh and Blood: Sex and Violence in Recent French Cinema." In *The New Extremism in Cinema: From France to Europe*, eds. Tanya Horeck and Tina Kendall, 18–25. Edinburgh: Edinburgh University Press, 2011.

Radford, Jill, and Diana E. H. Russell (eds.). *Femicide: The Politics of Woman Killing*. New York: Twayne, 1992.

Reardon, Kiva. "Subject Slaughter." *Cinephile*, vol. 8, no. 2 (Fall 2012): 18–25.

Restuccia, Frances. *The Blue Box: Kristevan/Lacanian Readings of Contemporary Cinema*. New York: Continuum, 2012.

Reyes, Xavier Aldana. *Body Gothic: Corporeal Transgression in Contemporary Literature and Horror Film*. Cardiff: University of Wales, 2014.

Richardson, Michael. "Torturous Affect: Writing and the Problem of Pain." In *Traumatic Affect*, eds. Meera Atkinson and Michael Richardson, 148–70. Newcastle upon Tyne: Cambridge Scholars Publishing, 2013.

Sachs, Rob. "Charlie Clouser's Scary Soundtrack for *Saw*." *Day to Day*, NPR, October 29, 2004, <http://www.npr.org/templates/story/story.php?storyId=4132853>

Sade, Donatien Alphonse François, Marquis de. *The 120 Days of Sodom and Other Writing*. Trans. Austryn Wainhouse and Richard Seaver. New York: Grove Weidenfeld, 1987.

Sanders, Barry. *Sudden Glory: Laughter as Subversive History*. Boston: Beacon Press, 1995.

Scarry, Elaine. *The Body in Pain: The Making and Unmaking of the World*. New York: Oxford University Press, 1985.

Scarry, Elaine. "'The Body in Pain': An Interview with Elaine Scarry." Interviewed by Elizabeth Irene Smith. *Concentric: Literary and Cultural Studies*, vol. 32, no. 2 (September 2006): 223–37.

Schaefer, Eric (ed.). *Sex Scene: Media and the Sexual Revolution*. Durham, NC: Duke University Press, 2014.

Schaefer, Eric. "Exploitation Films: Teaching Sin in the Suburbs." *Cinema Journal*, vol. 47, no. 1 (Fall 2007): 94–7.

Sconce, Jeffrey. "Spectacles of Death: Identification, Reflexivity, and Contemporary Horror." In *Film Theory Goes to the Movies*, eds. Jim Collins, Hilary Radner, and Ava Preacher Collins, 103–19. New York: Routledge, 1993.

Scott, A. O. "Torture or Porn? No Need to Choose." *New York Times*, May 12, 2011, <http://movies.nytimes.com/2011/05/13/ movies/a-serbian-film-directed-by-srdjan-spasojevic-review.html>

Self, Will. "The American Vice." In *Screen Violence*, ed. Karl French, 71–81. London: Bloomsbury, 1996.

Serres, Michel. *Genesis*. Trans. Geneviève James and James Nielson. Ann Arbor: University of Michigan Press, 1995).

Serres, Michel. *The Parasite*. Trans. Lawrence R. Schehr. Minneapolis: University of Minnesota Press, 2007.

Sharrett, Christopher. "The Idea of Apocalypse in *The Texas Chainsaw Massacre*." In *Planks of Reason: Essays on the Horror Film*, ed. Barry Keith Grant, 255–76. Lanham, MD: Scarecrow, 1984.

Sharrett, Christopher. "The Problem of *Saw*: 'Torture Porn' and the Conservatism of Contemporary Horror Films." *Cineaste*, vol. 35, no. 1 (Winter 2009): 32–7.

Shaviro, Steven. "Regimes of Vision: Kathryn Bigelow, Strange Days." *Polygraph*, 13 (2001): 59–68.

Shaviro, Steven. "Body Horror and Post-Socialist Cinema: Györgi Pálfi's *Taxidermia*." *Film-Philosophy*, vol. 15, no. 2 (2011): 90–105.

Shaviro, Steven. *The Cinematic Body*. Minneapolis: University of Minnesota Press, 1993.

Shin, Chi-Yun. "Art of branding: Tartan 'Asia Extreme' films." *Jump Cut*, 50 (Spring 2008), <http://www.ejumpcut.org/archive/jc50.2008/TartanDist/text.html>

Smith, Madeleine. "Monstrous Bodies and Gendered Abjection." In *To See the "Saw"*

Movies: Essays on Torture Porn and Post-9/11 Horror, eds. James Aston and John Walliss, 157–75. Jefferson, NC: McFarland, 2013.

Sobchack, Vivian. *The Address of the Eye: A Phenomenology of Film Experience*. Princeton: Princeton University Press, 1992.

Sontag, Susan. *Regarding the Pain of Others*. New York: Farrar, Straus, & Giroux, 2003.

Sontag, Susan. "Regarding the Torture of Others." *New York Times Magazine*, May 23, 2004, 24–9, 42.

Stam, Robert. *Subversive Pleasures: Bakhtin, Cultural Criticism, and Film*. Baltimore: Johns Hopkins University Press, 1989.

Strauven, Wanda, ed. *The Cinema of Attractions Reloaded*. Amsterdam: Amsterdam University Press, 2006.

Sylvester, David. Interview with Francis Bacon. *The Brutality of Fact: Interviews with Francis Bacon*. 3rd enlarged edn. Oxford: Thames & Hudson, 1987.

Taylor, John. *Body Horror: Photojournalism, Catastrophe and War*. New York: New York University Press, 1998.

Taylor, Paul A. Interview by Srecko Horvat. *International Journal of Žižek Studies*, vol. 1, no. 0 (2007): 1–7.

Thomsen, Bodil Marie Stavning. "*Antichrist*—Chaos Reigns: The Event of Violence and the Haptic Image in Lars von Trier's Film." *Journal of Aesthetics and Culture*, vol. 1 (2009): 1–10.

Tisdale, Sallie. "Graphic Novel," *New York Times*, April 16, 2009. Accessed February 22, 2015, <http://www.nytimes.com/2009/04/19/books/review/Tisdale-t.html?_r=0>

Tomkins, Silvan S. *Affect Imagery Consciousness: The Complete Edition*. New York: Springer, 2008.

Tumini, Angela. "Eros and Thanatos: The Murderous Struggle of Pain and Desire in Gabriele D'Annunzio's *Triumph of Death* and in Lars von Trier's *Antichrist*." In *Making Sense of Pain: Critical and Interdisciplinary Perspectives*, ed. Jane Fernandez, 165–71. Oxford: Inter-Disciplinary Press, 2010.

Tyler, Imogen. "'CHAV MUM CHAV SCUM': Class Disgust in Contemporary Britain." *Feminist Media Studies*, vol. 8, no. 1 (2008): 17–34.

Tyson, Gareth et al. "Demystifying Porn 2.0: A Look into a Major Adult Video Streaming Website." Paper presented at the Internet Measure Conference, Barcelona, October 23–5, 2013, 417–26.

Tziallas, Evangelos. "Torture Porn and Surveillance Culture." *Jump Cut*, 52 (Summer 2010), <http://www.ejumpcut.org/archive/jc52.2010/evangelosTorturePorn/>

Tziallas, Evangelos. "The Spectacle of Correction: Video Games, Movies and Control." In *To See the "Saw" Movies: Essays on Torture Porn and Post-9/11 Horror*, eds. James Aston and John Walliss, 45–72. Jefferson, NC: McFarland, 2013.

Wester, Maisha. "Torture Porn and Uneasy Feminism: Re-thinking (Wo)men in Eli Roth's *Hostel* Films." *Quarterly Review of Film and Video*, 29 (2012): 387–400.

Weiss, Allen S. *Phantasmic Radio*. Durham, NC: Duke University Press, 1995.

Wetmore, Kevin J. *Post-9/11 Horror in American Cinema*. New York: Continuum, 2012.

Williams, Linda. *Hard Core: Power, Pleasure, and "The Frenzy of the Visible."* Berkeley: University of California Press, 1989.

Williams, Linda. "Film Bodies: Gender, Genre, and Excess." *Film Quarterly*, vol. 44, no. 4 (Summer 1991): 2–13.

Williams, Linda. "Discipline and Fun: *Psycho* and Postmodern Cinema." In *Reinventing Film Studies*, eds. Christine Gledhill and Linda Williams, 351–78. London: Arnold, 2000.

Williams, Linda. *Screening Sex*. Durham, NC: Duke University Press, 2008.

Williams, Melanie. Review of *9 Songs*. *Film Quarterly*, vol. 59, no. 3 (Spring 2006): 59–63.

Wilson, Laura. *Spectatorship, Embodiment and Physicality in the Contemporary Mutilation Film.* New York: Palgrave, 2015.

Wolfe, Cary. "Introduction to the New Edition: Bring the Noise: *The Parasite* and the Multiple Genealogies of Posthumanism." In *The Parasite*, trans. Lawrence R. Schehr, xi–xxviii. Minneapolis: University of Minnesota Press, 2007.

Zimmer, Catherine. "Caught on Tape? The Politics of Video in the New Torture Films." In *Horror after 9/11: World of Fear, Cinema of Terror*, eds. Aviva Briefel and Sam J. Miller, 83–106. Austin: University of Texas Press, 2011.

Žižek, Slavoj. *For They Know Not What They Do: Enjoyment as a Political Factor.* London: Verso, 1991.

Žižek, Slavoj. "Kant with (or against) Sade." In *The Žižek Reader*, eds. Elizabeth Wright and Edmond Wright, 283–301. Oxford: Blackwell, 1999.

Žižek, Slavoj. "Camp Comedy." *Sight and Sound*, vol. 10, no. 4 (2000): 26–9.

Žižek, Slavoj. *Welcome to the Desert of the Real! Five Essays on September 11 and Related Dates.* New York: Verso, 2002.

Zuromskis, Catherine. "Prurient Pictures and Popular Film: The Crisis of Pornographic Representation." *The Velvet Light Trap*, 59 (2007): 4–14.

Filmography

2 Girls 1 Cup, Marco Fiorito, 2007, 1 min.
"8 Simple Rules for Buying My Teenage Daughter," *Family Guy*, Fox Network, Season 4, Episode 8, 2005, 22 mins
9 Songs, Michael Winterbottom, 2004, 71 mins
127 Hours, Danny Boyle, 2010, 94 mins
A Serbian Film [*Srpski film*], Srdjan Spasojevic, 2010, 104 mins
Act of Killing, The, Joshua Oppenheimer, 2012, 115 mins
Alien, Ridley Scott, 1979, 117 mins
All That Heaven Allows, Douglas Sirk, 1955, 89 mins
Andrei Rublev, Andrei Tarkovsky, 1966, 205 mins
Antichrist, Lars Von Trier, 2009, 108 mins
Audition [*Odishon*], Takashi Miike, 1999, 115 mins
Baise-Moi [*Rape Me*], Virginie Despentes and Coralie Trinh Thi, 2000, 74 mins
Battle Royale [*Batoru Rowaiaru*], Kinji Fukasaku, 2000, 114 mins
Beats of the Antonov, Hajooj Kuka, 2014, 68 mins
Benny's Video, Michael Haneke, 1992, 105 mins
Berberian Sound Studio, Peter Strickland, 2012, 92 mins
Blow-Up, Michelangelo Antonioni, 1966, 111 mins
Borat: Cultural Learnings of America for Make Benefit Glorious Nation of Kazakhstan, Larry Charles, 2006, 84 mins
Caché [*Hidden*], Michael Haneke, 2005, 117 mins
Calvaire, Fabrice Du Welz, 2004, 88 mins
Captivity, Roland Joffé, 2007, 96 mins
Carrie, Brian De Palma, 1976, 98 mins
Chained, Jennifer Chambers Lynch, 2012, 94 mins
Choose, Marcus Graves, 2010, 83 mins
Clinic, The, James Rabbitts, 2010, 94 mins
Clip [*Klip*], Maja Miloš, 2012, 102 mins
Cloverfield, Matt Reeves, 2008, 85 mins
Cold Fish [*Tsumetai nettaigyo*], Shion Sono, 2010, 144 mins
Confessions [*Kokuhaku*], Tetsuya Nakashima, 2010, 106 mins
Cut, Park Chan-wook, 2004, 48 mins
Deep Throat, Gerard Damiano, 1972, 61 mins

Deliverance, John Boorman, 1972, 110 mins
Devil's Rejects, The, Rob Zombie, 2005, 107 mins
Dexter, Showtime, 2006–2013
Diary of Anne Frank, The, George Stevens, 1959, 180 mins
Dumplings [*Jiao zi*], Fruit Chan, 2004, 38 mins
Dumplings [*Jiao zi*], Fruit Chan, 2004, 91 mins
Embarrassing Bodies, Maverick Television, 2008–13
Friday the 13th, Sean Cunningham, 1980, 95 mins
Frontière(s) [*Frontier(s)*], Xavier Gens (2007), 108 mins
Funeral Parade of Roses [*Bara no soretsu*], Toshio Matsumoto, 1969, 107 mins
Funny Games, Michael Haneke, 1997, 108 mins
Funny Games, Michael Haneke, 2007, 111 mins
Fuses, Carolee Schneeman, 1965, 22 mins
Helter Skelter [*Heruta sukeruta*], Mika Ninagawa, 2012, 127 mins
Hostel, Eli Roth, 2005, 94 mins
Hostel: Part II, Eli Roth, 2007, 93 mins
Human Centipede (First Sequence), The, Tom Six, 2009, 92 mins
Human Centipede II (Full Sequence), The, Tom Six, 2011, 88 mins
Hungry Bitches, Marco Fiorito, 2007, 62 mins
I Saw the Devil [*Ang-ma-reul bo-at-da*], Kim Jee-woon, 2010, 141 mins
I Spit on Your Grave, Meir Zarchi, 1978, 101 mins
I Spit on Your Grave, Steven R. Monroe, 2010, 108 mins
Imitation of Life, Douglas Sirk, 1959, 125 mins
"Informative Murder Porn," *South Park*, Comedy Central, Season 17, Episode 2, 2013, 22
    mins
In the Realm of the Senses [*Ai no korida*], Nagisa Oshima, 1976, 109 mins
Inside, Alexandre Bustillo and Julien Maury, 2007, 82 mins
Invasion of the Body Snatchers, Philip Kaufman, 1978, 115 mins
Irreversible [*Irréversible*], Gaspar Noé, 2002, 97 mins
Isle, The [*Seom*], Kim Ki-duk, 2000, 90 mins
Jackass 2.5, Jeff Tremaine, 2007, 64 mins
Jackass 3.5, Jeff Tremaine, 2011, 84 mins
Jackass Number Two, Jeff Tremaine, 2006, 92 mins
Jackass, MTV, 2000–2002
Jackass: The Lost Tapes, MTV, 2009, 104 mins
Jackass: The Movie, Jeff Tremaine, 2002, 87 mins
Ju-on: The Grudge [*Ju-on*], Takashi Shimizu, 2002, 92 mins
Kinatay, Brillante Mendoza, 2009, 105 mins
Lady Vengeance [*Chinjeolhan geumjassi*], Park Chan-wook, 2005, 112 mins
Leviathan, Lucien Castaing-Taylor and Verena Paravel, 2012, 87 mins
Love Exposure, [*Ai no mukidashi*], Shion Sono, 2008, 237 mins
Martyrs, Pascal Laugier, 2008, 99 mins
Monsters Inc., Pete Docter et al., 2001, 92 mins
Nymphomaniac Volume I, Lars Von Trier, 2013, 117 mins
Nymphomaniac Volume II, Lars Von Trier, 2013, 123 mins
Office Killer, Cindy Sherman, 1997, 82 mins
Oldboy [*Oldeuboi*], Park Chan-wook, 2003, 120 mins
Piano Teacher, The [*La pianist*], Michael Haneke, 2001, 131 mins
Rear Window, Alfred Hitchcock, 1954, 112 mins

[REC], Jaume Balagueró and Paco Plaza, 2007, 78 mins
Ring, The, Gore Verbinski, 2002, 115 mins
Ringu, Hideo Nakata, 1998, 96 mins
Romance, Catherine Breillat, 1999, 84 mins
Salò, or the 120 Days of Sodom [*Salò o le 120 giornate di Sodoma*], Pier Paolo Pasolini, 1975, 116 mins
Saw 3D: The Final Chapter, Kevin Greutert, 2010, 90 mins
Saw II, Darren Lynn Bousman, 2005, 93 mins
Saw III, Darren Lynn Bousman, 2006, 108 mins
Saw IV, Darren Lynn Bousman, 2007, 93 mins
Saw V, David Hackl, 2008, 92 mins
Saw VI, Kevin Greutert, 2009, 90 mins
Saw, James Wan, 2003, 9 mins
Saw, James Wan, 2004, 103 mins
Scream, Wes Craven, 1996, 111 mins
Skin, The [*La pelle*], Liliana Cavani, 1981, 131 mins
Slaughtered Vomit Dolls, Lucifer Valentine, 2006, 71 mins
Slumdog Millionaire, Danny Boyle and Loveleen Tandan, 2008, 120 mins
Sombre, Philippe Grandrieux, 1998, 112 mins
Sophie's Choice, Alan Pakula, 1982, 150 mins
Sounds Like, Brad Anderson, 2006, 58 mins
Stand By Me, Rob Reiner, 1986, 89 mins
Steel Trap, Luis Cámara, 2007, 89 mins
Stoker, Park Chan-wook, 2013, 99 mins
Strange Circus [*Kimyo na sakasu*], Shion Sono, 2005, 108 mins
Strangers on a Train, Alfred Hitchcock, 1951, 101 mins
Sympathy for Mr. Vengeance [*Boksuneun naui geot*], Park Chan-wook, 2002, 129 mins
Taxidermia, György Pálfi, 2006, 91 mins
Texas Chain Saw Massacre, The, Tobe Hooper, 1974, 83 mins
Thelma and Louise, Ridley Scott, 1991, 130 mins
Them [*Ils*], David Moreau and Xavier Palud, 2006, 77 mins
Thing, The, John Carpenter, 1982, 109 mins
Tosh.O, CBS Paramount Network Television, 2009–
Trainspotting, Danny Boyle, 1996, 94 mins
Trouble Every Day, Claire Denis, 2001, 101 mins
Turistas, John Stockwell, 2006, 93 mins
Twentynine Palms, Bruno Dumont, 2003, 119 mins
Watching "A Serbian Film" (Reaction Video), TwistedChimp, 2011, 2 mins
Wayward Cloud, The [*Tian bian yi duo yun*], Tsai Ming-liang, 2005, 112 mins
Wetlands [*Feuchtgebiete*], David Wnendt, 2013, 109 mins
Why don't you play in hell? [*Jigoku de naze warui*], Shion Sono, 2013, 129 mins
Window Water Baby Moving, Stan Brakhage, 1959, 13 mins
Wolf Creek, Greg Mclean, 2005, 99 mins

Index

EU Authorised Representative:

Easy Access System Europe Mustamäe tee 50, 10621 Tallinn, Estonia

gpsr.requests@easproject.com

Printed and bound by CPI Group (UK) Ltd, Croydon, CR0 4YY

22/05/2026

02116342-0002